STANDISH O'GRADY, Æ AND YEATS

For My Mother and Father

Standish O'Grady, Æ and Yeats

History, Politics, Culture

MICHAEL McATEER

Queen's University, Belfast

IRISH ACADEMIC PRESS
DUBLIN • PORTLAND, OR

First published in 2002 by
IRISH ACADEMIC PRESS
44, Northumberland Road, Dublin 4, Ireland
and in the United States of America by
IRISH ACADEMIC PRESS
c/o ISBS, 5824 N.E. Hassalo Street,
Portland Oregon 97213-3644

Website: www.iap.ie

British Library Cataloguing in Publication Data

McAteer, Michael
    Standish O'Grady, and Yeats: history, politics, culture 1.O'Grady, Standish,
    1864–1928 2. Authors, Irish – 19th century – Biography
    I.Title
    828.8'09

ISBN 0-7165-2734-0

Library of Congress Cataloging-in-Publication Data

McAteer, Michael, 1968–
    Standish O'Grady, Æ, and Yeats: history, politics, culture Michael McAteer.
      p. cm.
    Includes bibliographical references (p.) and index.
    ISBN 0-7146-2734-0 (cloth)
    1. O'Grady, Standish, 1846–1928—Knowledge—History. 2. Literature and
    history–Ireland–History–19th century. 3. Literature and history–Ireland–
    History–20th century. 4. Politics and literature–Ireland–History–20th century. 5.
    Russell, George William, 1867–1835–Political and social views. 6. Yeats, W. B.
    (William Butler). 1865–1939–Knowledge–History. 7. English literature–Irish
    authors–History and criticism. 8. O'Grady, Standish, 1846–1928–Influence. 9.
    Ireland–Intellectual life. 10. Ireland–In literature. 11. History in literature. I. Title.

    PR5112.O55 Z76 2002
    828'.809–dc21

2002017242

Typeset in 10.5/12pt Ehrhardt by FiSH Books, London WC1
Printed by MPG Books Ltd, Bodmin, Cornwall

'Educated Irishmen are ignorant of, and indifferent to, their history; yet from the hold of that history they cannot shake themselves free. It still haunts the imagination, like Mordecai at Haman's gate, a cause of continual annoyance and vexation.'
  Standish O'Grady, *History of Ireland: Cuculain and His Contemporaries*

'The Irishman's imagination never leaves him alone'
  George Bernard Shaw, *John Bull's Other Island*

'An endless feast, an endless war'
  W.B. Yeats, 'The Wanderings of Oisin'

Contents

Acknowledgements   viii

Introduction   1

1   Fathering the Revival: O'Grady's quest for origins   14

2   Lifting 'The Insane Mist': *History of Ireland: Cuculain and His Contemporaries*   36

3   Science, myth and history in *History of Ireland: Critical and Philosophical*, and other works   60

4   Towards a politics of paradox: *Toryism and the Tory Democracy*   86

5   A matter of ideals: George Russell's ideology of co-operation   104

6   'A sea-covered stone': O'Grady's influence on the young W.B. Yeats   126

Conclusion   149

Notes   154

Bibliography   187

Index   195

Acknowledgements

THE FOLLOWING WORK is the fruit of research carried out at the School of English, Queen's University Belfast between 1994 and 1998, generously funded by the Department of Education, Northern Ireland. Thanks are due to all the staff at the School of English, whose support was always forthcoming, particularly Dr Eamonn Hughes, whose advice and encouragement through the course of my research has been indispensable to this project. A work such as this develops from various branches of influence. While it is not possible to identify all of these, I wish to record my appreciation of the encouragement offered by the staff at the Department of English, Maynooth, during my years of undergraduate and postgraduate study there, particularly Dr Peter Denman. Acknowledgement is also due to 'The Red Stripe Collective' Reading Group at Maynooth, for creating a context for theoretical reflection in which some of the concepts developed in this book were addressed. For their support during the course of my research, warmest thanks are due to Patricia Houston and Bernard McKeown.

The library staff of Queen's University Belfast, particularly the staff at Special Collections, the Linenhall Library, Belfast Central Library, the National Library of Ireland and the British Newspaper Library at Edgware, London, have been most helpful during my research. Chapter 4 of this book is a modification of an essay published in the volume *Ireland in the Nineteenth Century: Regional Identity*, edited by Leon Litvack and Glenn Hooper (2000). Thanks are due to the editors for permission to reprint material here.

Introduction

SINCE THE ADVENT OF REVISIONISM and postcolonialism the question of historiography has acquired a high profile in Irish Studies, resulting in part in a questioning of traditional scholarly boundaries. Joep Leerssen's ground-breaking *Mere Irish and Fíor-Ghael* introduced a rigorous application of Saussurian theory and a new form of historical approach to literary texts that acknowledged their specifically literary form while situating them historically.[1] A theoretical approach to the question of literature and history is also found in David Cairns and Shaun Richards's application of Gramscian and Foucaultian concepts to the study of Irish literature.[2] Furthermore, a willingness by literary scholars to treat history on its own terms is exemplified in Terence Brown's *Ireland: A Social and Cultural History* and in W.J. McCormack's *From Burke to Beckett*.[3] In an inverse manner, R.F. Foster's *Paddy and Mr Punch* is a positive example of an Irish historian taking literary works seriously from a historian's perspective, notwithstanding the assumptions implicit in that perspective.[4] Other recent works exemplifying the desire to engage literature and history include Edna Longley's *The Living Stream*, Terry Eagleton's *Heathcliff and the Great Hunger*, Declan Kiberd's *Inventing Ireland*, Leerssen's *Remembrance and Imagination*, and Seamus Deane's *Strange Country*.[5] All of these works contribute enormously to illuminating the complex relationship between the historical and the literary, yet equally, all of them remain informed, to greater or lesser degrees, by the constrictions of the revisionism-postcolonial debate in Irish Studies today.

This book is attuned to the cultural and political forces energising that debate but it also seeks to articulate a form of critique beyond it. Far from eluding the specificity of those forces in the manner of a certain kind of deconstructive erasure of history, however, this critique aims to transcend the revisionist-postcolonial debate by pointing to a secret complicity between both schools resident at its centre. In its illumination of this complicity, the pressing need for a new assessment of the work of Standish James O'Grady and his influence on the Irish Literary Revival becomes apparent.

O'Grady may at first seem an odd figure to invoke in this context. Born in 1846, the son of a Church of Ireland Rector in County Cork, he was brought up in a tradition of strongly evangelical protestantism. First 'converted' to Irish literature and history by an encounter with Sylvester O'Halloran's *History of Ireland* (1778), he went on to produce works on Irish history and legend that were greatly

1

influenced by Thomas Carlyle's values of tradition, heroism and feudalism. Although W.B. Yeats bestowed the status of father of the Irish Literary Revival upon O'Grady, many of the writers who claimed to be influenced by him, including Yeats, also attempted to go beyond his limitations, particularly in relation to the moral conservatism informing his treatment of ancient Gaelic legend. A picture thus emerges of a writer who, if limited in creative ability by a conservative moral outlook, was important in mediating narratives of ancient Gaelic legend that would later receive a more satisfactory literary treatment in the hands of more skilled writers such as Yeats and Gregory.

This has been the persona O'Grady has come to acquire in studies of the Irish Literary Revival. Aside from the fact that it is derived in the first place from the image of O'Grady created by Yeats, it leaves in obscurity much about O'Grady's work that disturbs certain basic assumptions underlying contemporary revisionism and postcolonialism. Far from confirming the accuracy of this image, close consideration of O'Grady's main literary, historical and political works reveals a man of notable complexity whose writing carries an ideological import that is directly relevant to the most advanced current debates on questions of history, signification and gender.

Evidence of this complexity can, in the first place, be found by considering the phrase Augusta Gregory coined for O'Grady, a 'Fenian-Unionist'.[6] Whether or not the phrase is accurate, it is significant that O'Grady's politics have rarely been understood in this way subsequently. On the contrary, O'Grady has been placed by anti-revisionist critics on either side of the nationalist–unionist divide. Terry Eagleton, for example, refers to O'Grady as a 'militant unionist' yet Seamus Deane sets him alongside Padraic Pearse and Daniel Corkery in implicit opposition to Yeats and Synge.[7] In contrast, R.F. Foster is more attuned to the paradoxical persona that Gregory's description illuminates: 'And in fact O'Grady – Unionist, Carlylean, anti-democratic, at once scourge and champion of the landlord classes – was obsessed by what he called (a hundred years before Homi K. Bhaba) "the national narrative".'[8] While acknowledging that Foster's is the more informed response, the reference to Bhaba is a thinly disguised gibe at postcolonialism, a gesture that suggests Foster is interested in O'Grady as a precursor of anti-nationalist revisionism. Furthermore, if Foster argues that the complexity of O'Grady's nationalism has been strategically downplayed, it must equally be recognised that the complexity of his unionism needs to be addressed, given the fact that in the opening section of *Toryism and the Tory Democracy*, O'Grady claimed that the Act of Union was a disaster for Ireland.

The problems Eagleton, Deane and, to a lesser extent, Foster have in dealing with the paradoxical nature of O'Grady's work may be simply due to the lack of sustained critical attention he has received over the past thirty years in Irish Studies. More disturbingly, it suggests the impossibility of thinking the 'Fenian-Unionist' form within the terms of revisionism and postcolonialism in contemporary Irish Studies because of the extent to which these terms belie a

Celtic–Saxon binary opposition they purport to critique. Consequently, the vitriolic intensity of O'Grady's criticism of Irish landlords in his political work and his enthusiastic embrace of Gaelic legend and history is likely to be conceived as a cultural form of liberal unionism by revisionist criticism. Equally, any attempt to read O'Grady's work as part of the Irish nationalist legacy during the period of the Literary Revival must downplay O'Grady's recognition of the authority of constitutional monarchy and his deep hostility to rebellion during the period of the Land War and the movement for Home Rule in Ireland at the end of the nineteenth century. As a 'Fenian-Unionist' then, O'Grady calls to mind Derrida's notion of the absent centre.[9] As father of the Irish Literary Revival, his work stands at a point of origin for the ideological framework within which the Revival would develop subsequently; yet this point of origin is also the moment where this framework, structured along the binary opposites nationalist–unionist, Irish–British, or Celtic–Saxon, collapses.

The ramifications of this complexity in O'Grady's work and its influence on Æ (George W. Russell) and W.B. Yeats extend beyond considerations specific to his Irish–British context into the more general theoretical questions centred on the relationship of history to signification, made pressing over the past thirty years by the advent of postmodernism and its effect on empiricist and materialist conceptions of history. This is due to the fact that historiography emerges as the most crucial problem in O'Grady's engagement with ancient Irish mythology. His most important works, *History of Ireland: The Heroic Period*, *History of Ireland: Cuculain and His Contemporaries*, and *History of Ireland: Critical and Philosophical* are as much concerned with developing a concept of history appropriate to his objectives as they are with imparting narratives of ancient Irish history. The form of this concept and the contradictions frustrating its coherent realisation raise problems that have emerged forcefully in contemporary theory. Perhaps nowhere has the effect of developments in the field of contemporary theory been as profound as on the direction Marxist theories of history have taken over the past thirty years, an effect that has led to a seismic break from within the Marxist tradition that has taken the form of post-Marxism.

The theoretical focus of my analysis of O'Grady's work and its influence on Russell and Yeats concentrates around this transformation of Marxist theories of history in the light of poststructuralism or, more generally, postmodernism. It is a transformation that can be seen embryonically in work of O'Grady himself, in which there is a constant struggle between his sense of history as solid material fact and of the imagination as Other – spontaneous, magical and irreducible to material fact. The intellectual wrestling between Marxism and structuralism–poststructuralism has been intense over the past thirty years, particularly in the 1970s when Norman Geras was denouncing as 'idealist', Louis Althusser's project of transforming Marxist theory in structuralist terms.[10] Generally speaking, however, hard determinist Marxism has been retreating into an ever more defensive position since the 1960s and

3

it would not be oversimplistic to claim that the current fragmented condition of left-wing intellectualism within the academy may be attributed as much to an internal critique as it is to the broader geo-political developments that brought an end to the Soviet Union.

In any case, two general positions have emerged on the left out of the influence of contemporary theory, namely, neo-Marxism and post-Marxism. The first, a category described by Tony Bennett as neo-Althusserian, is distinguished by its attempt to incorporate concepts emanating from poststructuralism such as absence, textuality and discourse, into contemporary Marxist theory, without renouncing a commitment to Marxism.[11] The work of Antonio Gramsci and Louis Althusser forms the basis for much of the literature emanating from this category, supplemented by that of Pierre Macheray, Etienne Balibar and Nicos Poulantzas. The second category, post-Marxism, has developed from certain Marxist theorists entering the intellectual orbit of poststructuralism, consequently renouncing precepts fundamental to the Marxist tradition, yet continuing their theoretical analysis primarily with reference to Marxist thought.[12]

Throughout the volumes of *History of Ireland*, O'Grady struggled to articulate a concept of history appropriate to the kind of relationship between history and the imagination he wished to promote. The tensions and ambivalences that this involved, most evident in his hesitation between imaginative and empiricist conceptions of history, are emblematic of tensions in late nineteenth century intellectual culture generally, and they establish a pretext for the ambivalences (some might say the confusion), of contemporary left-wing theory in its concern to be rooted in material history but not reductionist. This is particularly evident in the blurred boundaries between neo-Marxism and post-Marxism. Matei Calinescu's criticism of Fredric Jameson, for example, reads Jameson's work as effectively post-Marxist rather than neo-Marxist.[13] Obversely, in identifying the necessity of the concept of universal history for 'the inauguration of posthistorical time' in the post-Marxism of Ernesto Laclau, Judith Butler highlights the extent of his indebtedness to the Marxist ideas he attempts to break away from, even in the realisation of that break.[14] Nevertheless, the features that define and distinguish neo-Marxism from post-Marxism remain valid and are concentrated on the relationship between history and signification. Whatever its shortcomings as a work of literary criticism, Fredric Jameson's *The Political Unconscious* remains a seminal work for the illumination of these features.

The theoretical introduction to *The Political Unconscious* is a clear example of neo-Marxism, revealing Jameson's indebtedness to Louis Althusser in the latter's determination to confront the challenges of structuralism, poststructuralism, and psychoanalysis, without abandoning a Marxist belief in history as the ultimate determinant of human consciousness. While poststructuralism's insistence on textuality and hermeneutic plurality is conceded, history nevertheless remains, in Jameson's view, 'the ultimate ground as well as the untranscendable limit of our understanding in general and our textual interpretations in particular'.[15] Reformulating Althusser, Jameson proposes 'that history is *not* a text, not a narrative, master or otherwise, but that, as an absent cause, it is inaccessible to us except in textual form, and that our approach to it and to the Real itself necessarily passes through its prior textualization, its narrativization in the political unconscious'.[16] The process by which Jameson attempts to integrate the poststructuralist concern for the autonomy of discourse (Foucault) or signification (Derrida) with a Marxist insistence on the determining force of history, rests on the movement Althusser makes away from the 'economism' of the base-superstructure analogy in classical Marxism to the concept of relative autonomy. Understood in terms of this concept, each social formation (cultural, juridical, political, economic) has its own internal discursive rules that cannot be reduced to those of any other social formation, including the economic. However, this autonomy is not absolute, since each social formation is a particular expression of the general mode of production (the global relationship obtaining between forces and relations of production), according to Althusser's theory.[17]

The primacy of the general mode of production to comprehending the dynamics of human history is central to classical Marxism. In Volume 1 of *Capital*, Marx writes that 'it is not what is made but how, and by what instruments of labour, that distinguishes different economic epochs'.[18] The mode of production is synonymous with history in Jameson's argument in *The Political Unconscious*. Just as history remains accessible only through textuality yet of itself is never reducible to that textuality, so the mode of production constitutes a global system of social relations within which individual modes of production specific to various social formations or 'levels', retain an internal discursive autonomy irreducible to any other level, according to the logic of Jameson's argument. History, in this sense, is only apprehensible in its trace or its symptoms – it is never present except as absence, as the sign of a totality the very signification of which registers itself as an absent cause.

One of the biggest challenges that Standish O'Grady's work poses for contemporary historical interpretation is the fact that the *transhistoricality* of his concept of history, effaced or underplayed in contemporary historical scholarship, becomes transparent in the volumes of *History of Ireland*. O'Grady's idea of 'great permanent relations', considered in the first chapter of this book, may be patriarchal in intention but, as a transhistorical interpretation of history, it disturbs the subject–object distinction upon which patriarchy, like empirical historiography, rests. By unveiling the transhistoricality of history, in other words, O'Grady not only subverts unintentionally his own patriarchal ideology, but also the credibility of any historical criticism that effaces its own transhistoricality. O'Grady's work reveals that all acts of historicisation are, in a sense, already transhistorical: in order to historicise, a concept of history is required that can only be subject to its own critique at the expense of collapsing the subject–object distinction that is the precondition for the act of historicisation in the first place. In contemporary Irish Studies, the revisionist interpretation of Irish history cannot 'revise' revisionism itself without collapsing its own analytical premisses. Equally, postcolonial criticism must preclude itself from its own critique if it is not to collapse in on itself. The concept of history, whether empirical, materialist or spiritual, remains outside the analytical process in order for the process to be effective. In this sense, it is always a transcendental concept, even if its analysis argues away from transcendence, as both revisionism (in attacking teleological nationalism) and postcolonialism (in undermining liberal rationality) would claim to do. It is significant, in the light of this, that one of the objections to Jameson's interpretation is that, in conceiving history as synonymous with the general mode of production, his concept of history is, in fact, transhistorical.[19] Alex Honneth's criticism of the strategy of Althusser's *Reading Capital* implicates Jameson on this point when he claims that Althusser ignored the historical specificity of *Capital* in attempting to make it the basis for an all-encompassing theory of history.[20]

Post-Marxist objections to the form of Jameson's analysis in *The Political Unconscious* centre on the credibility of his attempt to engage positively with concepts circulating around poststructuralism (textuality, absence, Other) and yet retain a commitment to the historical materialist basis of Marxist thought. From this perspective, the post-Marxist problematic is detectable in embryonic form in the work of O'Grady and in its trace in the co-operative ideology of Russell and the symbolist interpretation of history in the early Yeats. We find in O'Grady's *History of Ireland* a continual struggle between the view of history as empirical fact and of history as imaginatively created. Sometimes he leaned towards the former view, sometimes towards the latter, but for most of his literary career he tried to find a way of moving beyond the empirical–imaginative opposition. His influence on George Russell can be seen in a similar vacillation between pragmatism and idealism in Russell's ideology of co-operation and equally in Russell's attempt to transcend the subject–object binary opposition that defines these categories. The influence can also be seen in Yeats, whose attraction to symbolism in his work of the 1890s sometimes appeared as a complete surrender to the free-play of the imagination and the otherness of irrationality typical of the spirit of the decade and consonant with many of the themes in contemporary postmodernism. Equally, however, Yeats appeared interested in symbolism on other occasions as a form through which the arts could be rescued from the obscurity of aestheticism. Certainly, the view of symbolism as the transformation of the Victorian scientific view of history was never far from Yeats's thought, a view that echoes O'Grady's attempt to move beyond the empirical–imaginative opposition.[21]

There is a credible sense in which Jameson's treatment of history in his introduction to *The Political Unconscious* can be read as a late twentieth century theoretical version of the mythic form of historiography that O'Grady develops as a means to satisfying the historical and imaginative imperatives structuring his treatment of Gaelic legend, considered in Chapter 2 of this volume. Particularly in *History of Ireland: Critical and Philosophical*, O'Grady's mythic form is not so much an attempt at bringing together scientific and literary responses to history as it is an attempt to think of history beyond the opposition between the scientific and the literary, or at least to think of science itself as both factual and imaginative. Jameson insists that history is not reducible to the indeterminacy of signification as postmodernists such as Jean Baudrillard would argue, but this does not mean that his position is an empirical one, as Tony Bennett claims.[22] Empirical historiography rests on the assumption that valid evidence of past events forms the basis of what is understood as history; this view is certainly not expressed in *The Political Unconscious*; indeed, it is precisely the opposite view that Jameson expresses, that 'History can be apprehended only through its effects, and never directly as some reified force'.[23] This suggests, therefore, that Jameson, like O'Grady, is trying to conceptualise history beyond the division between empirical and imaginative models, albeit within the context of a very different theoretical discourse. If this suggests the appropriateness of Jameson's approach in analysing O'Grady's work, it equally indicates that this approach is not meta-theoretical (as contemporary theory likes to see itself) but has intellectual roots backdating to the nineteenth century.

The fundamental criticism Bennett makes of Jameson's approach centres on the concept of necessity. Indeed, it is precisely in their attitudes to the concept of necessity that post-Marxism and neo-Marxism go their separate ways. A refusal to entertain any longer the primacy of the concept of necessity in Marxist theory can be credibly identified as the instigating moment of post-Marxism, a refusal born in the context of postmodern instability within the intellectual world and the collapse of the Soviet Union in the political world. The advent of revisionism and postcolonial criticism within Irish Studies in recent decades is also to a large extent the product of an anxiety about the concept of necessity in cultural and political analysis of Ireland's history and contemporary condition. Revisionism has disputed the belief that Irish independence was rendered inevitable by its history, undermining the nationalist view that the country's history was indisputably colonial, that Ireland's 'national destiny' would one day be realised. For revisionism, this was 'not necessarily' the case, and it sees in postcolonial criticism, despite all its theoretical or para-theoretical protests, a teleological belief that it *was* necessary and, more pertinently, that it still is.[24]

Postcolonialism, on the other hand, adopts a critique of the concept of necessity from a different perspective. It identifies in revisionist strategies within Irish historical scholarship, the form of Enlightenment rationality in conflict with forces of desire, magic and the irrational. Seamus Deane comments that 'In the post-Enlightenment era, any system opposed to its [the state] regime of rationality, especially any counter-revolutionary system that appealed for its legitimation to forces or agencies that were not susceptible to rational analysis, was dismissed from consideration as a species of myth that was dependent for its survival on irrational procedures'.[25] The ideas of T.W. Moody, one of the founding members of contemporary Irish historical revisionism, exemplify this, according to Deane, in that his view of the scientific method in historical analysis aims to expose myth in nationalist accounts of Irish history and denigrate it as rhetoric.[26] In Deane's view, the onslaught of contemporary critical theory destabilises fundamentally the empirical, rational basis upon which revisionism rests. In consequence, the *necessary* relationship of the cause–effect logic structuring empirical rationality is broken. Implicit in Deane's argument is the view that, in so far as revisionism is conceived as the constant effort to be more scientifically accurate about the past, consistently revising the received view in a spirit akin to Karl Popper's falsifiability theory of scientific method, it remains enthralled to the concept of necessity.[27]

Bennett's criticism of Jameson's concept of history as necessity, therefore, impacts on revisionism and postcolonialism in Irish Studies in a manner relevant to assessing Standish O'Grady's work and its influence. Bennett comments:

> ...by making Necessity the ontological basis of, and therefore epistemological guarantee for, a Marxist narrativisation of History rooted in the category of the mode of production, this fundamental category is itself radically transformed: no longer an articulated combination of forces and relations of production, it becomes merely a specific expression and organisation of the relations between two ahistorical essences – Desire and Necessity – locked in an eternal and irresolvable antagonism.[28]

The criticism rests on the view that Jameson's understanding of the mode of production is distinct from his definition of history, the difference being that the former is historical while, ironically, the latter is not. The distinction Bennett draws here is challenged, however, by the fact that within Jameson's argument the mode of production, like history, can only be seen in its effects:

> If...one wishes to characterise Althusser's Marxism as a structuralism, one must complete the characterisation with the essential proviso that it is a structuralism for which only *one* structure exists: namely the mode of production itself, or the synchronic system of social relations as a whole. This is the sense in which this 'structure' is an absent cause, since it is nowhere empirically present as an element, it is not a part of the whole or one of the levels, but rather the entire system of *relationships* among those levels.[29]

In the light of this, the mode of production is synonymous with history conceived as that structural totality irreducible to particular linguistic and discursive forms, but only perceptible as a trace within those particular forms. Given that Jameson defines history as the experience of necessity, this implies that the mode of production only becomes apparent in the experience of necessity. This position is potentially a new reductionism, since it implies that desire conceals the mode of production, whereas necessity reveals it.

The consideration of O'Grady's work and its influence on Russell and Yeats in the following chapters indicates that Jameson's definition of history needs to be revised dialectically in order to render it compatible with the concept of the mode of production in a non-reductionist fashion. Thinking briefly of O'Grady's work in terms of Althusser's concept of relative autonomy, the basis for such a revision becomes apparent. In Althusser's concept, each discursive formation within a social structure corresponds to a particular 'level'; the relationship between all levels constitutes the mode of production, but no one particular level is reducible to another. These discursive formations are cultural, legal, political and economical and, of course, have subset levels within them, e.g. the discourses of aesthetics and anthropology within a cultural discursive formation. There are three broad levels within O'Grady's work; the literary, the historical, and the political. Each of these levels carries a degree of discursive autonomy: O'Grady's *History of Ireland: Critical and Philosophical* is historical rather than literary (though the concept of history is revised within the work). His novels *Lost on Du-Corrig* and *The Chain of Gold*, are clearly literary, though O'Grady's position on history and politics is imparted through them, while *Toryism and the Tory Democracy* is obviously political, though again, O'Grady's position on history and literature is implicit within the work.

My analysis in the following chapters indicates that to deny the autonomy of these levels in O'Grady's work is to fail to recognise the work's contemporary relevance. To read the volumes of *History of Ireland* simply as literary with no credibility as works of history is to leave unexamined the manner in which history is being conceptually revised in those volumes. Similarly, to read his novels exclusively as codifications of the political and economic circumstances of O'Grady's class at the end of the nineteenth century is to miss the significance of the literary transformation of myth in those works. History is *not* literature nor is literature politics in O'Grady's writing. No one level is reducible to the other. However, if any body of work supports the view that these discursive formations are relatively rather than absolutely autonomous, it is O'Grady's. To attempt to consider his concern with history without reference to the imaginative orientation predominant in his fictional work or his political ideology is simply impossible; each level is structurally interrelated.

This fact is reconcilable with the evident autonomy of history, literature and politics in O'Grady's writing when it is recognised that difference is a necessary prerequisite for this autonomy from the outset. The autonomy of history as a discursive formation in his work becomes pronounced when the distinctiveness of history from the imagination or from politics is emphasised, i.e. in those moments when O'Grady tries to present his method as scientific. In these moments, the imaginative and the political function as the Other of O'Grady's historical discourse. This Other of historical discourse simultaneously establishes its power and its limitations as a discursive formation; the power-urge driving its knowledge claims as an autonomous discourse and the confinement of these knowledge claims to that discourse. From the perspective of empirical historical scholarship, then, O'Grady appears unconvincing as a historian when his treatment of history appears literary and political but is more convincing when on those rare occasions his literary and political concerns do not intervene. The more the Other of historical discourse (literature, politics) manifests itself within the discourse itself, the weaker its epistemological authority becomes. The necessary presence of this Other as absence within O'Grady's historical discourse can be interpreted as the trace of the mode of production; conceived in this way, the mode of production becomes the ground of a dialectic of necessity and desire within this discourse. This indicates that Jameson's definition of history as necessity ought to be reformulated as the ground of necessity and desire, in order to make it compatible with his understanding of the mode of production. With such a reformulation, the apparent discrepancy between the concepts of the mode of production and of history in Jameson's argument ceases to exist because necessity and desire are inscribed in Althusser's concept of relative autonomy; they express the paradox of the autonomy of a discursive formation as simultaneously signalling its power and its limitation.

As illustrated in the consideration of O'Grady's influence on Russell and Yeats in Chapters 5 and 6, the reception of O'Grady's work confirms this view of discourse as relatively autonomous in structure. The literary mode by which Yeats advances upon O'Grady's writing involved dispensing with the Victorian features Yeats identified in it, particularly O'Grady's concern for empirical history. Implicit in this is Yeats's belief that O'Grady was restricted artistically by a need to make his literary treatment of Gaelic legend credible from an empirical historical perspective; O'Grady's attempt to assimilate a non-literary discourse to a literary one limited him aesthetically. Obversely, any *empirical* historical credibility that O'Grady's *History of Ireland* has is dissipated by the literary form of his approach to historical material; this 'literariness' limits his strengths as a historian, from the perspective of conventional historical scholarship. Autonomy, therefore, reveals the dialectical nature of discourse in so far as the epistemological coherence of any discourse (its claims of necessity) are inseparable from its epistemological limits (or contingency). Viewed from within the framework of academic specialisation (intensified throughout the twentieth century), the better O'Grady was as a historian, the worse he was as a creative writer and vice versa.

In a seminal work of post-Marxist thought, Ernesto Laclau and Chantal Mouffe's *Hegemony and Socialist Strategy*, the authors unwittingly affirm this dialectical interpretation of discourse while denying the validity of dialectics in their general argument. In arguing for the 'unfixity of the social' in their theory of hegemony, they claim that 'not only does the very category of necessity fall, but it is no longer possible to account for the hegemonic relation in terms of pure contingency, as the space which made intelligible the necessary/contingent opposition has dissolved'.[30] This argument is structurally dialectical, the category of necessity functioning as thesis, contingency as antithesis, and the space beyond the necessary/contingent opposition as synthesis. Furthermore, Laclau and Mouffe concede that this space is not intelligible within current theoretical categories and that the development of new categories that would make it so, 'constitutes a problem'.[31] If contingency is conceived in terms of its psychoanalytical corollary, desire (since both function as forms of absence denying the closure of necessity), then it is possible to conceive of the space beyond the necessity/contingency opposition as analogous to the concept of history as the ground of necessity and desire, a history not intelligible except in terms of its effects. Considered in this way, Laclau and Mouffe's argument comes very close to my reformulation of Jameson's definition of history as a dialectic of necessity and desire.

Laclau is forceful in his denial of the legitimacy of dialectics in the context of poststructuralism because he views it as an indubitably necessitarian form of thought. In *New Reflections on the Revolution of Our Time*, Laclau argues that the antithetical or negative moment in dialectics, corresponding to contingency, is structurally subordinate to the necessary character of the dialectic as a whole:

> The Hegelian notion of negativity is that of a necessary negativity and as such was conceived as *determinate* negation. That is to say that the negative is a moment in the internal unfolding of the concept which is destined to be reabsorbed in an *Aufhebung*, or higher unity... Contingency itself is absorbed as a moment in the self-unfolding of the necessary.[32]

It is precisely this necessity of contingency to dialectical thought, however, that indicates the fundamentally anti-determinist nature of the Marxist concept of history. Without contingency, only the empty metaphysical concept of self-identity remains. Even if, as in Hegel's presentation of dialectics, this metaphysical concept remains as its *telos*, the introduction of the negative moment as a necessary one splits self-identity and reveals necessity and contingency as a binary relationship in which both terms contradict yet depend on each other. In dialectics, therefore, necessity depends on contingency for its realisation and contingency exists under erasure as a moment necessary in its very contingency.

This necessity of contingency to the dialectical method reveals the necessity of the irrational to the form of rationality it embodies. Significantly, the shift from mysticism to rationality that, Marx argued, was the basis of the difference between his own and Hegel's dialectical method, involved the destructive force of a negativity that highlighted the necessity of contingency to dialectical rationality:

> In its rational form it [the dialectic] is a scandal and an abomination to the bourgeoisie and its doctrinaire spokesmen, because it includes in its positive understanding of what exists a simultaneous recognition of its negation, its inevitable destruction; because it regards every historically developed form as being in a fluid state, in motion, and therefore grasps its transient aspect as well; and because it does not let itself be impressed by anything, being in its very essence critical and revolutionary.[33]

That Laclau and Mouffe remain within this form of dialectical thought in an argument that denounces dialectics is revealed by the fact that the category of necessity must be retained in their articulation of an anti-necessitarian argument and that undecidability functions as a structural principle, thereby acquiring a necessary status in the act of subverting necessity.[34] Gerard Raulet argues that 'there is in Marx himself the outline of a complex relation between rationality and irrationality whereby modernization is both the accomplishment of reason and the height of irrationality since it remains dominated by a rupture...'[35] Acknowledging that it was Marx's intention to abolish this irrationality, Raulet nevertheless claims that 'already in Marx modernity is actually lived as a crisis of rationality', a point that becomes emphatic in the work of Walter Benjamin and Theodor Adorno.[36]

A definition of modernity as the inescapability of dialectics, then, emerges from a consideration of neo-Marxist and post-Marxist interpretations of the relationship of history to signification. This suggests that the postmodern celebration of absence, desire and contingency may be destined to mutate into the hermetic absolutism it has rightly despised in the totalitarian propensities of Enlightenment rationality (including that of scientific socialism) without attunement to *ressentiment*; the burden of presence, repulsion (Sartre's 'viscosity') and necessity without which non-identity cannot be thought. The pertinence of this for the revisionist–postcolonial debate in Irish Studies becomes apparent in the effacement of this dialectical form through the sublimation of nationalist tendencies (however subaltern–postmodern) within postcolonialism and in the sublimation of unionist tendencies (however liberal–modern) within revisionism.

This sublimation can be seen by paraphrasing the postcolonial argument as follows: the Irish nationalist tradition may have been flawed in many respects but, given the catastrophic legacy of British imperial conquest in Ireland, it has been a necessary one. In the light of this, revisionist attacks on the central elements of this tradition, however emancipatory those attacks might seem, can, with legitimacy, be suspected as part of a continuing strategy, backdated at least as far as 'killing Home Rule with Kindness', of suppressing counter-hegemonic forces within Ireland under a liberal, rational guise.[37] Equally, the revisionist argument may be paraphrased: the history of British involvement in Ireland has been greatly destructive, yet ultimately necessary as a modernising, liberalising force. From this perspective, Irish nationalism, even as a liberal Celtic Tiger, must always be subject to strong interrogation, given its legacy of communalist intolerance, reactionary hysteria and violence.[38]

Paraphrasing the application of postcolonial and revisionist readings in Irish Studies in this way does not do justice to the degree of variety within both discourses – Colin Graham's postcolonial critique of Irish nationalism is a case in point.[39] It is difficult not to accept, however, that Graham's use of postcolonial theory is the exception rather than the norm in Irish Studies to date and that historical and literary revisionism associate postcolonialism with a 'theoretical' embrace of Irish national identity. This being the case, the extent to which postcolonialism and revisionism oppositionally feed off each other becomes apparent, indicative of their effacement of the dialectical form I have identified with modernity.

O'Grady's work brings to the forefront a dialectical form of thought that subverts these discourses without eluding the conflictual energy out of which they have arisen. As a committed unionist dedicated to awakening a sense of Irish identity among the landed gentry, O'Grady is a contradictory personality living out the dialectics of history in a stark manner, igniting a cultural Renaissance that was marked with the imprint of his thought even when it was least acknowledged; whether he intended it or not, the complex nature of his work defies attempts to assimilate him to either side of the unionist–nationalist divide. The analysis offered in the following chapters is fuelled by a sense of the importance of this contradiction structuring his writing and its influence on George Russell and W.B. Yeats. The ideology of co-operation that Russell developed out of his involvement with the Irish Co-operative Movement and Yeats's treatment of history in his early work, both heavily influenced by O'Grady, reveal the extent to which their writing was structured by modernity conceived in its full dialectical sense. In the light of this, it might be said that the most important feature of the legacy of Standish James O'Grady was the capacity to think dialectically.

Fathering the Revival:
O'Grady's quest for origins

THE PROBLEM IN ATTRIBUTING AN ORIGIN to the Irish Literary Revival of the late nineteenth and early twentieth century is that it depends on how the Revival is understood. Was it primarily a literature of 'masculine' heroism focused on Cuchulainn, or a literature of 'feminine' subtlety, pathos and imaginative freedom? Was it driven by an epical impulse that became the cultural expression of a political movement towards national self-determination, or by a lyrical impulse that expressed a Romantic revolt against modernisation and the hegemony of instrumental rationality through which it developed? Was it driven by a desire to transcend the opposition between the epical and the lyrical, to infuse the grandeur of a national ideal with the subtlety of individualistic cosmopolitanism? (W.B. Yeats appeared to think so, certainly in his 1893 essay 'Nationality and Literature'.) The kinds of response offered to these questions inevitably bears upon the choice of location proposed for the origin of the Revival itself, thereby discrediting the belief that such a location could be established in an ideological vacuum, independent of any prior interpretation of what the Revival actually was. This is made starkly evident, for example, in the source Christopher Murray locates for the modern Irish theatre that emerged in the Revival – Duras House, on the Doorus peninsula in County Galway, where Yeats and Lady Gregory laid plans for the foundations of the Irish Literary Theatre in 1897. The location is symbolically appropriate for the nationalist form through which Murray views modern Irish drama. Of the environ, he remarks: 'Christian and pagan remains lie cheek by jowl; myth and history are intermixed. It is a landscape inscribed with thousands of years of culture.'[1] If the nation is to be the dominant, even exclusive, concern of modern Irish drama, as Murray believes it is, then its origins must be national; hence, the dramatic movement springs from a location where 'myth and history are intermixed'.

Seamus Deane identifies two Celtic Revivals in Irish literary history since the eighteenth century. The first, which included the writing of Charlotte Brooke, Lady Morgan, Thomas Moore's *Irish Melodies* and the musical scores of Edward Bunting, emerged in the latter half of the eighteenth century and was marked by an 'odd confusion of Teutonic, Celtic and "old British" elements'.[2] He claims that this was brought to an end by the Famine, the death of Daniel O'Connell and the failed rebellion of 1847, and that the path was already being cleared for the second Celtic Revival in the work of Carleton,

Mangan, Davis and *The Nation* ballads. Deane cites the first volume of Standish O'Grady's *History of Ireland* as the moment when the Revival got underway.³ In tracing the origins of the Revival in this manner, the seminal importance Deane attributes to the influence of Edmund Burke on Ireland's cultural history since the eighteenth century is accommodated and the more recent Revival is situated firmly within the framework of European Romanticism, a factor that becomes important for Deane's reading of Yeats in *Celtic Revivals*. Terry Eagleton also looks to O'Grady as a point of origin for the Revival, but also as a point of transition in the nineteenth century from the antiquarian/historical to the imaginative approach to Irish culture; O'Grady's work exhibits a shift from academic to creative writing and 'the major imaginative works which were never forthcoming from Young Ireland begin to appear'.⁴ Eagleton's claim here is illuminating, precisely because O'Grady's work is infused throughout with a tension between the historical and imaginative approach. In marking his work as the point of origin for the Revival, Eagleton implicitly concedes that although there is a shift to the imaginative, a concern for empirical historical fact characteristic of the historical approach might be said to reside within the unconscious of the Revival itself, thus problematising the view of the Revival as an imaginative 'flight' from historical reality.

Others have challenged the view of O'Grady as instigator of the Revival. Jerry C.M. Nolan comments that on the basis of George Russell's extraordinary testimonies to O'Grady's influence on him, 'E.A. Boyd, using a very narrow focus, misleadingly concluded that O'Grady was Father of the Literary Revival in Ireland'.⁵ Vivian Mercier turns to an antiquarian work, Eugene O'Curry's *Lectures on the Manuscript Materials of Ancient Irish History* (1861) as 'the prime source-text of the Literary Revival'.⁶ Certainly O'Curry's work, along with his *On the Manners and Customs of the Ancient Irish* (1873), jointly edited with W.K. Sullivan, and most importantly, Sylvester O'Halloran's *A General History of Ireland* (1778), were all important source material for O'Grady. His first encounter with this last work came as a new discovery that inspired an almost spiritual conversion to Irish history and legend.⁷ The notion, however, that the Revival had its origins in these works is misleading to the extent that the Revival itself represented a movement beyond the antiquarian, pseudo-scientific approach adopted by O'Curry, O'Halloran and others. O'Grady's early work is more satisfactory as a point of origin, because it is positioned at a critical moment in the movement from the empirical to the aesthetic treatment of Irish history and legend: more precisely, it involves an epistemological shift in which the distinctive categories empirical and aesthetic become objective and are thereby transformed.

Perhaps the most convincing alternative to O'Grady as a point of origin for the Revival is Samuel Ferguson. Ferguson had been writing for many decades before O'Grady, converting Irish manuscript source material into poetic and narrative forms. He anticipated the epic aspiration of O'Grady's *History of Ireland* in his epic poem 'Congal', which he first began working on in 1842 and completed, more or less, by 1861, though the poem was not published until 1872, six years before the first volume of O'Grady's work.[8] The work set a poetic precedent for the epic orientation of O'Grady's work, and Aubrey De Vere dedicated his own epical poetic effort *The Foray of Queen Maeve* (1882) to Ferguson, 'for Congal, and for many poems beside, that illustrate aright the legends of ancient Ireland'.[9] However, Ferguson's direct influence on O'Grady must not be overstated. Although, as Malcolm Browne notes, the young O'Grady was a regular visitor at Ferguson's residence, O'Grady claimed that he was never aware that Ferguson was 'a great Irish poet' during this time.[10] Nevertheless, it is impossible to underestimate the influence of a writer once described by Yeats as the 'greatest poet Ireland has produced, because the most central and most Celtic', notwithstanding Yeats's characteristic hyperbole.[11]

Some considerations, however, mitigate against the view of Ferguson as originating the Revival. M.A.G. O'Tuathaigh comments that 'before Ferguson's death, a younger man [Standish O'Grady], gifted with a livelier imagination and untroubled by the scholarly scruple of the older man, fell captive to the heroic sagas and sowed the seeds of a literary renaissance'.[12] A quality of scholarly refinement surrounds much of Ferguson's verse that lends it an aura of antiquity, far from the exigencies of the contemporary world. Certainly there are sublime, even gothic, moments in much of Ferguson's verse, particularly in 'Congal', but these are usually dissipated by this general sense of antiquity, a feeling for a Gaelic past the heroic sentiments of which are to be admired and the cultural artefacts of which are deserving of scholarly interest, but a past that exhibits values inappropriate in a society 'civilised' by the practice of objective reasoning. Peter Denman argues that Ferguson constantly sought a connection between the remote Gaelic past buried in the manuscripts from which he drew source material for his poetry, and his own age, domesticating rather than exoticising that past.[13] This act of domestication, however, ensured that whenever connections between antiquity and contemporaneity were made, they were couched in a framework in which the divisions and disruptions of the nineteenth century were distilled. Indeed, despite Denman's observation, it is not implausible to observe a certain displacement at work in Ferguson's treatment of Gaelic antiquity, in which the political turmoil of the nineteenth century is projected onto a far distant past rather than confronted in all its ugly immediacy. This worked to provide a pretext for distinguishing that past from the present in terms of barbarism and civilisation. David Lloyd observes this process in Ferguson's essays on Hardiman's *Irish Minstrelsy*:

> Ferguson's aim was to present a theory of the gradual development of the native Irish loyalties from the immediate clan to the idea of a

constitutional monarchy, obliging a transition from investment in the senuous to investment in the supersensuous. Knowledge thus becomes unifying rather than – as with Hardiman – divisive and sectarian.[14]

Traces of this propensity to civilised order are evident in O'Grady's work. He shared with Ferguson much of that Victorian disposition observed by Peter Denman in the latter's treatment of old Irish sagas.[15] However, much more overtly than in Ferguson's *œuvre*, the anxieties residual in that same disposition become manifest in O'Grady's writing, thereby opening up a space for a radical rethinking of categories presumed in Ferguson. Furthermore, because O'Grady sought direct connection between Gaelic antiquity and contemporary Ireland, the impact of these latent anxieties becoming manifest became culturally and politically disturbing. Far from simply seeking to present Irish legend as an antique curiosity that would act as a symbol of cultivation in a land judged backward by many English commentators, O'Grady sought to go further than Ferguson, to render the Irish cultural legacy a vehicle of cultural and political renewal.[16] From this perspective, the contrast between Ferguson and O'Grady might be compared to that between Matthew Arnold the rational liberal and Thomas Carlyle the rhetorical radical. Unlike Ferguson, O'Grady made explicit his hope that his work would instigate a cultural renaissance in Ireland:

> I would also add when I consider the extraordinary stimulus which the perusal of that [Irish bardic] literature gives to the imagination, even in centuries like these, and its wealth of elevated and intensely human characters, that, as I anticipate, with the revival of Irish literary energy and the return of Irish self-esteem, the artistic craftsmen of the future will find therein and in unfailing abundance, the material of persons and sentiments fit for the highest purposes of epic and dramatic literature and of art, pictorial and sculptoral.[17]

That this clarion call was responded to in varying degrees is shown in the range of writers who acknowledged their debt to O'Grady, including Æ, T.W. Rolleston, John Todhunter, Aubrey de Vere, Austin Clarke and W.B. Yeats.[18] Although many of these writers exhibited a lyric rather than an epic sensibility in their literature, O'Grady's influence came through in the epic characters and events of Gaelic legend they chose as subject matter.

In addition, O'Grady's claims as a historian distinguish him from Ferguson. Particularly in Ferguson's essays on James Hardiman's *Irish Minstrelsy* that were published in the *Dublin University Magazine* in 1834, a Hegelian view of history is implicit in much of Ferguson's cultural endeavours.[19] However, the potentially radical aspect of this view of history, later exploited by Marx, remained confined to the subject matter of Gaelic antiquity in Ferguson's work. Denman comments that the 'major thrust of his life's activities, as poet, antiquarian, and archivist, was to gather, decipher and record the traces of the Irish past'.[20] In this endeavour, however, empiricism, or what O'Grady would describe as the 'archeological' approach to the past, remained largely unquestioned. Though a quiet but uneasy dialogue between them is maintained throughout his career, Ferguson's practical 'Head' remains master of his romantic 'Heart'.[21] O'Grady, however, shifted the perspective on the Gaelic past, seeking to bring his particular version of it into contact with contemporary history in order to transform the social and political landscape. In the process, the disinterestedness characteristic of the empirical approach to history was brought into disrepute, making it virtually impossible to return to the security of the antiquarianism. The imaginative appropriation of history in the Literary Revival that followed O'Grady's early writing is testimony to the major shift that takes place in that writing.

History of Ireland: The Heroic Period and *History of Ireland: Cuculain and His Contemporaries* were O'Grady's most influential works; given the importance of his influence, the principles upon which his bardic histories are based take on great significance. Of such principles, the most ostensible is O'Grady's notion of history culminating in art, which he outlines in *History of Ireland: Critical and Philosophical*:

> Romance, epic, drama and artistic representation are at all times the points to which history continually aspires – there only its final development and efflorescence. Archeology culminates in history, history culminates in art.[22]

This idea contains in embryo O'Grady's attitude to history and the imagination that pervades *History of Ireland*. In viewing art as the fullest expression of history, he attempts to break from a purely empirical historiography in which a pursuit of fact using methods broadly conceived as scientific forms the starting point for any investigation of the past. In rejecting this approach, it is tempting to view O'Grady's position on history and art as anticipating the argument made by Oscar Wilde in 'The Decay of Lying' of 1889 for life as an imitation of art.[23] However, if O'Grady's idea opposes a purely empirical approach to history, it also opposes an aestheticist eliding of history. If his position is an implicit rebuke to Matthew Arnold's notion of the Celt as one who reacts against the despotism of fact, it is also a rejection of Oscar Wilde's celebration of this notion.[24] The idea expresses the belief that historical fact is as inseparable from the imagination as the imagination is inseparable from historical fact and O'Grady's endeavour throughout *History of Ireland* is to illustrate that this is the case. This belief was shared by Friedrich Nietzsche who, four years before the publication of *History of Ireland: The Heroic Period*, expressed an idea remarkably similar to that of O'Grady:

> Anything that constrains a man to love less than unconditionally has severed the roots of his strength: he will wither away, that is to say, become dishonest. In producing this effect, history is the antithesis of art: and only if history can endure to be transformed into a work of art will it perhaps

be able to preserve instincts or even evoke them. Such a historiography would, however, be altogether contrary to the analytical and inartistic tendencies of our time, which would indeed declare it false.[25]

Most of all, however, the idea revealed the enormous influence of Thomas Carlyle on O'Grady's thought. Throughout his writing career, Carlyle criticised twin features of contemporary England that he regarded as corrosive – empirical science and its intellectual off-shoot, utilitarianism, and dilettantism, conceived as a disengagement of artistic culture, co-terminous with the disengagement of the aristocracy, from contemporary historical reality. He viewed history as highest among the arts in his own time, but was deeply critical of the scientific tendency in historical practice in which history was treated as something that could be calculated in an empirical fashion, a practice that he believed to be on the wane in Europe, influenced as he was by the rise of Hegel's philosophy of world history in Germany during the 1830s:

> However, that class of cause-and-effect speculators, with whom no wonder would remain wonderful, but all things in Heaven and Earth must be computed and 'accounted for;' and even the Unknown, the Infinite in man's Life, had, under the words *enthusiasm, superstition, spirit of the age* and so forth, obtained, as it were, an algebraical symbol and given value, have now wellnigh played their part in European culture;[26]

Carlyle is equally scathing of a literary culture disengaged from all sense of historical reality, writing of dilettantes as 'looking out through those blinking smoke-bleared eyes of theirs, into the wonderfulest universal smoky Twilight and undecipherable disordered Dusk of Things; wholly an Uncertainty, Unintelligibility, they and it'.[27] Carlyle believed that utilitarianism, of which the purely empirical approach to history was one form, existed dialectically with dilettantism, as opposing forms of what he regarded as the general malaise of society in nineteenth-century industrial Britain. In the following passage, Drudgism expresses the mechanical nature of society emerging during the Industrial Revolution, Dandyism the retreat of aristocratic culture from engagement with historical reality in the face of the predominance of science:

> Or better, I might call them two boundless, and indeed unexampled Electric Machines (turned by the 'Machinery of Society'), with batteries of opposite quality; Drudgism the Negative, Dandyism the Positive: one attracts hourly towards it and appropriates all the Positive Electricity of the nation (namely, the Money thereof); the other is equally busy with the Negative (that is to say Hunger), which is equally potent.[28]

Although O'Grady's concept of history appears to be typological in the volumes of *History of Ireland*, an argument for permanence through change, the influence of Carlyle indicates that it is dialectical in structure. If 'art' is the culminating point in O'Grady's concept of history, 'archeology' is, nevertheless, its bedrock, and the attempt to disengage historical fact from the imagination feeds into the malady that Carlyle's concept of history, like O'Grady's after him, is designed to expose, just as destructively as the utilitarian denial of the relevance of the imagination.[29]

The dialectical structure governing O'Grady's idea of history culminating in art is manifested throughout *History of Ireland: The Heroic Period*, in a relentless pursuit of a unified vision of history and the contradictions that surface in the process. The first fifteen chapters of the book develop from vague speculation, in which O'Grady grapples with the 'archeological' fragmentation of Irish pre-history, to confident assertion, whereby he locates the festival of Tara as the point of origin for Irish history proper, an assertion that announces the beginning of his epic narrative. He opens with a reflection on the origins of the Irish race, arguing that of the eight distinct races of man, the two most important were the Turanian, from the northern regions, and the Scythian, from the south. He argues that civilised society originated in the latter, 'the Mediterranean and Semitic peoples', believing that the northerners exhibited a compulsion to destroy their society throughout ancient history.[30] O'Grady extrapolates an argument for the superiority of Irish among northern peoples from this premise, contending that Irish blood was a mixture of southern Basque and northern Celt, the former injecting a quality of civilisation otherwise absent.[31] This view provides the basis for his distinction between what he regards as the imaginative southern Irish and the militaristic Ulster Irish. The argument is a subtle refutation of Matthew Arnold's Celticism, for it transposes Arnold's concept of civility from the Saxon to the Latin temperament. Irish culture, from O'Grady's perspective, is not an anarchic phenomenon in need of the civilising force of Saxon rationality, but the source of a unique combination of civility and barbarism that might refine a will to destruction he associates with the ethnic origins of northern races.

This illustrates how Gaelic legend acquires Hellenistic status for O'Grady. If the superiority of Greek culture was defined by a combination of measure and excess, as Arnold conceived it was in *On The Study of Celtic Literature*, then Gaelic culture would acquire equal superiority if it could be shown to possess this combination also.[32] O'Grady's determination to show that this combination *was* present in the Gaelic bardic material indicates the extent to which he sought to turn Arnold's presentation of Celticism on its head. It is clear that O'Grady's argument was also directed against the historian and biographer of Thomas Carlyle, James Anthony Froude, whose attitude to Ireland in *The English in Ireland in the Eighteenth Century*, first published in 1872, fully endorsed Arnold's gendering of the Celt as feminine in, for the most part, an extremely condescending and negative tone. Froude describes the Irish as 'the spendthrift sister of the Arian race'.[33] He writes of the 'incompleteness' of Irish character, the Irish lacking, in his view, 'the manliness which will give strength and solidity to the sentimental part of their dispositions'.[34]

However, if O'Grady's combination of Turanian and Sythian in Gaelic civilisation could be presented as a justification of its cultural superiority, it might also be presented as evidence of the uniquely contradictory nature of that civilisation. His attempt to establish the unity of the Gael, as a combination of 'barbarous' north and 'civilised' south, magnifies the division it seeks to overcome in the very act of imagining a resolution of it. Considered analogous to his historiography, O'Grady's racial theory illuminates the contradiction in his treatment of the imagination and history; he tries to combine the 'barbarous' north of empirical fact with the 'civilised' south of imagination but fails to overcome the contradiction between both. This becomes clear as his work progresses, in the sense that the more earnestly he seeks to overcome the dichotomy of empirical history and imaginative flight from history, the more inexorable that dichotomy appears.[35]

O'Grady's speculations on the ethnic origins of Gaelic history prefigure the dichotomies that emerge in the course of *History of Ireland*, but at this juncture in the work it appears that O'Grady invokes them to illustrate the inadequacy of an empirical approach to uncovering the earliest facts of history. Following the ethnic discussion, he turns to an eleventh century historian, Tierna, in grappling with the problem of historical fact in this context. O'Grady cites Tierna in claiming that Irish history began as late as the twelfth century BC, with the kingship of Kimbay MacFiontann at Emain Macha: '…behind Tierna's point of departure, his *fons et origo* of Irish history, lies a vast silent land, a land of the dead, a vast continent of the dead, lit with pale phosphoric radiance'.[36]

This highlights a crisis of origin besetting O'Grady's historiography from the outset. By conceiving of Emain Macha as the site of the origin of Irish history, O'Grady presumes that its pre-history is a form of death, of non-origin. The historical credibility that O'Grady attributes to Emain Macha as such a site, therefore, is subject to the destabilising contingency that this pre-history introduces. Michel Foucault argues that such splitting is the condition of origin; traditionally conceived, the origin was always superseded by the Fall, and in contemporary times 'a new cruelty of history…compels a reversal of this relationship and the abandonment of "adolescent" quests: behind the always recent, avaricious, and measured truth, it posits the ancient proliferation of errors'.[37] Therefore, the spectre of death, revealed here as the contingency underlying the necessary status of Emain Macha as the site of historical origin, lies within O'Grady's historiographic project from the outset, a spectre that becomes overt in Yeats's response to O'Grady's work.[38]

O'Grady argues that from Emain Macha onwards, Irish history evolved through the transformation of chaos into order, an order whose principles were aristocratic, both aesthetically and politically. He writes of the satisfaction derived from tracing the growth of kingship in Ireland as akin to contemplating the gradual formation of warring tribes into a united people:

the chaos of confusion and aimless strugglings concentrate gradually into the wise and determined action of a nation, fulfilling its part in the great national confraternity of the world.[39]

The unity associated with the concept of the nation presented here is a further instance of the structure of O'Grady's method; the 'aimless strugglings' pointing to the atomistic, fragmented nature of history when conceived from a purely empirical perspective, and their transformation into national history suggesting the imaginative forming of an otherwise fragmented history that O'Grady's *History of Ireland* undertakes. However, the crisis of origin that all dialectical structures of thought necessarily involve is also introduced in the process; the unity that O'Grady aspires to is already split, the order he pursues existing in a necessary dialectical relationship to the anarchy it attempts to transcend.[40] This emerges during *History of Ireland* as a crisis of gender, in which O'Grady's pursuit of order and unity reveals itself as a struggle for masculine authority over the feminine Other, a struggle that the attempt to unify historical fact and imagination embodies.[41]

Running parallel to this emergence of a nation out of the fragmentation of pre-history is the emergence of the hero, aesthetically personified in chapter eleven by the figure of Fionn McCool whose delight it was 'to sleep by the cataract of Assaroe, to hear the scream of the sea-gulls over Eyerus, to listen to the blackbird of Derry Carn'.[42] As someone personifying the emergence of epic heroism within history, Fionn enjoys extensive treatment in *Finn and His Companions*, published in 1892, but O'Grady employs him at this point of *History of Ireland* to introduce the heroic value-system underlying his narrative treatment of Cuchulainn, the most important character in his work as a whole. Before he embarks on that narrative, however, O'Grady concludes the preamble that began with the speculations on ethnic origins of Gaelic civilisation by focusing on the festival of Tara, the historical emergence of which, he claims, was evidence of the development of a quasi-national aristocracy in ancient Ireland. He discusses the importance of the 'feis' in early Irish society, not just for sporting contest, with which it has most often been associated, but also for its political and commercial purposes. Claiming that the feis of Tara was the most important in the country, O'Grady argues that the history of Ireland begins in earnest with the conflicts between rival tribes to hold the throne of Tara. Tara became a binding place where the chieftain lent 'dignity and authority to the fair, and the importance of the fair extended the influence and renown of the chieftain'.[43] His perspective shapes the festival of Tara as a meeting point of chaos and order; the divisive rivalries of the tribes analogous to the fragmented nature of Irish pre-history and the authority of the chieftain analogous to the emergence of nationhood as fragmented history 'authorially' formed. O'Grady as author thus creatively moulds his narrative in terms of what he perceives to be the historical basis of patriarchal authority. Although this view of Tara is conditioned by the Victorian conservatism informing O'Grady's work throughout *History of Ireland*, it reflects Mikhail Bakhtin's claim that medieval festival occasions were ones of transgression *and* renewal; if authority is contested, as it is in O'Grady's presentation of the feis, so is there continuity: 'Bare negation is completely alien to folk culture'.[44] Once more, however, O'Grady's pursuit of unity amplifies the division it seeks to overcome; the 'necessity' of monarchical authority exists in a necessary relationship to the 'contingency' of tribal contest; the festival is a pre-requisite for the establishment of the unifying *telos* of nationhood, yet it also bears witness to the division that rivalry and contest reveal.

In chapter fifteen O'Grady brings his discussion of Tara to a close and begins the main narrative of *History of Ireland*, the saga of Cuchulainn. Echoing Milton in his prologue to *Paradise Lost*, O'Grady invokes the spirits of the ancient Gaelic bards and the spirits of the soil of Ireland to guide him in this 'epic' endeavour to create an epic version of ancient Irish history:

> Spirits of the ancient bards, my ancestors, and ye sacred influences that haunt for ever the soil and air of my country, nameless now and unworshipped, but strong and eternal, be with me and befriend, that in circles worthy so glorious singing their praise upon whom nations looked back as upon their first and best, with a flight unfailing I may rise to regions where no wing of laborious ollav or chanting shanachie ever yet fanned that thinner air.[45]

Although, in a manner similar to Carlyle's *History of the French Revolution*, O'Grady hoped to create an epic of Irish history that might attain Miltonic, or even Homeric, status, this invocation is more than simply an attempt to imitate these canonical figures. Nor is it just a conventional literary device employed to end the prologue and begin the main narrative. It is symbolic, introduced to signal the meaning behind the content of the chapters preceding it. As noted above, the first chapters, in which the chaotic and impenetrable nature of Irish pre-history is confronted, are included by O'Grady to illustrate his belief in the inadequacy of a purely empirical approach to Gaelic pre-history. The chapters following these focused on the beginnings of Irish history as accessible chronology and connected this to the emergence of heroism and aristocratic society in the bardic chronicles. The invocation represents the culmination of O'Grady's delineation of this development from archaeology to history, from formlessness to form, and from history to art. It stands at the border not just between the fragmentation of Irish pre-history and the unity of Irish history formed as national history; it also mediates O'Grady's quasi-empirical historical method of the opening chapters and his literary method of the rest of the book. Thus, the invocation highlights the inseparability of structure and subject matter in *History of Ireland*, a redemptive moment, in Walter Benjamin's sense, articulating a transcendence of the split between history and the imagination, fundamentally the split between subject and object.[46] The invocation becomes its own object, just as the form of the *History of Ireland* becomes its subject-matter. By invoking the spirits of the ancient bards and the 'sacred influences' of his country, O'Grady envisages not just an epic-heroic epoch confined to the age of Cuchulainn, he *invokes* a new era in which the ancient spirits of Ireland, 'nameless now and unworshipped', might once more become a felt presence in the nation's affairs. In his concern to name these spirits, O'Grady expresses the view of sound as at once spirit or *nous* (breath), and as name, a view that Benjamin recognises as evidence of the magical quality of language.[47] A clear precedent is thus established for Yeats's later use of invocation, most notoriously in 'Easter 1916', a poem that adopts a messianic relation to history.[48]

Following the invocation, O'Grady begins his historical narrative by recounting the origins of the city of Emain Macha, centre of the Red Branch Knights whose greatest hero was Cuchulainn. The city was named after the wife of Kimbay MacFiontann, Macha the red-haired warrior queen, who turned into a 'beautiful maiden' to become Kimbay's wife. The story that follows this illustrates how *History of Ireland* is structured in terms of a dialectic of necessity and contingency that takes the form of the interrelationship of authority and rebellion.

In O'Grady's narrative, after the death of Kimbay's foster-son, Ugainey More, a gathering of kings decide that a character named Lorc should succeed him. Lorc's brother, Corac, is furious and plots to overturn his brother's monarchy. He sends a messenger to Lorc, falsely informing him that he, Corac, has died. Upon hearing this, Lorc travels immediately to his brother, who lies in wait and kills him when he arrives. Following this Corac gathers his forces to storm the city of Dun-Rie, slaughtering all of Lorc's sons except Lara, who avoids death by feigning insanity. Lara is taken into the protection of an old man for whom he works as a labourer. Later on, Lara and his master are taken into the protection of an enemy of Corac, the king of Shiel, who reigned in Slieve Mish.

O'Grady interrupts this story by introducing the legend of the arrival of the Milesian clan in Ireland, a legend full of supernatural incident, closely relating ancestry, providence and the activities of gods. He regularly interrupts one narrative with another in this way throughout *History of Ireland*, a strategy that raises the question of the epic form he employs and its relationship to history. Eric Auerbach makes a useful distinction in relation to this between two kinds of epic; that of Homer's *Odyssey* and that of the Old Testament. In making this distinction, Auerbach focuses on a crucial moment in the *Odyssey* in which the housekeeper Eurycleia recognises Odysseus by a scar on his thigh; this recognition is followed by an interruption in the narrative in which a detailed history is given of how Odysseus acquired the scar. Auerbach argues that this interruption is not employed to heighten the suspense in the narrative, but to relax the tension. He claims that it illustrates how, in Homer's epic, everything lies on the surface of the narrative, resulting in a virtual excess of detail; this being the case, even the smallest details cannot be omitted. Unlike the epic form of the story of Abraham's sacrifice in the Old Testament, he argues, there is no temporal deep structure to the *Odyssey*; events in the narrative have no meaning beyond themselves.[49] Furthermore, Auerbach argues that the epic form of the *Odyssey* is wholly legend, whereas the epic form of the Abraham story tends towards history.[50] O'Grady's interruption seems to meet the conditions of the Homeric form of epic as defined by Auerbach in that the interruption, by virtue of its length, relieves rather than heightens suspense in the narrative. Furthermore, the characters referred to in the story of Lara and Corac are not presented with any psychological depth. However, in placing the legend of the arrival of the Milesian clan within the story of Corac and Lara, O'Grady mythologises history through use of the place-name Slieve Mish; Slieve Mish is the point of contact in both stories and, as a site of worship, it invests the story of Lara and Corac with a spiritual significance it otherwise lacks, lending a meaning to the story beyond the simple redaction of events. The interruption, therefore, suggests that O'Grady's form of epic stands between those of Homer and of the Old Testament as described by Auerbach; if action rather than personality is given priority in character depiction, it is also true that action is given a significance beyond itself in *History of Ireland*.

According to the legend that O'Grady recounts in the digression, the Milesians sailed to Ireland, bringing with them an ancient magical stone called the Lia Fáil, 'which the Clanna Gaedhil in the ancient days had brought with them to Espân, and ancestral prophesies had foretold that the sovereignty of the Gaeil should not cease around it', indicating his view that the Milesian clan had Gaelic origins.[51] O'Grady writes that at the time, Ireland was controlled by the Tuatha De Danann gods who scattered the Milesians on the sea by causing a great storm. A number of the Milesian families survived and one of them, the family of Heber, arrived at Slieve Mish. There Heber and his people witnessed a vision of the Tuatha and 'the ever-living Shee that attended her'. O'Grady writes that she promised to protect the children of Heber until the end of time. After the vision, Heber established Slieve Mish as the capital of his kingdom.

In his introduction to this first volume of *History of Ireland* O'Grady makes the following instructive comment:

> I remember some remark of Horace to this effect, 'Hence it happens that we see, as in a picture, all the life of the old man.' This has been my object to represent, as in a picture, the state of society which obtained in this country in ancient times, which, though distant in one sense, are near in many others. It is the same sky that bent over them, which shines or darkens over us. The same human heart beat in their breasts as beats amongst us to-day. All the great permanent relations of life are the same.[52]

This idea of permanence within change is articulated in the link that Slieve Mish represents between the Milesian legend and the story of Lara and Corac. The idea reveals the influence of Carlyle's *Past and Present*, in which the author celebrates what he regards as the fundamental spiritual permanence uniting past, present and future:

The past is a dim indubitable fact: the Future too is one, only dimmer; nay properly it is the *same* fact in new dress and development. For the Present holds it in both the whole Past and the whole Future; as the LIFE-TREE IGDRASIL, wide-waving, many-toned, has its roots down deep in the Death-kingdoms, among the oldest dead dust of men, and with its boughs reaches always beyond the stars; and in all times and places is one and the same Life-tree![53]

As a place made sacred by the presence of the Tuatha De Danann, Slieve Mish is the site of those 'great permanent relations' of which O'Grady writes. In chapter twenty the form of those relations is shown in the *Aireachta* or tribunal of Slieve Mish in which the ollamh (judge) administers justice amongst the people. Unlike the society created by the rebellious King Corac at Dun-Rie, in which the status of the ollamhs and bards is not recognised, Slieve Mish is feudal rather than autocratic. O'Grady presents it as a place where justice is based on the notion of the common good and where the king's authority is unquestioned, but also where the king recognises the power of ollamh and bard. From O'Grady's perspective, therefore, it is natural that Slieve Mish is the site of restoration of the social order disrupted by the rebel Corac. Furthermore, in introducing the legend of Slieve Mish at a point in the narrative when the social order it embodies has fallen into disarray as a result of Corac's rebellion, O'Grady suggests that the moment of final disintegration of the feudal patriarchal order contains the seeds for its restoration; exiled from Dun-Rie, Lara finds himself in Slieve Mish from where the reversal of Corac's rebellious victory will begin.

During his time in Slieve Mish, Lara falls in love with the king's daughter, Moreea. The king eventually agrees to give his daughter's hand in marriage and he prepares an army for Lara to attack Corac's fortress at Dun-Rie. O'Grady writes that on the eve of the lunar feast of Samhain, Craivetheena, poet and harpist of Slieve Mish, struck magical notes on the ramparts of Dun-Rie, causing all the warriors within to fall into a slumber, after which Lara entered the fortress and killed his brother Corac.[54] The fortress is destroyed and Moreea then becomes Lara's queen 'and from them proceeded a race of monarchs and legislators whose fame was great amongst the Gaeil'.[55]

The structural determination of history as dialectical in O'Grady's work becomes manifest at this point in the clash between two forms of history. The role Slieve Mish plays in the narrative appears to indicate that O'Grady interprets history in a cyclical form. Lara's exile there is evidence of the disintegration of feudal patriarchal order but it is also the place where the restoration of that order begins. In this sense Slieve Mish symbolises the cyclical form of history in Nietzsche's idea of eternal recurrence and in Yeats's idea of the antithetical moment in the interpenetrative movement of gyres structuring his interpretation of history in *A Vision*.[56] However, Slieve Mish also appears to exemplify the typological form of history in O'Grady's idea of 'great permanent relations'. The place links Lara, who personifies the patriarchal order of Emain Macha, to the ancient Milesian aristocracy, the implication being that the essence of history is conditioned by the heroic, patriarchal form they embody.

The emergence of cyclical and typological forms of history here, indicate that the archetypes O'Grady champions throughout *History of Ireland*, in this case Slieve Mish as the site of patriarchy, exist in a necessary dialectical relationship with their opposites; Dun-Rie, as the site of Corac's rebellion, foregrounds Slieve Mish as the site of tradition and restoration. O'Grady's affirmation of a typological historiography in *History of Ireland* is, therefore, always already in crisis. The recourse he takes to the cyclical is the sign of this crisis because it reveals his need for the contingency of rebellion to illustrate the necessity of order. The gender aspect of this crisis is indicated in Julia Kristeva's observations on the gendering of temporality. Kristeva suggests that female subjectivity characterises both cyclical and typological concepts of time, through *repetition* and *eternity*, but that whereas the former facilitates vorticity and *jouissance*, the latter abstracts the body from its somatic contingencies, as in cult of the Virgin mother. While Kristeva is concerned with the manifestation of hysteria (in a sense specific to her theoretical vocabulary) that these forms of temporality signify when colliding with linear, teleological history, the distinctions she draws between the cyclical and the typological (in her word, the monumental) reveal the gender form of this problem of historiography in *History of Ireland*.[57]

In the story of Lara and Corac, then, rebellion is presented as evil not simply because it disrupts the continuity of the social order, but because it inverts the system of gender relations upon which that social order is based. The social order of Emain Macha as presented by O'Grady rests on the authority of masculinity in the form of paternal kingship, an authority the maintenance of which requires femininity to be controlled institutionally. This accounts for the importance of the institutions of bard and druid to the maintenance of patriarchal order in *History of Ireland*. The male poet and harpist, Craivetheena, paves the way for the restoration of Lara's authority, not with a sword but with a sleep-inducing harp, exemplifying the manner in which the patriarchal order in the narrative accommodates a forgetfulness it designates as feminine in order to retain an authority over femininity. Mirroring this, the warrior goddess Macha is transformed into a 'beautiful maiden' in order to be accommodated within the patriarchal structure of Kimbay MacFiontann's monarchy. In contrast, Corac's disregard for ollamh and bard leads to the rise of women's political power and the weakening of the marital institution. The manner in which the story is presented suggests O'Grady's belief in the necessity of public institutions, the prerogative of which rests on the association of order and patriarchy; without these, the domestication of woman, a consequence of which is her confinement to subjectivity, conceived as emotion and irrationality, is undermined, and woman

27

then emerges as a political rebel, as is shown later in O'Grady's depiction of Queen Maeve.[58] On the other hand, a consequence of the maintenance of the patriarchal order is a prefiguration of the land as feminine. Slieve Mish exemplifies this, where the vision of a Tuatha De Danann goddess designates the place as a source of patriarchal order and myth.

Following the story of Lara and Corac, O'Grady skips over a long period of history to set the scene for the introduction of Cuchulainn. He continues his narrative at the point of the death of Rury the Great, a descendant of Kimbay MacFiontann, whose followers in southern Ireland dropped their allegiance to Emain Macha after his death, 'entering into local confederacies and alliances in which the interests of the ancestral race and the elder branch were not regarded'.[59] As a result of this, O'Grady writes, the strength of the descendants of Ugainey More grew in the east of Ireland and eventually they seized the kingship of Tara and ordered the Temairian festival, an event which O'Grady compares to the festival of Olympus in ancient Greece. O'Grady depicts 'Yeoha Faydleeah' as the most noteworthy king among these descendants because he fathered Queen Maeve, the most important woman in *History of Ireland*.

Maeve's origins as narrated by O'Grady forebode disorder and rebellion, indicative of the manner in which femininity functions as the Other in *History of Ireland*, the space of imaginative freedom and desire subordinated yet potentially disruptive of patriarchal order and necessity. It is unsurprising that O'Grady presents her entry onto the stage of ancient Irish history in the context of political uncertainty and of the destructive impact of the 'other'world on the family institution. Her father Yeoha, who came to power during an era of increasing division in Ireland, marries a woman named Eadâne who, after the birth of Maeve, is taken away by a figure from the otherworld. Thereafter Yeoha's life turns tragic and his three sons are killed. Maeve grows up to marry a Connaught prince Aileel More, portrayed later in O'Grady's narrative as a man of weakness.

This account of Maeve's background is a microcosm of the dynamics of gender structuring *History of Ireland*. From the outset it is clear that O'Grady is attempting to forge a connection between the imagination and history, but his patriarchal ideology requires that the opposition between the imagination and history is retained. His maintenance of this ideology requires that the imagination must remain Other to history as femininity must remain Other to masculinity. Therefore, the relationship that O'Grady is attempting to establish must not be allowed to go too far, to reach a point where the opposition between the imagination and history is entirely collapsed. That, in effect, would represent the feminisation of masculinity and the masculinisation of femininity, creating emasculated men (Aileel More) and politically powerful women (Maeve). The account O'Grady gives of Maeve's background indicates his belief that rebellion allows the 'otherworld' of feminine subjectivity to enter into the fabric of history and, in consequence, to subvert the patriarchal order that designates it as Other. Co-terminous with the fact that Maeve's father descends from a group of warriors who broke away from the authority of Emain Macha in Ireland is the fact that his wife Eadâne descends from the otherworld of the Tuatha De Danann. In giving birth to Maeve, therefore, she is giving birth to the Other within history, to the non-identical free-play of imaginative desire within the identical closure of historical necessity. In historiographic terms, Maeve represents the possibility of conceiving history in accordance with my reformulation of Fredric Jameson's definition of history as necessity, namely, as the ground of necessity and contingency/desire. One criticism made of Jameson's definition is that it reveals a patriarchal form of thought because desire cannot be accommodated within it.[60] Maeve personifies imaginative freedom *within* history, thereby transforming the concept of history itself.

Having introduced the character of Maeve in this way, O'Grady next turns his attention to her diametric opposite in *History of Ireland*, Cuchulainn. From the outset, he stands out as the embodiment of the heroic sentiments that lie at the heart of O'Grady's literary endeavours. Having described his first heroic exploit when he defeated a group of young nobles at a game of hurling, O'Grady writes:

> This was the debût and first martial exploit of the great Cuculain, type of Irish chivalry and courage, in the bardic firmament a bright particular star of strength, daring and glory, that will not set or suffer aught but transient obscuration till the extinction of the Irish race.[61]

In *On Heroes, Hero-Worship and the Heroic in History*, Thomas Carlyle considers the attributes of what he sees as the heroic in human history. He contends that the Old Norse hero Odin evoked a spontaneous admiration and adoration in those around him and although Odin himself had long passed away, 'there is this huge Shadow of him which still projects itself over the whole History of his People'.[62] O'Grady invests Cuchulainn with the same magnitude throughout *History of Ireland*. Cuchulainn's heroism is not simply the manifestation of his personality, but O'Grady presents it as the basis of a social order. He is presented as emblematic of a society based on nobility, cohesion and integrity; he only appears as an individual in circumstances where this form of society has been overthrown in rebellion. Carlyle claims that society is founded on hero-worship:

> All dignities of rank, on which human association rests, are what we may call a Heroarchy (Government of Heroes), or a Hierarchy, for it is 'sacred' enough withal. The Duke means *Dux*, leader; King is *Kon-ning*, Kan-ning, Man that *knows* or *cans*.[63]

Believing that the integrity of the hero is vital to this form of society, Carlyle asserts that a determination to confront life in its starkest reality is the mark of such integrity:

> I should say sincerity, a deep, great, genuine sincerity, is the first characteristic of all men in any way heroic... The great Fact of Existence

is great to him. Fly as he will, he cannot get out of the awful presence of this Reality. His mind is so made, he is great by that, first of all.[64]

Carlyle's view of heroism, therefore, equates patriarchal hierarchy with historical fact; to disrupt the former is to obscure the latter.

In deferring to this perspective, O'Grady's determination to present *History of Ireland* as historically factual reveals his patriarchal hierarchical ideology. However, as his concept of 'great permanent relations' is, as noted above, always already in crisis, so this perspective on history is subject to the problem of femininity within patriarchal discourse. This problem is manifested in two primary conflicts, one internal and the other external, in *History of Ireland*. Throughout the narrative Fergus MacRoy endures an inner struggle between his loyalty to Maeve and his admiration for Cuchulainn. This conflict is externalised in the enmity between Cuchulainn and Maeve.

The gender form of these conflicts becomes more pronounced as the narrative progresses. Fergus MacRoy is a crucially contradictory character in this regard because the patriarchal traits of his personality, his nobility and integrity, demand that he rebel against the king of Emain Macha, Concobhar MacNessa, thereby dividing the Red Branch Knights, upholders of the heroic code. Fergus, therefore, contradicts the Carlylean scheme of things; as a hero, his actions ought to solidify patriarchy and continue tradition but in fact they result in division and the ascent of Maeve to a position of political authority.

The context within which Fergus rebels highlights the gender form of this contradiction. The source of this contradiction lies in O'Grady's account of the legend of Deirdre, Concobhar MacNessa's daughter, in *History of Ireland*. Following standard versions of the legend, O'Grady narrates how the druid Cathvah prophesied on the occasion of Deirdre's birth that she would be the cause of division among the Red Branch Knights; how, frightened by the prophecy, Concobhar put Deirdre into the care of the old woman Lowcram who was instructed to keep her within a remote tower until her death; how Deirdre grew into a beautiful woman and eventually left the tower.

Fergus is described by O'Grady as 'the great sheltering tree of all the noblest and best knights', presented as a paternal figure for the three sons of Usna, the knights Naysi, Anly and Ardan.[66] His version of the Deirdre legend continues with an account of how she fell in love and escaped to Scotland with one of the sons of Usna, Naysi. When the news of this reached King Concobhar he 'passed sentence of perpetual banishment and exile against the clan, for he feared the words of the prophet prophesying the Red Branch divided against itself'.[66] O'Grady describes how Fergus's persistent pleading on behalf of the sons of Usna eventually procured a reversal of Concobhar's sentence. He contrasts the reaction of elation of the sons of Usna to the news with that of Deirdre, who 'uttered three cries of lamentation, and shed tears of sorrow, for she said that evil was impending over the children of Usna'.[67] Her forebodings prove well-founded, as Concobhar disregards his promise to reverse the sentence, travelling north to meet the arrival of Deirdre and the sons of Usna, ensuring that Fergus was delayed further south at Dun Kermah. O'Grady then describes the slaughter of the sons of Usna and how Fergus went into rebellion against Concobhar when news of this reached him, drawing over two-thirds of the Red Branch Knights to his side. He states that after he was eventually defeated by Concobhar, Fergus moved to the kingdom of Maeve and Aileel More west of the river Shannon.

Edward Hagan notes the problem Fergus presents: 'The character of Fergus is intriguing: he is very noble, but he pays no heed to the bards or the druids.'[68] Accounting for the contradiction of a noble figure involved in rebellion, Hagan suggests that its source may lie in this indifference. But he also recognises that Standish O'Grady's own attitude to the druids is ambivalent:

> At times he treats them as an institution to be respected; at other times he shares Fergus's contempt for them. O'Grady was suspicious of any species of priestcraft. On the other hand, he would brook no contempt for the bards, as the entire *History* makes clear.[69]

Plausible though these observations are, they do not entirely resolve the problem of Fergus because they do not account for the complexity of gender within the story of the sons of Usna. O'Grady's ambivalence towards the druids embodies the dichotomy of his patriarchal ideology, in which the construction of masculinity as objective and rational necessitates the construction of femininity as subjective and libidinal. If this ideology controls femininity by domesticating it as irrational, it also concedes masculine identity's dialectical dependence on the 'irrational' feminine and, therefore, concedes that masculine identity has the possibility of its own collapse inscribed within it. Hélène Cixous identifies the masculine–feminine split as the ground of all binary oppositions within discourse as it embodies the subject–object split that is the condition for discourse in general.[70] Toril Moi points out, however, that Cixous's deconstruction of this split does not abolish the categories specific to the phallogocentric logic of patriarchy but traces 'the way in which each signifier contaminates and subverts the meaning of the others'.[71]

In O'Grady's account of the story of Lara and Corac, Craivetheena's music – lulling Corac's rebel forces into a slumber – is representative of the manner in which the bardic institution reveals femininity, constructed as 'passive', contributing to the restoration of patriarchal order. The druidic institution functions in a similar manner in *History of Ireland* but more obviously than the bardic, it contains within it the threat of the destruction of patriarchy. The existence of a priestly institution like that of the druid indicates a fear of the unknown which, although constructed as feminine within patriarchal ideology, remains to be *deciphered*.[72] As magicians, the druids possess this power, thus acting as the guardians of an esoteric knowledge. O'Grady expressed his fascination with this esoteric knowledge in an article on druidism published in 1875.[73] The Ogham letters referred to in the manuscript sources of the Táin Bo Cuailgne provide O'Grady with evidence of this form of knowledge in pre-Christian Celtic culture. In claiming that these letters originated in the east, he suggests that druidic knowledge foregrounded the hieroglyphic nature of language, a characteristic effect of oriental languages which, Jacques Derrida claims, are structurally ideogrammatic rather than phonetic, thus remaining outside what Derrida identifies as the logocentric tradition of western languages, in which writing is a debased image of the self-presence of speech. The Ogham letters, therefore, indicate that the esoteric knowledge of the druids rests on an insight into the opacity of signification. This opacity, insofar as it is Other to occidental logocentricism, points to the Other of the feminine in the patriarchal structure governing that logocentricism; femininity, therefore, is encoded in the esoteric knowledge of the druids, simultaneously the opaque Other necessary to the constitution of language as transparent, and the subversive force threatening to overturn the structure of patriarchy within which it is encoded.[74] The esoteric knowledge of the druids, therefore, reveals the *necessity* of the contingency of femininity to the formulation of masculine identity as self-identical presence within the structure of patriarchy. This indicates that O'Grady's ambivalence to the druids is more than intentional; it manifests the structural crisis of *History of Ireland*, where the assertion of history as patriarchal necessitates the Other of femininity that contains the possibility of subverting the system within which it is constituted. This interpretation is reinforced by O'Grady's belief that both eastern and western traditional language forms, identified by Derrida as ideogrammatic and phonocentric, were contemporaneously present in ancient Ireland.[75]

To the extent that the druids possess this esoteric knowledge, they exist beyond the power and control of the king; Concobhar fears Cathvah's prophesy over Deirdre because it engages a language not available to him. Consequently his capacity to control femininity is undermined. Significantly, Deirdre also possesses the prophetic knowledge of the druids in her ability to accurately decipher Concobhar's real intentions in relation to the sons of Usna. Woman as threateningly desirable, old hag or powerful warrior are metonymies that recur throughout *History of Ireland*, re-inforcing the construction of femininity as the threatening Other. By virtue of their immersion in what Julia Kristeva identifies as the 'hysteria' of the feminine within the structure of patriarchy as designated in Lacanian psychoanalyis, the druids inspire fear and suspicion, as the case of Concobhar illustrates.[76] When Fergus discounts the authority of the druids, therefore, he transgresses an unspoken agreement between the outer world of politics and the inner world of psyche structured within patriarchy. As a hieratic order, the druids are a vital link between patriarchy and its Other – the world of female subjectivity. In breaking the link, the hero, embodiment of militaristic masculinity, ceases to authorise his destiny and the destiny of his gender. It is no surprise, therefore, that Fergus finds himself subordinate to a politically powerful woman, Maeve.

In O'Grady's narrative, the death of the sons of Usna and Fergus's ensuing revolt create the circumstances that make Maeve's political intrigues and the magical connivance of the druids possible. O'Grady presents her as threatening in her duplicity to the male order embodied by Cuchulainn, undermined by the spell that has been cast on the Red Branch Knights. The spell results from the refusal of the people of Coalney to lend their prize bull to Maeve, provoking her anger. O'Grady writes of a 'maiden of divine aspect' appearing to her with a warning about Cuchulainn. The visionary figure tells Maeve that she will 'spread amazement' in Ulster: 'They [the Red Branch Knights] shall not return to their right mind for a season.'[77] The spell recalls, ironically, that cast by the poet Craivetheena on the forces of Corac at Dun-Rie centuries earlier. Whereas that earlier spell contributed to the reinstatement of patriarchy, this one aids its decline, indicative of the problem druidism represents for O'Grady in *History of Ireland*. The scenario of supernatural forces assisting Maeve's rebelliousness suggests that a hitherto domesticated feminine subjectivity is entering the broader political arena. Fergus recognises this and his address to Maeve in chapter thirty is a revealing demand for the domestication of woman:

> Fitter were it for thee, O Queen, to have remained in thy own Dun and seen to the government of thy household, than to march upon this foray with thy lord, silly from age, and thy son, Orloff, silly from youth. At home in thy own palace thou shouldst have remained with these, for here thou art a disturbing influence, and partest from me the authority over the loose array of this great host.[78]

Patriarchy is illustrated here in the implication that Maeve's political involvement is the result of the weakness of Aileel More as a husband and a father and in Fergus's assertion that Maeve should confine herself to 'the government of thy household', revealing his desire to restrict femininity to interior, subjective space. Maeve evokes both fear and desire, fear in Fergus because her sexual desirability among the clans of Aileel More undermines his own authority; 'for with thy fair face and thy stature beyond women, and thy shining shield, thou hast bewitched them, and also the far coming kings of the south...'[79]

A corollary of Maeve's ascent to political power is a development in the characterisation of Cuchulainn. Cuchulainn is presented by O'Grady not just as a heroic figure, but also as the embodiment of feudal patriarchy. However, as that form of society goes into decline, his heroism becomes more distinctive, appearing more as an individual than as a social phenomenon, climaxing in his solitary defence of Ulster against the forces of Maeve. Individuality moves from being a contingent to a necessary condition of heroism and O'Grady develops the character of Cuchulainn in terms of heroic individualism. Cut off from the Red Branch Knights, who remain stricken by 'the insane mist', he emerges as the final embodiment of everything they represent and he defeats every warrior Maeve sends to challenge him.[80] Having bound herself to an agreement whereby her forces could not cross the river Dia to invade Ulster until Cuchulainn was subdued in single combat, Maeve connives to get former companions of his to fight against him, knowing how this would split his loyalty. Meanwhile, Cuchulainn's military prowess becomes more manifest as he defeats his challengers in increasingly heroic fashion. In making him drunk, Maeve finally connives in getting Fardia, a former companion of Cuchulainn's and the most skilful swordsman among her forces, to agree to challenge him.

History of Ireland: The Heroic Period culminates in the battle of Cuchulainn and Fardia in which Cuchulainn is depicted at his most heroic. On the morning of the battle he is juxtaposed against the vast multitude of Maeve's armies in an image that both recalls the feudal model of communal heroic society and recognises its absence both in the historical moment in which the battle takes place, and, implicitly, in the historical moment in which O'Grady is writing:

> Then arose Cuculain, the unconquerable, striding through the forest, and he wondered which of the great champions of Maeve should be brought against him that day; and when he came out into the open, he beheld the whole south country filled with a vast multitude, as it had been at the AEnech of Taylteen or the great feis of Tara when the authority of the Ard-Rie is supreme, and all the tribes of Erin gather together with their kings.[81]

Pathos is added to Cuchulainn's military might, the sight before him reminding him of a former time when all the tribes were gathered under the high kingship of Tara. That what actually stands before him is a vast army of soldiers, many of them former comrades, intent on destroying him, fills him with sadness. When Fardia implores Cuchulainn to discontinue his resistance he replies:

> My people have indeed abandoned me and conspired for my destruction; but there is no power in Erin to dissolve my knightship to the son of Nessa and my kinship with the Crave Rue. Though they hate me, yet I cannot eject this love out of my heart.[82]

In O'Grady's account of the epic battle that follows, Fardia is killed by Cuchulainn but the victory is hollow. Upon his death 'a great sorrow overwhelmed him, and he lamented and mourned over Fardia, joining his voice to the howl of the people of Fardia'.[83] Furthermore, the wounds inflicted in the previous conflicts have been compounded in this final combat and Cuchulainn appears to be verging on death. His lifelong companion, Laeg, learns of his condition and travels to meet him. Before the conclusion of the narrative, a bard recounts to Laeg the story of the sons of Usna and how Cuchulainn, upon learning of Concobhar's slaying of them, went to Emain Macha to destroy it.

In this account, Cuchulainn did not enter the city, however, because in order to do so he would have had to pass three naked women on the bridge leading into Emain Macha. This incident presents femininity as the ultimate threat to the heroic code and it is significant that it is recalled so close to the end of the narrative when Cuchulainn appears to verge on death. It is the one sexually 'explicit' incident that O'Grady does not edit out from his sources.

Laeg finds the wounded Cuchulainn and with this the spell falls from the Red Branch. This signals the start of the wars of the Táin Bo Cuailgne dealt with in the second volume of *History of Ireland*. A vast litany of historic and divine figures appear to the hero, forming a thematic conclusion to the book. By chanting such a vast number of names in a bardic fashion, O'Grady gives a reminder of the invocation that initiated the narrative, indicating once more the phonocentric form of his epic project. This litany is employed to signal the 'great permanent relations' that Cuchulainn embodies and his resurrection to god-like status. He does not die after these visions but falls 'into a deep sleep, without a dream, that lasted for the space of a day and a night'.[84] The resurgence of the Red Branch Knights upon the passing of Cuchulainn is more evidence of the cyclical model of history disrupting the typological view embodied in O'Grady's concept of 'great permanent relations', a disruption that reveals the dialectical structure of history governing O'Grady's narrative. Cuchulainn's passing represents the furthest point of the degeneration of feudal patriarchy and also the original moment of its restoration. The permanence of the relations that Cuchulainn embodies, therefore, is contradictory in that those relations exist in a necessary relation to the degeneration of patriarchy.

History of Ireland: The Heroic Period must be considered in relation to the second volume, *History of Ireland: Cuculain and His Contemporaries*, for a full assessment of its value, as the latter develops the style and completes the narrative of the first volume. Nevertheless, it is an important work in its own right because it establishes the conceptual terrain for O'Grady's subsequent literary–historiographic work. Because it narrates the fragmentation of patriarchal order, it reveals the anxieties latent within the project O'Grady initiates, anxieties that arise from the contradiction inherent in the typological form of historiography he advocates and the dialectical structure within which it is articulated. Fergus's contradictory attitude to the druids and the division in loyalties that Cuchulainn experiences in his battle with Fardia are indicative of the contradictions informing *History of Ireland: The Heroic Period*, contradictions O'Grady attempts to efface with a more homogeneous triumphalism in the second volume.

Lifting 'The Insane Mist': *History of Ireland: Cuculain and His Contemporaries*

T HE INITIAL RESPONSE TO O'GRADY'S *History of Ireland: Heroic Period* was not what the author had hoped for. It failed to ignite any immediate enthusiasm for bardic literature amongst the artistic community. Critical reviews of the book were positive but they interpreted it as a historical romance rather than a genuinely historical work.[1] Although he held to the view that history culminated in art, this was certainly not how O'Grady intended the work to be read. He wished to convince his audience that the literary presentation of bardic material did not imply that it was not historical but that, on the contrary, the craft of bardic narration could communicate a sense of the lived experience of people in ancient Ireland in a way that purely empirical historiography could not. Furthermore, O'Grady appears to have felt that the first volume, considered on its own, misrepresented his intentions. He believed that this occurred because of the difficulties he encountered in the management of his source material, resulting in the narrative appearing to be exclusively imaginative. This stylistic problem illustrates that the inadequacy of the first volume from O'Grady's perspective centres on the question of gender:

> All the borders of the epic representation at which, in the first volume, I have aimed, seemed to melt, and wander away vaguely on every side into space and time.[2]

His attempt to present the bardic material as historical is expressed here in a manner resonant with the Old Testament presentation of the act of creation as lending form to chaos. In identifying the lack of 'a clear historical frame' in the first volume, therefore, O'Grady draws a necessary relation between history and form.[3] Furthermore, the biblical analogy indicates that form is conceived by O'Grady as the sign of his authorship *as* authority; the success or failure of his *History of Ireland* depending on the control he exerts over his source material.[4] This will to authority reveals the manner in which history is conceived in patriarchal terms by O'Grady. The attempt to render the source material historical, therefore, indicates that the problems besetting the first volume express the crisis that femininity poses for him. On the one hand, the construction of femininity as subjective and irrational is necessary to the presentation of masculinity as order and authority within *History of Ireland*. On the other hand, this construction reveals the dialectical interdependence of masculine order and feminine chaos within the structure of patriarchy, an interdependence that threatens to undermine the structure as a whole. O'Grady's attempt to incorporate the imagination into history, therefore, is fraught from the outset with the possibility of history evaporating into pure imaginativeness. In the light of the lack of 'a clear historical frame' in the first volume that O'Grady identified, it is not surprising that a reviewer in *The Celtic Magazine* referred to it as a 'magnificently brilliant historical romance'.[5]

To counter the suggestion that his work was purely imaginative, O'Grady published *Early Bardic Literature, Ireland* in 1879, which was republished as an extended introduction to the second volume of *History of Ireland* the following year, in which he argues fervently for the historical veracity of his material and the need for Irish people to take an interest in their own history. He reinforces Carlyle's idea of history culminating in art by asserting a necessary relationship between historical fact and artistic representation in order to defend his belief that the superhuman aspects of early Irish bardic history were not simply products of the imagination. He claims that Ireland's ancient history passed relentlessly into the realm of literature; 'the history of one generation became the poetry of the next, until the whole island was illuminated and coloured by the poetry of the bards'.[6] This is presented as analogous to Carlyle's claim in *On Heroes, Hero-Worship and the Heroic in History* that the hero of one epoch became the god of the next, 'until the formation of the Tuatha De Danann, who represent the gods of the historic ages'.[7]

In order to make these claims convincing, O'Grady considers why Irish bardic material had come to be regarded as purely imaginative. He starts by reflecting on what he views as the great divide within this material, a divide that reflects the split between history and the imagination he perceives in his own era, indicative of how O'Grady constructs the past from his contemporary perspective:

> On the one hand the epical, a realm of the most riotous activity of thought; on the other, the annalistic and genealogical, bald and bare to the last degree, a mere skeleton. They represent the two great hemispheres of the bardic mind, the latter controlling the former.[8]

He traces this division to an entry in the *Annals of the Four Masters*, dated 1499 BC: 'The Fleet of the Sons of Milith came to Ireland to take it from the Tuatha De Danann'.[9] This refers to the legend of the arrival of the Milesian clan in Ireland, that O'Grady treated in the first volume of *History of Ireland*. This entry, he claims, is the source of the division between 'the mythological or divine on the one hand, and the historical or heroic-historical on the other'.[10] Such a claim, arbitrary though it is, illustrates the dialectical structure of O'Grady's historiography. If, as he believes, the history of one generation is mythologised in the next, then the cumulative histories of successive generations must result in a qualitative transformation of the relationship between myth and history in general. Figure 1 illustrates this transformation.

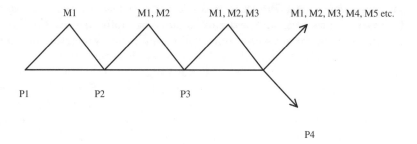

M1   M1, M2   M1, M2, M3   M1, M2, M3, M4, M5 etc.

P1   P2   P3

P4

P1 = Historical Period 1.   M1 = Myth 1.

Figure 1

Extrapolating from O'Grady's argument, a point in history must be reached (P4) where the accumulation of mythic narratives is so great that mythology itself is transformed from a more or less transparent narrative of the past to an essentially self-reflexive category, though one still rooted in history. At this point, myth separates from chronicle.[11] O'Grady selects the earliest reference he knows to the Tuatha De Danann as his starting point, since the Tuatha fitted this model perfectly. He claims that they were the imaginative product of a long history of mythologising heroic historical figures; at some point in ancient history the accumulation of so much mythology created a belief in the existence of a god-like clan in Ireland and so the Tuatha was born in the imagination of the people.

O'Grady proceeds to identify the root for the dismissal of Irish bardic literature as unhistorical in the failure of medieval scholars to recognise this distinction between myth and chronicle. The result, he claims, was a deflation of mythic grandeur and a corruption of historical fact:

> The conjectures of the present century are founded upon mediaeval attempts to reduce to verisimilitude and historical probability what was by its nature quite incapable of such treatment. The mythology of the Irish nation, being relieved of the marvellous and sublime, was set down with circumstantial dates as a portion of the country's history by the literary men of the middle ages.[12]

O'Grady's argument implies a twofold negative effect of the medieval scholastics' treatment of the bardic material; Irish bardic history lost its factual credibility and Irish mythology came to be viewed as artistically impoverished. From this perspective it is unsurprising that, as Hagan remarks, 'O'Grady seems to have been fighting an Irish intellectual current which dismissed the early literature as poetic fancy'.[13]

O'Grady, then, sought to re-establish the distinction between myth and chronicle in Irish bardic literature that, he believed, had been obscured by medieval scholars. Yet he also wished to make the historical factuality of his literary enterprise manifest in the second volume of *History of Ireland*. This apparent contradiction is compounded by the similarity between the narrative of both volumes, as Hagan notes:

> Chapter II resumes the narrative [from volume one], and despite all the talk about historicity, the rest of Vol. II resembles the narrative sections of Vol. I. If anything, O'Grady becomes more proficient at the literary devices which plunge the reader into a story and dull any concern that he or she might have for absolute historic fact.[14]

This apparent anomaly, however, rests on Hagan's own disagreement with O'Grady's argument in the introduction to the second volume. Implicit in his criticism is the assumption that because O'Grady's narrative involves myth, for the most part, it is necessarily divorced from actual historical events, an assumption to which O'Grady does not subscribe. For him, the mythic events in his narrative *were* historical in the sense that they illustrated life-patterns whose historical constancy had raised them to the level of archetypes. He sees these archetypes as barometers of the social order that produced them, yet he never considers the superhuman antics of Cuchulainn, for example, as historical from an empirical perspective. O'Grady posits a manner of reading history alternative to what he regards as rigid factual historicism, appealing for a new perspective on the past eliding that of empirical historiography, an approach indebted to Carlyle's *Past and Present*. In this work, Carlyle attacks the 'Dryasdust' approach to the past for its failure to capture its lived experience. As with O'Grady, Carlyle sees this failure as the reason for the lack of popular interest in history. He parodies the 'Dryasdust' method of explaining the significance of the monastic ruins of St Edmundsbury:

> ... that the Monks were of such and such a genus, such and such a number; that they had so many carucates of land in this hundred, and so many in that; and then farther that the large Tower or Belfry was built by such a one, and the smaller Belfry was built by etc. etc. – Till human nature can stand no more of it; till human nature desperately takes refuge in forgetfulness, almost in flat disbelief of the whole business, Monks, Monastery, Belfries, Carucates and all![15]

Rejecting this empirical approach, he boldly asserts: 'These old St Edmundsbury walls, I say, were not peopled with fantasms; but with men of flesh and blood, made altogether as we are.'[16] In focusing on the history of St Edmundsbury, Carlyle insists on this lived reality as the basis of his writing. He grounds the heroism and sainthood attributed to the landlord Edmund in the generations that followed him to the martyrdom he enacted in refusing to submit to Danish invaders. For Carlyle, the importance of such a gesture and the honour it subsequently enjoyed lay in the evidence it provided of a society where the hero enjoyed a god-like status. So, as with O'Grady's Cuchulainn, the myths surrounding St Edmundsbury were, Carlyle argues, grounded in history in a manner that empirical historiography could never convey. Carlyle's attitude emerges clearly in O'Grady's attack on archaeological examinations of sacred neolithic tombs scattered throughout Europe:

> For after the explorer has broken up, certainly desecrated, and perhaps destroyed those noble sepulchral raths; after he has disinterred the bones laid there once by pious hands, . . . and after the savant has rammed many skulls with sawdust, measuring their capacity, and has adorned them with some obscure label, and has tabulated and arranged the implements and decorations of flint and metal in the glazed cases of the cold gaunt museum, the imagination, unsatisfied and revolted, shrinks back from all that he has done.[17]

W.J. McCormack compares this approach unfavourably with that of O'Grady's cousin, Standish Hayes O'Grady, whom he describes as 'a meticulous Celticist'. He acknowledges the value of Standish James's work, however, judging his strength to be what he calls 'a kind of style', but the praise is dwarfed by McCormack's disdain for what he perceives as O'Grady's lack of a materialistic historical sensibility:

> He admires the heroic gesture of Cuchulainn, and is uninterested in the distinction between myth and chronicle. The validity of words is established by the memories they evoke; time is essentially conceived as the barrier between inner and outer worlds rather than the index of change and process in an objective social existence.[18]

Contrary to this, O'Grady insists on the need to distinguish between myth and chronicle, as noted above. He argues, however, that this does not mean that myth is completely separate from history. On the contrary, O'Grady argues, following Carlyle, that a purely factual approach is as inadequate as a purely aesthetic attitude to conveying historical reality. The fact that O'Grady's argument is informed by the crisis of gender that the dialectical structure determining his historiography reveals is no basis for McCormack's criticism which, like Hagan's, is collusive with the empirical side of the template it criticises as unempirical.

The concept of history that interests O'Grady, then, is not one of chronicle, but of the historical patterns informing mythic narratives, patterns whose historical constancy, in his view, give rise to myth in the first place. From this perspective, the myth of Cuchulainn's superhuman endeavours is ultimately sourced in some heroic historical individual, whose memory became embued with supernatural status as generations passed. From the nature of the myth, i.e. the heroism and loyalty informing Cuchulainn's supernatural feats, O'Grady deduces that the social order in which it emerged was based on a heroic value-system. His concept of myth, therefore, is inseparable from his concept of history.

In his approach to *History of Ireland: Cuculain and His Contemporaries* O'Grady intends:

> to reduce that blank, sheer wall of ignorance, apathy, and prejudice which stands between Irishmen and their birth-right – the history of the land in which they are born, and of the ancestors from whom they have sprung, and to lessen their all but invincible repugnance to believe themselves members of the ancient nation to which we have the honour to belong.[19]

When he resumes the narrative from volume one at chapter two, certain changes are apparent that reflect this increased concern for history, and particularly the historical integrity of his narrative. His authorship has become more 'authoritative', reflected in the improved pace of the narrative and increased realism of characterisation. Furthermore, certain concerns implicit in the first volume are now brought to centre stage. Foremost among these is the role O'Grady attributes to the bards. The verbal exchanges centring around this question in chapter six, 'The Mor Reega', and chapter twelve, 'Queen Maeve and her Courtiers', illuminates his understanding of the role of the bardic institution in patriarchal society and why Maeve's denigration of their status is presented by him as unacceptably transgressive. After one of the bards sings in praise of her enemy, Cuchulainn, she gives vent to her anger, admonishing the bards for their 'womanlike' qualities:

> Effeminate, unwarlike, resembling women, whose weapon is their intemperate tongue; worse than women, for they give birth to warriors, but you, laws to impoverish noble clans, lying tales, and pedigrees. Forsooth, you chronicle the past.[20]

These accusations are particularly transgressive within the terms of O'Grady's patriarchal ideology, since the bardic songs and chronicles are the prime instrument for passing on the heroic code, a role vital to the sustenance of patriarchy. From O'Grady's perspective, Maeve's description of the bards as effeminate corrupts the gender purity of the code and by relating this effeminacy to the persona of a historian she travesties the relationship between past and present. This indicates O'Grady's belief that the loss of a sense of historical continuity is concomitant with the destruction of institutions that negotiate the space between a masculinity constructed as public and ordered, and a femininity constructed as private and anarchic. He characterises the attitudes and actions of Maeve as duplicitous in his narrative to convey the view that these effects are caused by woman achieving political authority. Maeve's denigration of the bards as effeminate may bear testimony to her own 'Amazonic' qualities but more importantly, it suggests the superfluity of the role of the bards in a scenario where femininity is no longer constructed as exclusively private.[21] O'Grady presents Queen Fleas, the wife of Aileel Finn and a personification of passive femininity, responding to Maeve in a manner that celebrates the importance of the bards, with the suggestion lurking within her speech that *History of Ireland* itself, as a bardic work, might act as an inspirational flame igniting the minds of contemporary people:

> Thee to asperse the singing men of Eire! who guard with rhymed tuneful words the wisdom of all the wizards of ancient times, together with the heroic deeds of our ancestors, and the ramifications of the tribes and noble clans, who inflame with heroic thoughts the minds of youthful warriors, and cause the aged to forget their shrunken limbs...and who but know the words of power which draw down the Tuatha De Danann from their mountains to our aid, or form their mounded grassy palaces and stone-girt Duns?[22]

In his account of this dispute O'Grady presents the relationship between bard and historian as an essential one; as creators of mythic narratives, the bards perpetuate the forms of a heroic past. Furthermore, in depicting ancestral heroism as a source of inspiration for the people of ancient Ireland, he implies that his own rendition of the Cuchulainnite saga will have a similar effect.

This dispute over the status of the bards illustrates O'Grady's rejection of what he identifies as the Wordsworthian idea of the poet; one who is preoccupied exclusively with nature in an imaginative way. In the dispute, Queen Fleeas bemoans how the bards only sing of military and heroic topics but not of the music of the blackbird and 'the beautiful aspects of the changing day', in keeping with O'Grady's depiction of her as an example of the passsive form of femininity. In contrast, Maeve's attitude is presented as one of complete indifference, other than her insistence that the bards should have no involvement in the establishment of laws. O'Grady has her magician Cailitin argue that the legal role of the bards would eventually lead to a situation of peace and, consequently, bardic songs would only be concerned with 'the mild and beautiful' as heroes would have passed into oblivion.[23] Cailitin, who is clearly presented by O'Grady as disreputable, expresses a view here that suggests the emasculating potential of the passive form of femininity dominating Victorian patriarchal discourse. While the passive views of Queen Fleeas, endorsed by Cailitin, initially appear less threatening to patriarchal ideology than Maeve's, the potential for that passivity to enter the realm of masculine heroism and etherealise it is suggested in Cailitin's view. This potential is later articulated in Yeats's 'The Wanderings of Oisin', considered in Chapter 6 of this volume, in which Niamh's realm of forgetfulness etherealises the masculine heroism of Oisin. It is evident, therefore, that the view expressed by Cailitin is cited by O'Grady to make the case that the passive form of femininity, necessary to the constitution of male authority, has the potential to 'leak' into the male persona and sedate the power urge of heroism.

Inevitably, O'Grady introduces a perspective into the discussion at this point that attempts to reconcile the passive feminine disposition of Queen Fleeas with an ethos of hero-worship. The warrior Ahrimail rejects Cailitin's views, asserting that the heroic is both beautiful *and* continues throughout history: 'We in our life imitate the immortal gods of Erin...'[24] Through the voice of Ahrimail, O'Grady rejects Cailitin's idea that the bards would one day be exclusively concerned with natural beauty because of O'Grady's belief that if this situation were to develop, poetry would have no connection to history. He is concerned to refute what he views as Wordsworthian principles because of the way in which they appear to sever an essential connection between historical fact and the imagination.

In rejecting these principles, O'Grady gives reasons why they have gained acceptance in modern European culture. In the introduction to *History of Ireland: Cuculain and His Contemporaries*, he argues that in the ancient history of Europe all its nations had a druidic and bardic culture but these survived only in Ireland. Due to the absence of the literature of this culture in the rest of Europe, he argues, modern philosophy explains the ancient gods on Wordsworthian grounds, 'which derives them directly from the imagination personifying the aspects of nature'.[25] He believes that the existence of Irish bardic literature, in which the connection between Irish gods and the raths and cairns around the country is 'almost universally insisted upon', provides evidence to the contrary: 'The scene of the destruction of the Firbolgs will be found a place of tombs, the metropolis of the Fomorians a place of tombs, and a place of tombs the sacred home of the Tuatha along the shores of the Boyne.'[26] In making this observation, O'Grady implies that these god-like tribes had roots of some kind in ancient Irish history; they were not simply the products of the imagination.

This argument illustrates O'Grady's awareness of the debate over the causes of mythic beliefs in contemporary pre-industrial and ancient societies that preoccupied philologists and thinkers in the newly emerging discipline of anthropology during the 1880s. O'Grady's rejection of the Wordsworthian view in favour of a historical understanding of myth anticipates the opinion of one of the pioneers of anthropology, Andrew Lang. In the 1880s, Lang rejected the highly influential theory of myth developed by the Oxford philologist Max Müller, whose interpretation of the source of beliefs in myth among ancient peoples corresponded to the interpretation O'Grady attributes to Wordsworth. Müller argued that a 'misunderstanding' lay at the centre of the development of beliefs in mythological gods in ancient European and Middle Eastern societies. On the basis of his specialist knowledge of the ancient Aryan language of Sanskrit, Müller claimed that this arose when a people who personified the natural world in imaginative ways handed on their language to a more literal minded generation, who mistook these personifications as referring to historical beings.[27] Julie Sparks examines Lang's parody of Müller's argument in his short piece 'The Great Gladstone Myth' collected in *In the Wrong Paradise and Other Stories* (1887). In this piece set in a far-distant future, Lang presents a scholar, Prof. Boscher (a thinly disguised image of Müller), arguing that the name Gladstone did not refer to any real historical person in the nineteenth century, but that it meant 'sun-hawk', an epithet for the sun.[28]

While Lang did not subscribe to the Carlylean 'heroic' view of history adopted by O'Grady, his strategy of combining the imaginative approach of literature with the scientific approach of anthropology in his study of myth and folklore is a close parallel of O'Grady's attempt to combine imaginative and empirical approaches in *History of Ireland*. Lang's piece on Gladstone entertains the view that we judge ancient beliefs as purely imaginative at the risk of our contemporary beliefs being equally judged to be without historical foundation by future generations. One important implication arises from this that Lang did not fully embrace, given his belief in myth as a product of a civilisation in its earliest stages of development, though it unconsciously structures his method of interpreting folklore in literary and scientific modes. Lang recognises the need to acknowledge that the myths of pre-industrial society have roots in history if contemporary history is not to be dismissed as purely imaginative by future generations. However, this affirms the belief that mythology can be viewed as a vessel for communicating facts about the past. In conceding this view, Lang unintentionally entertained the possibility that contemporary historical facts were, in some sense, also mythological. This not only reveals the proximity of O'Grady's thought to that of Lang, it also suggests the Carlylean view supported by O'Grady that purely imaginative and purely scientific approaches to the past were complicit with one another. From this perspective, it is hardly coincidental that the argument rejected by both O'Grady and Lang is associated by the former with Wordsworth, champion of the imagination, and by the latter with Müller, champion of the scientific method. Both figures could legitimately be regarded as embodiments of the divergence between literature and science accelerating during the nineteenth century. On the question of ancient mythology, however, the Wordsworthian view, as presented by O'Grady, corroborates with that of Müller, as presented by Lang. The suggestion arises that indifference to historical fact exhibited in much Romantic literature relied on an empirical scientific rejection of the value of the imagination as a vessel of historical fact.

The discussion between Maeve, Fleeas, Cailitin and Ahrimail in the second volume of *History of Ireland* reveals the importance O'Grady attaches to the view of the bards as historians, a view illustrating his belief that his own work was both imaginative and historical. It also brings Maeve's personality to the fore more emphatically than in the first volume, in order to convey O'Grady's concern at the effect of feminine subjectivity entering the public arena of political authority. Maeve rarely expresses herself openly in the first volume of *History of Ireland* but in the second volume she unashamedly dismisses the legal authority of the bards, as noted above, and she seduces Cormac Colingas.[29] Furthermore, her alliance with the magician Cailitin is perceived by O'Grady as further evidence of her unfitness for rule. Regarding Cailitin Hagan remarks, 'O'Grady makes perfectly clear that a vile character has appeared on the scene, and Cailitin's agreement with Maeve serves only to reflect great discredit on her.'[30] Cailitin was responsible for maintaining the spell that was cast over the Red Branch in the first volume and his alliance with Maeve in the second volume further underlines the alliance of esoteric druidism and feminine subjectivity that led to the destruction of patriarchal order in the first volume of *History of Ireland*.

It is possible to consider Maeve's open flouting of the heroic code as evidence of an advancing incapacity to control his text that left O'Grady feeling dissatisfied with *History of Ireland: The Heroic Period*. However, considering his determination to provide a 'clear historical frame' in the second volume which he felt was absent in the first volume, it is unlikely that his construction of femininity as subjective and anarchic would subvert his patriarchal ideology more thoroughly in the second volume. After all, the narrative of *History of Ireland: Cuculain and His Contemporaries* records the resurgence of the Red Branch Knights and the return of Cuchulainn. It is more plausible to consider O'Grady's more liberal exposure of Maeve's personality as a strategy for hastening her demise. Implicit in this strategy is the belief that once her hitherto subliminal propensity to seduction and social transgression attained political centre-stage, the inevitability of her political demise becomes self-evident. Allied to this is O'Grady's more pronounced demonisation of all forms of magical practice as 'enchantment'. Whereas his attitude to Cathvah the druid, who foretold the destruction of the Red Branch in the first volume, is ambivalent, seeing his role as necessary yet portentous, O'Grady's view of the magician Cailitin in the second volume is clearly negative. Chapter thirteen, entitled 'The Enchanter', refers to Cailitin and his role as 'enchanter' of the Red Branch. References to enchantment permeate the second volume and always in a negative context.

O'Grady's shift to this more clear-cut attitude reflects two interconnected motives of his; his desire to edit out mythic elements of his narrative that could not be presented as grounded in historical reality and his need to categorise assaults on tradition as engagement in unreality. He considers his patriarchal heroic version of history throughout *History of Ireland* as an antidote to enchantment because he believes that it can situate the imagination in historical reality. O'Grady's warnings against enchantment were made throughout his literary career, most strikingly in the section from *Toryism and the Tory Democracy* entitled 'The Great Enchantment', (later published episodically in the *All-Ireland Review*) and its application in *History of Ireland: Cuculain and His Contemporaries* illustrates the importance of the change in approach from the first volume. It reflects his aim of making his preoccupation with Irish bardic history relevant to the political environment of his own day. The influence of Carlyle on O'Grady becomes evident once more in this aspiration. Throughout *Past and Present* Carlyle alludes to 'enchantment', the manifestation of which he sees in the industrialised regions of England where values of heroism and nobility have been superseded by the 'phantasms' of wage-labour and *laissez-faire*:

In the midst of plethoric plenty, the people perish; with gold walls, and full barns, no man feels himself safe or satisfied. Workers, Master Workers, Unworkers, all men, come to pause; stand fixed, and cannot farther. Fatal paralysis spreading inwards, from the extremities, in St. Ives workhouses, in Stockport cellars, through all limbs, as if towards the heart itself.[31]

O'Grady believed that the political events of Ireland since the Act of Union indicated that the nation had become shrouded in the 'insane mist' that had beset the Red Branch Knights, a mist that lay particularly heavy on the class for whom he was most concerned, the landed gentry. His political writings are examined in Chapter 4 of this volume, but it is worth noting here that his major complaint against Irish landlords was their failure to *see* political reality as he understood it, a failure he puts down to a misperception of their relationship with the country of their origin. O'Grady sees their lack of knowledge of Irish history as the cause of this misperception. Their smug belief that, because of what they saw as their ethnic connection with the English landed aristocracy, the British Parliament would always act in the interests of their class in matters Irish, was, according to O'Grady, a product of enchantment. Only by turning their attention to indigenous Irish history and forging a leadership connection with the Irish populace could the landlords, he argues, secure their survival in an increasingly unpredictable and hostile environment. O'Grady's view was that the demise of the landed gentry would be rendered inevitable if they remained in the thrall of enchantment, just as Maeve's enthralment with the wizard Cailitin would eventually destroy her power.

In the light of this negative attitude to enchantment and the clear relation it has to feminine subjectivity in *History of Ireland*, the advance of Maeve's political influence in the second volume suggests that the patriarchal order represented by Emain Macha has been destroyed and madness has descended upon its society. However, rather than confirming O'Grady's failure to resolve the problem of gender that blighted his attempt in the first volume to present his narrative as both literary and historical, the sovereignty of rebellious femininity is depicted in order to begin the restoration of patriarchal order in the narrative. The dialectical structure of gender within patriarchy that worked against O'Grady in the first volume works for him in this instance. If his attempts to depict a history structured according to the logic of patriarchy were undermined by his failure to efface the necessary dependence of masculine self-identity on the Other of feminine subjectivity in the first volume, then the ascent of this subjectivity to the arena of political authority neutralises the libidinal force of femininity in the second volume.

Within the patriarchal framework through which history is gendered in *History of Ireland*, femininity is structured as subjective and irrational, and as contingent to the necessary self-identity of masculinity. However, this contingency can never become an absolute as it is a relational term; the absolute sovereignty of feminine subjectivity is equally as subject to contradiction as the notion of absolute masculinity because both are defined through a necessary relationship to their opposites. In the transference of feminine subjectivity from the private world of libidinality to the public world of politics, represented by Maeve's movement into a position of political authority, the restoration of patriarchy gets underway at the zenith of its degradation. In achieving absolute authority, feminine subjectivity, conceived as anarchic and ahistorical, ceases to be definable against masculine objectivity (which it has destroyed), conceived as ordered and historical; at this point feminine subjectivity becomes total, which is to say that it ceases to be feminine subjectivity, a necessarily relational idea. The all-pervasiveness of the 'insane mist', therefore, corresponds to the absolute of non-identity and irrationality, a moment Theodor Adorno identifies as fascist.[32] O'Grady's ostensible concessions to Maeve's subjectivity and its link to increased references to druidism in *History of Ireland: Cuculain and His Contemporaries* is, therefore, not a case of his formal and, consequently, historiographic design being destroyed by the otherness of a femininity conceived as anarchic; it indicates, rather, O'Grady's belief in a process by which the restoration of patriarchy necessarily emerges from its degradation. The cyclical form of history inscribed in this process strengthens O'Grady's claims about 'great permanent relations', unlike in the first volume, where it undermines those claims: in the first volume, claims for the permanence of patriarchal history are undermined in the revelation of its dependence on feminine subjectivity that the cyclical model foregrounds; in the second volume, however, the zenith of its degradation becomes the origin of patriarchal restoration, the cyclical model intimating, therefore, that if patriarchy can never be established absolutely, neither can it ever be destroyed entirely.[33]

This whole dynamic is highly ironic, particularly in view of O'Grady's strenuous efforts to marshal the imaginative looseness of his source material in the first volume of *History of Ireland*, a formal looseness O'Grady associates with that moral looseness he attributes to Maeve (a 'loose' text might be as dangerous as a 'loose' woman). If the concession to rather than the suppression of a libidinal imaginative free-play gendered as feminine is the process through which patriarchy is restored in O'Grady's text, then the affirmation of libidinality as emancipatory becomes problematic. The difficulty centres on the consequences arising from the transference of contingency and the irrational from the margin to the centre of political structures. The dynamic of O'Grady's narrative reveals how this transference produces despotism rather than liberty and inevitably results in the reconstitution of masculine authority. As personification of the lawlessness of the libidinal, Maeve's authority cannot make appeal to tradition and order for its justification; it is, therefore, an arbitrary assertion of power, a power from which the masks of tradition and order have been removed. In addition, however, this arbitrariness is itself a mask because it is doubly inscribed with contradiction. A return to the freedom of the imagination that Maeve's authority represents is always illusory, in that it is parasitic upon the law and order of patriarchy for which it is Other – it is always already alienated. It follows that the sensuousness and contingency of Maeve's 'feminine' power, presenting itself as a return to Nature, to the pre-Oedipal, is actually a step further away from it than the patriarchal order of rational necessity. The alienation of the latter from pre-Oedipal is taken as given, but Maeve's alienation is concealed and, therefore, doubly contradictory. This contradiction in the significance of Maeve's rise to power in O'Grady's narrative points to the contradiction within the glorification of the irrational and the contingent that would dominate the Celtic Twilight movement of the 1890s; her revelation of contingency as the thinking of the pre-rational somatic, the opposite of thought.

The implications of this contradiction for the affirmation of contingency in contemporary postmodern theory are important, particularly for post-Marxism, as the latter is predicated on the view of contingency as politically radical. This is evident in the seminal work of post-Marxism, *Hegemony and Socialist Strategy*, in which Ernesto Laclau and Chantal Mouffe sideline the category of historical necessity, central to the Marxist tradition, in their description of society:

> The incomplete character of every totality necessarily leads us to abandon, as a terrain of analysis, the premise of *'society'* as a sutured and self-defined totality. 'Society' is not a valid object of discourse...The irresoluble interiority/exteriority tension is the condition of any social practice: necessity only exists as a partial limitation of the field of contingency. It is in this terrain, where neither a total interiority nor a total exteriority is possible, that the social is constituted. For the same reason that the social cannot be reduced to the interiority of a fixed system of differences, pure exteriority is also impossible. In order to be *totally* external to each other, the entities would have to be totally internal with regard to themselves: that is, to have a fully constituted identity which is not subverted by any exterior.[34]

Ironically, in this passage the category of necessity acts as a pre-requisite for articulating an argument in which necessity is presented as a mere check on contingency. At the outset we are told that the incomplete nature of all totalities 'necessarily' leads to an abandonment of the concept of society, only to be told later that necessity is just a partial limitation of contingency.[35] Furthermore, the attempt to avoid relativism by checking contingency with necessity is highly dubious. Laclau and Mouffe state that absolute exteriority (pure contingency) is as impossible as an absolute interiority (self-identity) of objects, because in order for objects in a determinate relationship to be totally external in relation to each other, they would need to be totally self-identical in relation to themselves. While this is logically valid, it avoids the problem of how any element of an object can retain self-identity in a relationship in which context determines identity, as in a relation of equivalence as described by Laclau and Mouffe (see Introduction to this volume).

This problem cannot be resolved by conceiving of necessity as an unavoidable check on contingency or, in the words of Laclau and Mouffe, the unfixity of the social. Necessity and contingency are unavoidably dialectical terms, mutually defining by force of opposition. Laclau and Mouffe reveal in their argument how absolute contingency is a contradiction in terms, yet they grossly understate the necessary character of necessity to the contingency they vehemently champion. As a result, their argument for an interpretation of hegemony in terms of the relative non-fixity of the social is rescued from a collapse into infinite regress only by an arbitrary appeal to necessity as a partial limitation of contingency. It is not incredulous to find in this arbitrary appeal a trace of Maeve's arbitrary assertion of authority, despite her symbolising the anti-authoritarian free-play of the imagination that O'Grady associates with femininity.

O'Grady's conscious deployment of the dialectical method in depicting Maeve's rise to and subsequent fall from power indicates, therefore, the restorational possibility of dialectics. His narrative is intended to show that although the forces of the imagination have the potential to overthrow the political structures of patriarchy, they cannot replace these structures with anything but decadence, thus making the restoration of political order inevitable. Adorno highlights this conservative possibility of the method when he observes that dialectical thought includes not only the Marxist doctrine of proletarian revolution, 'but also the joke that... without Louis XVI there would never have been a revolution, so that he is to be thanked for the rights of man. Negative philosophy, dissolving everything, dissolves even the dissolvent'.[36] Rather than taking this as a cue to abandon the method, Adorno takes this to reinforce it, viewing the restorative possibility of the dialectic (exemplified in O'Grady's treatment of Maeve) as evidence of the need to dialecticise dialectics, to be aware of how it is both true and untrue; true, in this instance, in its revelation of the necessary relationship between subjectivity structured as feminine, and objectivity structured as masculine; false in the implication that because of this, patriarchy is ultimately the indestructible form of gender organisation in human society.[37] The realisation of the restorative possibility of the dialectical method in *History of Ireland* would be viewed by Adorno as a strategic deployment of the method rather than a surrender to it:

> The harm is done by the *thema probandum*: the thinker uses the dialectic instead of giving himself up to it. In this way thought, masterfully dialectical, reverts to the pre-dialectical stage: the serene demonstration of the fact that there are two sides to everything.[38]

For Adorno '[D]ialectics is the consistent sense of non-identity': if the seeds of patriarchal restoration are already sown in Maeve's assent to power, so too are the seeds of revolt already sown in that restoration.[39] The only certainty in history, therefore, is the impossibility of stability.

O'Grady's depicts enchantment in *History of Ireland: Cuculain and His Contemporaries* as a form of misperception: given the fact that enchantment represents for him a disconnection from historical reality, this indicates the ontological importance he attributes to perception, or vision. Hagan sees in O'Grady's ability to shift point of view the vehicle for his masterful use of suspense in the second volume.[40] This reinforces his authorship, as it suggests his capacity to see situations from all perspectives. Furthermore, an interchange between blindness and vision is characteristic of the second volume: this actualises a cyclical model of history in which the epoch of rebellion, when Maeve achieves political authority, is overtaken by a period of restoration, when the Red Branch awakens from its enchantment. This process is brilliantly evoked in chapter fourteen, 'Descent of the Red Branch', when, through the nebulous mist and vague sounds that surround her, Maeve gradually discerns the sign of her doom, the Red Hand of Ulster:

> I can hear, or hardly hear, voices as of gods or giant heroes, and a faint ringing as of brass amid the mysterious mist, and now more clearly I distinguish the flashings, and the stars, and the rapid fires. Amid the mist there is the beckoning of a gigantic hand, blood-red, and around it, as it were, lightnings. It is the Fomorah, or the people of Mac Erc, raised by sorcerers from their tombs, or the high gods of Erin descending visibly out of Tir-na-n-og, and the realms of the dead.[41]

Maeve's movement from blurred to focused vision is simultaneous with the Red Branch's awakening from the 'insane mist'; both illustrate a movement from the nebulosity of feminine subjectivity to the clarity of patriarchal history that O'Grady conceives as firm reality. Furthermore, Maeve's vision is not in the manner of empirical observation but is replete with symbolic force. This *Weltanshauung* is structured according to Maeve's mythological inheritance, her perception of reality, as understood by O'Grady, being conveyed in mythological terms. This reinforces O'Grady's argument that myth and history are not antinomial but that, on the contrary, history can only be truly perceived through its mythic forms.

The dialectic of blindness and vision recurs in chapter eighteen, entitled 'Not Yet', (illustrative of the suspense O'Grady uses to heighten the impact of Cuchulainn's return). The Red Branch are suffering heavily at the hands of Maeve, but just as they are about to be defeated, Cuchulainn appears as a god-like figure to destroy her army. Ironically, it is a blind man, the aged husband of Maeve, Aileel More, who first recognises the figure as Cuchulainn.[42] O'Grady characterises Aileel as a man of weakness throughout the *History of Ireland*. He portrays his blindness as a symptom of his incapacity to assume the authority of his ordained role as king, instead allowing Maeve, who, according to Fergus MacRoy in the first volume, should have been confined to 'the government of thy household', to dictate political affairs.[43] The ability of the blind Aileel to recognise Cuchulainn in this instance reinforces the connection O'Grady draws between patriarchy and true perception.

The return of Cuchulainn, then, symbolises the advent of a new era of patriarchal restoration. In chapter twenty-two, he overcomes the enchantment of druidism:

> Long had they laid the hero under spells, fairy-stricken and enfeebled by the force of druidic arts. But now, as out of the caves of death, he arose again in his invincible might, shaking off that magic sorrow and the oppression of the enchanters.[44]

He resolves the conflict between Fergus and Concobhar who, from O'Grady's perspective, were corrupted and set against each other because of the disruption of patriarchy; when they hear the voice of Cuchulainn, the antagonism between both subsides.[45] Cuchulainn does not return as the individual figure he was at the end of *History of Ireland: the Heroic Period*, when, because the country was governed, as O'Grady presents it, by the 'insane mist' of feminine rule, he alone remained the embodiment of patriarchal heroism in its purest form. He appears instead as a representative figure not just of Red Branch heroism but also the heroism of the Gaelic race, a change crucial to an understanding of his role in O'Grady's thought. As he prepares to do battle against the dark forces of Cailitin, Ioldana says to him: '"Not alone for the Red Branch shalt thou now fight, but for all the nations of Eire, who, thee beaten, will no longer yield men and heroes, and fair and peaceful fields, but her fens shall be enlarged, and dragons shall dwell there..."'[46] Following this, O'Grady describes the god Lu spreading a vision of Ireland before Cuchulainn that touches upon the folklore attaching to the island's rivers and mountains. The vision conveys the all-pervasiveness of Cuchulainn's fame and the heroic code his name embodies:

> And Cuculain saw her warlike tribes dwelling afar, and heroic forms in all the territories, and over Eire all the peoples raising to him high memorials, and hymning his name in songs. Also, the god caused him to see strange lands with mightier streams and fiercer suns, and the race of the ancient Gaedil there dwelling, and his name there renowned.[47]

The vision conveys O'Grady's desire to depict Cuchulainn as the embodiment of feudal communality. It indicates that the relationship between communality and Cuchulainn is reciprocal; the integrity of the community is guaranteed by respect for the memory of Cuchulainn and, in turn, this memory is informed by the communal propensity of Cuchulainn's heroism revealed in his selflessness. Therefore, the vision reveals the prescriptive basis of O'Grady's historiography. As the embodiment of the patriarchal order of Emain Macha, Cuchulainn symbolises the 'great permanent relations' that O'Grady interprets as history in its essence. By making selflessness a necessary attribute of the heroic personality, therefore, he implies that selfishness is a form of madness disengaged from historical reality.

51

Through this characterisation of Cuchulainn, O'Grady makes the relationship of individualism to community pertinent to the project of integrating the imagination and history that governs *History of Ireland*. The nature of this relationship in O'Grady's characterisation is difficult to ascertain because of the complexity of the terms involved.[48] For example, it appears self-evident that O'Grady presents Cuchulainn as anathema to the form of atomistic individualism that was advocated in the utilitarian philosophy of Jeremy Bentham during the nineteenth century.[49] Wên-Kuei Liao has argued, however, that Bentham maintained that claims for the interests of the community must refer back to the concept of individual interest as the notion of interest originates in the concept of the individual.[50] From a Benthamite perspective, therefore, Cuchulainn's indifference to his personal welfare in his concern for the interests of the community he represents is merely another form of hedonism. Similarly, Raymond Williams observes that although John Locke, described by Owen Chadwick as the father of liberal political thought in nineteenth century Europe, saw co-operation as natural, he believed, in line with Hobbes before him, in 'separate individuals who create society by consent or contract, for the protection of their individual interests'.[51] These observations indicate the precariousness of establishing a clear demarcation between individualism and communality. In recognising this, Williams nevertheless argues that the distinction is indispensable for articulating experiences as difficult to express precisely as they are irrefutable.[52] In the light of this (but acknowledging the difficulties surrounding the terms), it can be said that Cuchulainn's individualism embodies a conflict of feudal and modern social value-systems in the second volume of *History of Ireland*, rather than expressing a unique personality. Georg Lukács contends that the epic hero is only an individual to the degree to which he is estranged from the outside world; without such estrangement, his individuality vanishes:

> The epic hero is, strictly speaking, never an individual. It is traditionally thought that one of the essential characteristics of the epic is the fact that its theme is not a personal destiny but the destiny of a community.[53]

This claim is supported in *History of Ireland: The Heroic Period* by the fact that Cuchulainn's individuality only emerges when the social order he embodies goes into decline with the ascent of Maeve to political authority. This is reinforced in chapter twenty-three of *History of Ireland: Cuchulain and His Contemporaries*, 'In the City of Ath-a-Cliath', that follows immediately after the final battle of the Táin Bo Cuailgne when Maeve's forces are defeated by Cuchulainn and she is forced to return the bull of Coolney to the clans of Ulster. In this chapter, O'Grady transfers Cuchulainn to contemporary Dublin in order to draw a negative contrast between the heroic world of antiquity and the modern industrial age. In this instance, Cuchulainn appears individualistic because the feudal heroic order he is depicted as representing has disappeared; his grandeur arises from the juxtaposition of this order against the impoverishment of contemporary urban life:

Cuculain was dejected when he looked upon the people, so small were they, and so pale and ignoble, both in appearance and behaviour; and also when he saw the extreme poverty of the poor, and the hurrying eager crowds seeking what he knew not. But they, on the other hand, were astonished at the heroes, the greatness of their stature, the majesty of their bearing, and their tranquillity; also, at the richness and brightness of their apparel, the whiteness of their skin, and their long hair, parted in the middle and rolling over their shoulders. For, amongst the citizens of Ath-a-Cliath, they seemed like scions of some mighty and divine race long since passed away.[54]

This contrast suggests that Cuchulainn's individualism emerges as aristocratic only in the context of the supersession of feudalism by capitalism; he appears as *das Übermensch* in the eyes of the masses to whom he seems exceptional.[55] The contrast Lukes draws between the negative *Individualismus* articulated during the French Enlightenment, associated with *laissez-faire* economics, pecuniary atavism and social atomism, and the *Individualität* of German Romanticism appears to be borne out in the contrast.[56] However, a dialectical relationship between both is also indicated in the fact that Cuchulainn's heroism requires the banality of contemporary industrial society as depicted by O'Grady in order to appear as individual and, consequently, as aristocratic. Williams's claim that the abstract concepts of the individual and of society/community emerged simultaneously as separate entities with the Reformation and the beginnings of capitalist economy, supports the argument that individualism only emerges in Cuchulainn during the displacement of the feudal social order he embodies.[57] Cuchulainn's individualism, therefore, is contradictory. It represents the heroic order O'Grady associates with feudalism in which the imagination and history, subject and object, are united; yet it also signifies *qua* the exceptionality that defines it as individual, the absence of this unity. In the light of this, it needs to be recognised that O'Grady's depiction of Cuchulainn stands between two forms of Romantic individualism as defined by Lukes. To the extent that he appears as exceptional, Cuchulainn embodies the subjectivity of the Romantic individual, but as a symbol of feudal patriarchy, he represents the organic communalism that is expressed in the Romantic nationalism of nineteenth-century Europe.[58]

The image of Cuchulainn in the city not only depicts his individuality as aristocratic, it also pre-empts Yeats's denigration of Dublin in poems such as 'September 1913', in attacking what O'Grady sees as the degenerative materialism of the city. O'Grady complained that *laissez-faire* economics increased the gap between rich and poor, creating the conditions for anarchic revolt and, hence, a return to the obscurantism of enchantment. In his political works, he links this aversion towards materialism to his criticism of the Irish landlords in two ways; first, he claimed that they had rarely acted as a political group in the affairs of state since the Act of Union, instead setting their personal interests above the interests of their class; second, he argued that on those rare occasions when they did act as a group, their unique position in Irish society that they believed was guaranteed by the English connection inevitably overrode any sentimental relationship of leadership they might have forged with the rest of the Irish population. O'Grady viewed the individualism illustrated in these attitudes as a negative mixture of aristocratic and economic. The aristocratic nature of this individualism was negative to the degree to which it was exclusively egotistic, divorced from any sentimental connection to an organic community characteristic of the understanding of feudal society in the work of Victorian intellectuals such as Carlyle, Ruskin and Morris.[59] This negativity was exacerbated by the influence of *laissez-faire* economics that O'Grady saw in the tendency of the landlords to prioritise their personal interests above the interests of their class. O'Grady saw individualism consistently triumphing over communality in the political machinations of the Irish landlords. In 'Ireland and the Hour' from *Toryism and the Tory Democracy* (1886) he implores the landlords to abandon this individualism in favour of an inclusively feudalist model: 'You will find, too, that like your feudal ancestors, you must avoid modern exclusiveness. There will be no gulf between you and your men'.[60] O'Grady's understanding of Cuchulainn's aristocratic individualism is far from individualist, either in the Romantic sense of a retreat into complete subjectivity or in the utilitarian sense of the primacy of individual interest; it arises because the social order he represents, structured according to a heroic feudal value-system, is absent in the contemporary era of industrial capitalism. Also implicit in the image of Dublin confronting Cuchulainn is the view that what the poor cherish most about the heroes is what they lack most, namely, a sense of that individuality that O'Grady sees eroded in the homogenising effects of large-scale urbanisation. Therefore, O'Grady concurs with the view that the rise of bourgeois individualism, manifested in the political doctrine of liberal democracy and the economic doctrine of *laissez-faire*, has produced an alienation symptomatic of the loss of authenticity in contemporary society.[61]

In a work that illuminates those tensions characteristic of O'Grady's treatment of individualism in *History of Ireland*, Lawrence Stone defines the term in two ways; on the one hand, as an interest in the self that is marked by introspection and, on the other, as a concern for personal autonomy and a corresponding respect for the personal autonomy of others. He traces the rise of individualism in both senses, the first developing in the sixteenth and seventeenth centuries with the idea of the uniqueness of the individual (an idea Stone traces to Puritanism) and the second developing in the seventeenth and early eighteenth centuries when the first idea developed into an abstract political doctrine that would culminate in Paine's *Rights of Man*.[62] He examines the many forms in which the rise of individualism manifested itself, in terms of community, patriarchy and the question of property.

In considering the decline of community between the sixteenth and eighteenth centuries, Stone focuses on the weakening of kinship and clientage as powerful vehicles of social organisation. He notes the decline of 'hospitality' among the aristocracy during the seventeenth century as one sign of this, a decline that he explains in terms of

> ...a major reorientation of consumption patterns, caused by the growth of a more inward-looking, more private and more urbanized life-style for the aristocratic family...It was characterized by the withdrawal of the family from the great hall to the private dining-room and by the increasing habit of residing for long periods in London to enjoy the 'season'.[63]

Stone sees the main function of this hospitality, expressed in open-handed generosity to kin relatives and clients, the retaining of hordes of largely idle servants and 'the keeping of an open table for all comers' as largely symbolic, ensuring the maintenance of the status of the aristocratic patron. It expressed a social order where hierarchy and community were in tandem, and where the notion of family extended beyond the particular boundaries of the nuclear model.

Banquet scenes reflecting this 'hospitality' recur throughout both volumes of *History of Ireland*. Their importance is denoted by the fact that key developments in O'Grady's narrative take place during them. For example, in the first volume in the story of Lara's triumph over his corrupt uncle Corac during their struggle to gain the throne of Emain Macha, the sequence of events that lead to patriarchal restoration begins during a banquet given by the king of Slieve Mish. Lara openly declares his love for the king's daughter Moreea during the banquet and her reciprocation initiates the processs of Lara's restoration of the patriarchal lineage of Kimbay MacFiontann disturbed by Corac.[64] The banquet scene recurs again in the second volume, given by Maeve on this occasion:

> There, then, the great warriors of the Tân feasted, rejoicing in themselves and their matchless Queen. But when they had made an end of eating, the slaves removed the remnant of the banquet and the instruments of the first feast, and went round again distributing abundantly the ruddy, exhilarating ale...[65]

In the context of this banquet Maeve reproves her bard, a gesture that provokes the dispute between Queen Fleeas, Cailitin and Ahrimail about the role of the bards considered above.

These occasions and others in the *History of Ireland* make vivid an idea O'Grady expresses later in 1886 in 'Ireland and the Hour' in *Toryism and the Tory Democracy*. He writes in praise of the feudal landlord who 'dined with his people and saw his ale go round, in days before men had learned to prate about Liberty and Equality'. Contrasting this with what he regards as the tokenist gesture of the contemporary landlord, he remarks: 'The landlord of old times did not feed in selfish and savage isolation, giving a big dinner once in a way to his tenantry – an ugly and hypocritical farce, as I can't help regarding the practice'.[66] In emphasising this idea, O'Grady even goes as far as citing an instance from Eugene O'Curry's *Manners and Customs of the Ancient Irish*, where a High-King of Ireland actually dines with his swine-herds.[67] His point is that close contact with his men brings the landlord into contact with what O'Grady regards as the *facts* of life:

> The feudal chiefs and barons had the secret, and well practised it in their stone halls or rude wattled palaces, eating and drinking with their men, so taught, not by historians and students, but by facts and close actual acquaintance with men and things.[68]

Of these facts, two remain uppermost in O'Grady's mind, rank and birth:

> Rank and birth are very solid facts, which you will not ignore, because as a matter of fact men, your men, are born, not in the white ideal of eternity, but in the many-coloured, varied, complicated practicalities of time, and the modern Irishman, in spite of all his political rhodomontade, does very deeply respect rank and birth.[69]

In advocating the communality of feudalism, therefore, O'Grady is not simply trumpeting community for its own sake; he values it because, in its feudal form, it complements hierarchy and he considers hierarchy an ineluctable fact.[70] In this obsession with fact, he pays homage once more to Carlyle, who considers the ability to discern fact as the most distinctive feature of the hero:

> A Hero, as I repeat, has this first distinction, which indeed we may call first and last, the Alpha and Omega of his whole Heroism, That he looks through the shows of things into *things*.[71]

O'Grady, of course, conceives these *things* as, in their essence, hierarchical and patriarchal. Stone points out that what was important in the sixteenth century idea of hospitality was not so much the idea of community as the particular form of community in which status was invested in the patron; the capacity to be hospitable conferred status not upon the beneficiaries but upon the purveyor. The decline of the practice threatened that status, helping to create the conditions wherein the authority of the king or landlord over his people diminished in their eyes.

The decline of kinship exemplified by the demise of aristocratic hospitality resulted, according to Stone, in a move from 'lineage' to 'civil' society, the former, regionalist, and the latter, universalist; kinship came to be replaced by loyalty to an emerging nation-state.[72] He argues that in order for the transformation to be effected without the threat of anarchic revolt, great emphasis was laid on authority and obedience in the pamphlets of the late sixteenth and early seventeenth centuries, an emphasis particularly directed at the authority of the male as husband and father.[73] Stone observes that this solidification of patriarchy within the emerging model of the nuclear family continued largely unabated until the last decades of the seventeenth century, arrested in 1689 with the publication of John Locke's *Two Treatises on Government* written in response to Robert Filmer's *Patriarcha* which drew upon the analogy of the father in the family to support an argument for the authority of the king in the state. In this work Locke refutes an essentialist, patriarchal model of marriage in favour of a utilitarian, contractual one. Summarising Locke, Stone writes that the power of the father over his child was 'only a limited and temporary authority, which automatically ends when the child grows up'.[74] This indicates that Locke saw patriarchy in terms of a pre–capitalist state of affairs that was rapidly becoming obsolete with the consolidation of the nation–state in the latter half of the seventeenth century in England.

As we have seen throughout both volumes of *History of Ireland*, patriarchy is central to O'Grady's thought. Edward Hagan notes that he advised the reader to take the second volume as factually superior to the first.[75] This was not simply due to increased accuracy of source material, but, more importantly, to its narration of the restoration of patriarchy in the resurgence of the Red Branch Knights and the return of Cuchulainn. Cuchulainn is O'Grady's supreme model of feudal patriarchy, since he is the heroic defender of the social order under attack from Maeve in alliance with the wizard Cailitin.

This patriarchalism that Cuchulainn personifies is structured according to a dialectic of general modes of production analogous to the dialectic of gender it instantiates; a social system of communal ownership is set in contrast against one of private ownership, the former grounded in an organic contact with 'the soil' and the latter in a mechanistic dislocation from it. This contrast is suggested in the image of Cuchulainn in contemporary Dublin referred to above but it is more explicit in a scene from the latter stages of the narrative in volume one. Cuchulainn has been wounded after his defeat of Fardia and Laeg, his life-long friend, travels to procure help for him. He stops at a certain house to seek assistance in mending his broken chariot and to rest his exhausted horse but the owner, Croothean, initially refuses to help him: 'It was not by the lavish entertainment of those who passed by this way that I have become rich and great as thou now see'st me, but by prudence and attention to my several affairs.'[76] The story of Croothean's rise to wealth reveals his resourceful and calculating personality and provides another illustration of O'Grady's view that the political authority of femininity was destructive. Croothean was a slave to Brigamba but, with her consent, entered into a pact with other 'fudirs' like himself, thereby acquiring communal rights before the brehon. He became the chief of the guild of which he was a member and eventually acquired more land from Brigamba to attain a position of wealth. Laeg's attitude to Croothean is one of disgust:

> An evil time, indeed, will it be for the Gaeil if the ollavs in their wisdom concur to plant among us such shrubs of deadly poison as thyself, O vile

and avaricious stranger, without gratitude or nobleness or love for aught save the miserable accumulation of thy sorry pelf.[77]

Laeg's use of the word 'stranger' here indicates the fragmentation of society accompanying the rise of capitalism that O'Grady symbolises through Croothean's rise to wealth. Croothean is a stranger to Laeg by not being of heroic lineage and by the strangeness of his selfishness to someone reared in the heroic and hospitable code of the Red Branch. Furthermore, Croothean represents a society of atomistic individuals in which everyone is a stranger to each other, unlike the feudal society that Laeg represents, where the identity of the individual is synonymous with that of the community. The dialectical nature of the relationship between the feudal and capitalist modes of production as indicated in this instance, however, manifests a contradiction analogous to that within O'Grady's patriarchal ideology in *History of Ireland*. The feudal communalism he advocates exists in a necessarily antithetical relationship to the bourgeois individualism he attacks, indicating that it is a concept always already in crisis as its identity is dependent on its opposite. Cuchulainn's individualism illustrates this in that it becomes apparent only in the absence of the feudal communalism it signifies – its significance contravenes its occurrence.

History of Ireland: Cuculain and His Contemporaries indicates that capitalism can function on either side of the subject–object, imagination–history, feminine–masculine binaries informing O'Grady's project. As the condition for the rise of class difference, social atomisation, the mutually opposed romantic and economic forms of individualism, the capitalist mode of production corresponds to the anarchic fragmentation O'Grady associates with pure femininity and the imagination unrestrained by the forms of historical reality. As the condition for the displacement of superstition by scientific rationality, the superscession of sentiment by calculation and the domestication of affective relations by mechanistic social structures like administrative bureaucracy, the capitalist mode of production corresponds to the concern for fact O'Grady associates with pure masculinity and unimaginative empirical history. Both interpretations feed into the feudal model that O'Grady juxtaposes against capitalism; his desire to circumscribe imaginative freedom with a concern for historical fact is a response to capitalism in the first sense and his desire to integrate the imagination into history is a response to it in the second sense. Thus, the unity of the feudal communalist model that O'Grady presents Cuchulainn as representing has the subject–object split it attempts to transcend inscribed within it. Whether O'Grady conceives capitalism in its drive towards individual freedom as the descent of human society into the formless chaos of femininity, or as a loss of the regenerative spontaneity of femininity in its drive for systematicity, this feudal unity exists in a necessary dialectical relationship to it as its Other and is therefore already a disunity.

To conclude, *History of Ireland: Cuculain and His Contemporaries* brings into sharp relief the manner in which the dialectical form structuring O'Grady's treatment of the relationship between history and the imagination in both volumes eludes his authorial control. It has been observed that this dialectical form emerges in O'Grady's need for a cyclical model of history to illustrate his typological ideal of history and that whereas this dialectical form worked against his intentions in the first volume, it works for them in the second. However, the reinstatement of patriarchy by Cuchulainn's triumph over Maeve at the end of the second volume fails to close the dialectic with a vision of history reunited to the imagination; that utopian vision emerges out of the *di-*vision of imagination and history, the divided, specialised forms of perceiving history and the imagination as divided and specialised. O'Grady's need to contrast Cuchulainn's stature with that of an impoverished Dublin crowd for the purposes of illustrating his heroism underlines the extent to which the dialectic remains outside his control. Nevertheless, his utopian vision, for all its flaws, remained an affront to the epistemological claims of aesthetics and empirical history that were developing into more discursively autonomous fields of study at the end of the nineteenth century. For this reason, O'Grady's last major attempt to integrate history and the imagination, *History of Ireland: Critical and Philosophical*, is a work of importance not just for revealing the paradigm that dominated attitudes to history and the imagination during the period of the Literary Revival in Ireland, but also because it was published at a time when a Victorian belief in the possibility of reconciling the imaginative and scientific movements of the century was caving in to a more intense consciousness of the subject–object split their divergence exemplified.

Science, myth and history in *History of Ireland: Critical and Philosophical* and other works

O'GRADY'S TREATMENT OF BARDIC MATERIAL IN *History of Ireland: The Heroic Period* and *History of Ireland: Cuculain and His Contemporaries* is beset with difficulties arising from his determination to present the works as historical and literary. As a counterweight to the narrative form of these volumes *History of Ireland: Critical and Philosophical* (1881) attempts to deal with the relationship between the imagination and history analytically, yet by the end of the book the tension between them remains. In this work, O'Grady moves between imaginative–literary and empirical–historical arguments for the validity of Irish bardic literature. At one point he states: 'To express the whole nature of a race or nation the artist needs that absolute freedom which is only supplied by a complete escape from positive history and unyielding despotic fact.'[1] Yet elsewhere in the book O'Grady employs the deductive logic of conventional empirical historiography.

The tension between imaginative and empirical approaches to history reaches a critical point in the racial beliefs O'Grady expresses in this work. The early chapters of the book repeat those dealing with prehistoric Ireland in the opening chapters of *History of Ireland: The Heroic Period* in which the argument was put forward that the Gaelic race was a mixture of 'barbarous' north and 'civilised' south. In *History of Ireland: Critical and Philosophical* O'Grady attributes the physical features associated with the Aryan race to the Celts; tall, blue-eyed and yellow-haired. He describes the races who invaded Ireland from southern Europe as 'dark, small, oval-faced.'[2] These physiological claims display the general influence of Darwin in heightening the physiological interests of ethnographers during the latter half of the nineteenth century. Within this context, the physiological references illustrate O'Grady's concern to attribute some degree of scientific credibility to his work.

Equally, however, his racial pronouncements are employed to justify the literary value of ancient Irish legend. In arguing that the Irish race was a mixture of northern Celt and southern Basque, for example, O'Grady equates the bardic literature of Ireland with some of the most renowned works of European culture:

> The Edda of Snorro, the Niebelungen Lied, and the Irish bardic literature, especially that priceless portion of it which deals with the age of Cuculain and the Ultonian Knights of the Red Branch, would doubtless never have reached us at all, nor would the elements of which

they are composed have been moulded into even the rudest epic forms, but for influences stealing into the North of Europe from the civilised South.[3]

O'Grady's racial views are also used to equate the bardic literature with the work of Homer:

> In the times of which Homer sang, the Greek nobles had yellow hair and blue eyes. At the time when the heroic literature of Ireland was composed, the Irish nobles had yellow hair and blue eyes. Athene seized Achilles by the yellow locks, while she herself was a blue-eyed goddess.[4]

The use O'Grady makes of racial theory, to convey the belief that his work had both scientific and cultural value, is the ultimate instance of his general concern to reconcile empirical and imaginative approaches to the past. It advances upon Matthew Arnold's attempts to reconcile science and literature by suggesting that, in relation to history, the empirical and the imaginative were, in a sense, merely modal variations of the same phenomenon. To this extent O'Grady's thought was closer to Nietzsche than to Arnold in *History of Ireland: Critical and Philosophical*, with the qualification that O'Grady is less self-consciously ironical in connecting imaginative and empirical approaches to the past.

This is borne out in the genealogical method that structures the book. O'Grady refers to the line of descent traced by medieval scholastic writers from Adam to the Milesians, the first inhabitants of Ireland who arrived from Spain with the Lia Fáil (the Stone of Destiny). He rejects this genealogical ladder, however, on the basis of his belief that it arose from the determination of medieval scholastics to Christianise the line of descent of Irish kings. He then traces a line of descent from the god Milesius to the establishment of Emain Macha under the kingship of Kimbay MacFiontann, the first historically verifiable city in Ireland; from Kimbay O'Grady traces a line of descent to the establishment of Tara as the first centre of national authority in Ireland, ruled in the first instance by Tuatha Techtmar; finally he traces a line of descent from Techtmar to Niall of the Nine Hostages, the first Irish king referred to in the book whose historical existence was factually indisputable.

This line of descent is not traced by O'Grady in an arbitary fashion. He supports his claims with critical reference to an array of sources, mostly from ancient Greece and Rome and from Irish medieval scholastics. In arguing for the historical importance of Emain Macha, for example, he refers to the map of Ireland drawn up by the classical Greek writer Ptolemy, on which 'Regia' was marked in the middle of Ulster.[5] In support of his belief that, through the Milesians, the Irish had roots in Spain, he quotes from an early Roman geographer, Festus Rufus.[6] Furthermore, he provides a credible explanation for the existence of heroic and divine cycles in the annals of Irish legend that is consistent with his understanding of the relationship between history and the imagination. He argues that in ancient Ireland bards from local regions, working in dialogue with one another, evolved ideas of heroism and nobility around the tombs of great kings and warriors in their locality. These bards communicated with those of other regions and in co-ordinating 'the topical traditions and local results of imagination, evolved a cycle of such champions banded together by some unifying principle of interest or race, such as the Ossianic cycle of Finn and his warriors, the Ultonian cycle of Cuculain and the Knights of the Red Branch'.[7] O'Grady argues that with the passing of the age in which the memory of the historical life of the warriors remained vivid in the minds of the bards, the status of these heroes grew until the bards eventually depicted them as equal in power to the gods of their age. He claims that this paved the way for a new divine cycle in which the heroes superseded the old gods to become the gods of a new age.[8]

On this basis, it is clear that O'Grady's genealogical method was intended to be scientific, within the less specialised nineteenth century sense of that term. *History of Ireland: Critical and Philosophical* is informed by a method of tracing ancestral origins and classifying characters O'Grady encountered in his source material in terms of the various cycles he identifies and with cognisance of the methodology he observes in the medieval treatment of that source material. This method of tracing and classification became definitive of the scientific method during the nineteenth century and produced its most radical consequences in Darwin's *On the Origins of Species* (1859) and *The Descent of Man* (1871). O'Grady's use of the method in his book is not always consistent and the conclusion he reaches of an ancestral line of descent running from the Milesian clan down to Niall of the Nine Hostages is hardly plausible, yet to dimiss *History of Ireland: Critical and Philosophical* as purely speculative is to ignore one of its most telling insights, namely, the proximity of science to myth in the genealogical method.

If this method is evidence of O'Grady's pretensions to empirical, scientific crediblity, it is also evidence of his subscription to the mythical concept of the Tree of Life, central to Celtic and Kabbalistic mystical traditions. On the basis of the traces of parenthood in a race or species under observation, the genealogical method builds up a family tree the branches of which multiply the further one pursues the origin of that race/species, given the doubling of parentage with each generation; theoretically, there is nothing to prevent the tree branching out infinitesmally, once a belief in the unique origins of a species is abandoned, as it is in Darwin. Implicit in the genealogical mapping of *History of Ireland: Critical and Philosophical* is the suggestion of a correspondence between the tree of evolution and the 'LIFE TREE IGDRASIL' venerated by Carlyle.[9] In the primacy he attributes to race, O'Grady, unconsciously at least, suggests an inverse correspondence between the empirical method of Darwin and the myths of origin it was intended to supplant.

In the Kabbalist mysticism of such nineteenth-century writers as

Swedenborg or William Blake, the material condition of contemporary man was evidence of the degree to which he had fallen from an original state of immaterial perfection. In Darwinism, however, the monumental complexity of man relative to the earliest species from which he evolved was evidence of his development in the direction of material perfection; theoretically, the infinite variety of natural forms was traceable in the genealogical tree of man and thus the whole history of the earth was written within him. In this sense, Darwinism paved the way for the Nietzschean claim that the realisation of man as *Übermensch* was coterminous with the death of God, a reversal of Christian incarnation.[10] To accept this, however, is to recognise that Darwin's method of empirical reason, of trace and classification, contributed to creating the conditions in which the irrationalism of the mythic hero and of racial suprematism was generated.

The tension in Darwinism between the empowering view of man as the god-like embodiment of the whole evolutionary process and the humiliating view of him as descendant of the ape comes through in *History of Ireland: Critical and Philosophical*. This is evident in a contradiction that undermines O'Grady's attempts to expound a general thesis that accommodates science and myth. O'Grady's attitude to a legend he encountered in his source material, the Gadelian legend, is one expression of this contradiction. The problem that the legend presents to him is that it breaks the line of descent he traces from Milesius to Niall of the Nine Hostages by not deriving the Milesian pedigree from the Tuatha De Danann or Fomorian clans. He argues that this legend was composed by medieval scholastics in order to dissociate Irish nobles from pre-Christian ancestry. He claims that this ignored the historical reality of pure pre-Christian ethnic traditions of which the legend was originally a part, uncontaminated by scholastic ideas.[11] He supports this by claiming that although the history of Milesius and of his Gadelian ancestors was laden with scholastic notions, no such concepts entered the Gadelian legend, recorded within this history. He also observes that the legend is treated in a factual rather than epic manner, indicative of the poetical limitations of the medieval scholastics.[12] In short, O'Grady claims, on the basis of empirical historical analysis, that the Gadelian legend was a medieval *myth*. In dismissing the legend on this basis, he is dismissing one myth in the service of another, the myth of a continuous genealogical line of descent from Milesius to Niall of the Nine Hostages. Because he adopts an argument for this purpose that is empirically historical in form, O'Grady reopens the gap between myth and science, between imagination and history.

This contradiction is also evident in O'Grady's treatment of the story of the Atticottic revolution in *History of Ireland: Critical and Philosophical*, which he describes as 'the massacre of the aristocracy of Ireland by the plebeians'.[13] According to his version of this legend, after the victory of the Milesian clan over the Fir-Bolgs and the Nemedians, the subject peoples decided to revolt against the Milesian aristocracy and establish their own Atticottic aristocracy.

The revolt failed and the subject peoples were scattered by the Milesians into separate parts of the country. O'Grady is keen to deny the historical accuracy of this story. His grounds are threefold. First, he contends that the very intensity of detail given by the scholastic authors of the Annals of the Four Masters to this story is an indication of its non-historicality. A pattern appears, he argues, where events of the far-distant past (and so less likely to be historically true) contain more descriptive detail than events of more recent times. Second, he points out that the possibility of a trans-tribal, national, plebeian revolt was extremely implausible in a society so heavily defined by tribe and locality. Third, he claims that a democratic spirit covered Ireland during the age of St Columba:

> Thenceforward, the patrician bards and monkish settler writers would be aware of the existence of servile discontent, and when the divine character of these Atticottic personages was forgotten, the notion that they were a servile race, usurping the place and privileges of the Milesian aristocracy, would naturally arise.[14]

As with the Gadelian legend, O'Grady provides historically plausible arguments for dismissing the Atticottic revolt as a myth, once again opening the gap between myth and science in his treatment of the past. This is another instance of one myth being dismissed by O'Grady in the service of another; the myth of a permanent patriarchal order in Gaelic history.

O'Grady's need to reopen the gap between myth and science in his treatment of the Gadelian and Atticottic legends provides evidence of the political bias behind the alternating perspectives of history that he takes in *History of Ireland: Critical and Philosophical*. Writing at a time when the land movement was, under the leadership of Parnell, the dominant force in Irish political life, O'Grady could not envisage the possibility of bardic literature setting a precedent for a revolt against the landed gentry, as the Atticottic revolt did. Were he to do so, the *raison d'être* of *History of Ireland*, forging a sentimental connection of nationhood between the landlords and the rest of the population, would be undermined. In addition, O'Grady needed to prove to the landed gentry that Ireland was an ancient and noble civilisation, despite its desperate condition in the wake of the Famine, if he was to convince them of the efficacy of committing themselves wholly to Ireland while adopting a position of leadership: 'Ireland is now, as I write, poor and weak. She was once strong and renowned. She will be strong and renowned again.'[15] His need to discredit the Gadelian legend becomes self-evident in the light of this political aspiration. This illustrates that in looking back to Ireland's far distant past, O'Grady is attempting to influence its present condition with a view to determining a future that will reflect the nobility of that past. Reflecting, for example, on the nebulosity of the dawn of Irish history, he comments:

> The legends represent the imagination of the country; they are that kind of history which a nation desires to possess. They betray the ambition and

ideals of the people, and in this respect, have a value far beyond the tale of actual events and duly recorded deeds, which are no more history than a skeleton is a man.[16]

The 'kind of history' that O'Grady desires Ireland to possess is one in which his ideal of a patriarchal community led by the landed gentry would be realised.

This being the case, the question of genre is highly relevant to an interpretation of *History of Ireland: Critical and Philosophical*, since the prophetic function O'Grady assigns to history is expressed in terms of the epic:

And thus, regarding the whole from a point of view sufficiently remote, a certain epic completeness and harmony characterises the vast panoramic succession of ages and races.[17]

In his analysis of epic poems by Tennyson, Samuel Ferguson and Edwin Arnold, Colin Graham elucidates aspects of Bakhtin's theory of epic from *The Dialogic Imagination* pertinent to *History of Ireland: Critical and Philosophical* because of the significance O'Grady attributes to the epic form. Graham focuses in particular on the connection Bakhtin draws between the epic, nation and temporality. Graham observes that Bakhtin does not conceive of the temporality inscribed in the epic in terms of linear history, but as a past prescriptively constructed and valorised above contemporaneity:

['The national epic past'] is...'a world of "beginnings" and "peak times"', 'a world of "firsts" and "bests",' a selective history which, because the epic poem is continually 'about' the past, places a past world hierarchically above the present.[18]

The prescriptive nature of O'Grady's epic history validates Bakhtin's view of the past specific to the epic world view as 'a specifically evaluating (hierarchical) category'.[19] Furthermore, O'Grady's pre-requisite of 'a point of view sufficiently remote' for the perception of 'epic completeness and harmony' supports Bakhtin's view of the epic past as 'walled off absolutely from all subsequent times...'[20]

However, it is clear that O'Grady's *History of Ireland* was published with the intention of impacting upon the cultural and political circumstances of late nineteenth-century Ireland; rather than eliding the contemporary, O'Grady aspires to transform it. An engagement with contemporaneity always runs the risk of disturbing epic 'completeness and harmony' however; the pre-determining necessity of the past may be split by the contingency of the present.

Bakhtin makes a distinction between contemporaneity for its own sake and contemporaneity for the future that is relevant here. He associates the former with the celebration of temporal flux characteristic of genres lower than the epic, genres that eventually developed into the novel form. The latter, in contrast, refers to his notion of future memorialisation, whereby the epic selects its materials with a view to their preservation in the memory of descendants; thus, this future is not open-ended but fixed in advance, underwritten in O'Grady's case by the notion of 'great permanent relations':

> The valorized emphasis is not on the future and does not serve the future, no favors are being done it (such favors face an eternity outside time); what is served here is the future memory of the past, a broadening of the world of the absolute past, an enriching of it with new images (at the expense of contemporaneity) – a world that is always opposed in principle to any *merely transitory* past.[21]

This argument points to the prescriptive nature of O'Grady's argument for the historicity of his work in his introduction to the second volume of *History of Ireland* when he suggests that the legend of Cuchulainn originated in some heroic historical individual. The memory of this individual was preserved and narrated among his descendants because he personified a heroic value-system; this memory valorises such a system and carries its own perpetuation as an imperative inscribed within its form.

The value-system encoded in O'Grady's idea of the epic corresponds to Bakhtin's theory to the extent to which his idea of 'great permanent relations' is prescriptive. However, the process by which O'Grady selects and forms from his source material is not only governed by this prescriptive imperative but also by the need to convey his work as factually historical; in fact, this prescriptive imperative is indelibly bound up with this historical imperative, as O'Grady's belief that history is always patriarchal conveys.[22] His philosophy of the epic involves a selection process that aspires to empirical historiographic *and* aesthetic credibility. His treatment of the legend of the Atticottic revolt is a revealing example of the ideological specificity of this selection process. O'Grady decides that the scholastic interpretation of this legend as a plebeian revolt is an historically relative judgement rendered erroneous by the particular intellectual bias of the medieval period, his interpretation motivated in this instance by his belief that acceptance of such a judgement would disturb the epic completeness his bardic history aspires to. This decision to discount the scholastic interpretation of the legend, therefore, is informed by pretensions to scientific objectivity and aesthetic necessity.

Graham sees a direct relation between the selection process Bakhtin views as part of epic construction, and the political ideology of nationalism:

> Nations then filter the past ideologically, producing an 'antiquity' which can be considered 'glorious' by Renan, 'selective' by Gellner, and an 'image' by Anderson. And the crossover with Bakhtinian epic again becomes clearer; it similarly reads the past ideologically, stressing 'peak times' of national (subsequently epic) history, becoming interwoven with (rather than merely parallel to) the ideological processes of nationalism.[23]

Undoubtedly, the process governing O'Grady's selection from his sources is designed to produce an epic picture coloured with the strains of an antique, heroic nationality. However, the imaginative and historiographic imperatives informing this enterprise ensure that this aim is fraught with difficulties that reveal the extent to which his epic deviates from Bakhtin's theory and, in terms of the symbiotic relationship Graham draws between epic and nation, the manner in which nation becomes an unstable notion in his *History of Ireland*.

Graham considers how Samuel Ferguson problematises aspects of Bakhtin's thesis:

> For Ferguson, the preservation of epic distance is necessary to prevent, rather than initiate, comment on contemporaneity. Ferguson's epic thus becomes stretched and revealing in the theoretical area in which epic and nation coalesce: because Ferguson himself tries to intervene in and adjust this relationship, his epic's discourse moves interestingly from Bakhtinian norms.[24]

Graham states that Ferguson, unlike Tennyson, had no immediate epic tradition with which he could identify with relative ease; the same could also be said of O'Grady. However, far from seeking to elide contemporaneity, O'Grady was largely directed towards it. Furthermore, O'Grady's desire to influence the political and intellectual climate in Ireland through *History of Ireland* raises an important issue that the manner in which Graham deploys Bakhtin's concept of the epic does not address. This concerns the artistic and historiographic imperatives informing his epic project. O'Grady's artistic treatment of Irish legends must meet the demands of the epic form; in examining his treatment of source material in *History of Ireland: The Heroic Period* the immensity of this problem can be seen. On the other hand, O'Grady does not want to present this literary endeavour as purely imaginative. He must stake a claim of historical veracity for his enterprise if it is to have the political and intellectual influence he desires. However, both imperatives conflict with one another, unveiling contradictions that O'Grady finds insurmountable. The evidence of the difficulties they provoke is found in the fact that he felt the need to write *History of Ireland: Critical and Philosophical* at all, since it constitutes an attempt to reconcile these conflicting requirements. Noted above is his attempt to surmount the problem in his introduction to *History of Ireland: Cuculain and His Contemporaries* by invoking Carlyle's idea of myth as the keeper of authentic history, contrasting it with the 'Dryasdust' historiography of the academic. The failure of this attempt is indicated by O'Grady's irresolution in choosing between artistic and empirical perspectives of history and the dependence of the former upon the latter in his philosophy of the epic. His treatment of the Gadelian and Atticottic legends are examples of this.

Another example is O'Grady's deployment of the Homeric analogy in his argument for the aesthetic suitability of Irish legend. This argument rests on the assumption that whereas a record of the indigenous history of other nations begins with Christianity, such a record predates it in Ireland. Consequently, he claims, Irish historians are presented with difficulties not encountered by other nations, in that the imaginary nature of pre-Christian literature makes it impossible to separate fact from fiction. O'Grady emphasises this argument by drawing an analogy with literary works universally respected. He points out that some of the most learned minds have applied themselves to the nature of the authorship of the *Iliad* and the *Odyssey* on the question of whether these works had one or more authors. Their inability to solve the issue with reference to 'the far less copious and less varied heroic literature of Greece', underlines the view that 'surely it would be madness for any one to sit down and gaily distinguish true from false in the immense and complex mass of the Irish bardic literature, having in his ears this century-lasting struggle over a single Greek poem and a single small phase of the semi-historic life of Hellas'.[25] The obvious intention in making this comparison is to equate the epic status of Irish bardic literature with the Homer's world-renowned epic, but of greater significance is the fact that the comparison rests on an act of critical historiography. O'Grady, in other words, bases an aesthetic judgement on the validity of Irish bardic literature not upon aesthetic considerations but upon historiographic ones: he takes recourse to an historiographic argument in seeking to justify an analogy between the literary value of Homer's work and that of Gaelic legend. This indicates that O'Grady's indirect refutation of Matthew Arnold's claim that Celtic literature was inferior to classical Greek literature (the paradigm for literary excellence in Arnold's view) was motivated not by purely literary considerations but by a determination to establish a relationship of equality between Irish and English culture.

This falling back upon the methodology of empirical historiography at a point where O'Grady argues away from 'the despotism of fact' reveals the tension at the heart of the genealogical structure of *History of Ireland: Critical and Philosophical*. It clearly exposes the ideological motivation behind O'Grady's valorisation of the epic form: it reveals the lack of aesthetic autonomy of O'Grady's epic and the inconsistency with which tests of historical validity are applied in the book. More fundamentally, however, it brings into focus an anxiety at the prospect of barbarism that the genealogical structure, ironically, was employed to neutralise. This can be traced to the indirect influence of Darwinism in *History of Ireland: Critical and Philosophical*. In mirroring both the biological tree of evolution and the mythical tree of life, the genealogical structure identifies a point of contact for O'Grady between the opposites of science and myth, thereby providing the conceptual framework for a vision of history and imagination united. However, the genealogical structure also has the immanent capacity to branch out infinitesimally, a potential that is realised in Darwin's discovery of the nature of man's relationship to the natural world. O'Grady tries to curtail this branching out because it undermines the purity of the bloodline he wishes to trace. His desire to identify this purity arises from a need to establish a primary separation of civility and barbarism. Therefore, he dismisses as mythical source material that identifies a break in the line of descent he traces but claims historical credibility for myths that identify continuity in this line of descent. This is shown by the fact that O'Grady identifies a historical basis for ancient Celtic gods like the Tuatha De Danann, but dismisses the historical basis for the Gadelian and Atticottic legends. The former contribute to the smooth tracing of a continous heroic tradition but the latter disrupt it. However, O'Grady is forced to open a gap between science and myth in this process, in direct contrast to his general objective of integrating them: in his determination to maintain a pure heroic bloodline, he is compelled to admit the division he identifies as evidence of the decadence of contemporary civilisation.

This contradiction within O'Grady's method can be traced in part to Darwin himself, who recognised the anxiety that would be generated by his claim that human origins were animal rather than angelic. Darwin attempts to dilute this anxiety by asserting that once it was accepted that primitive human society was barbaric, the notion that humans could have descended from some lower organised form would not be so difficult to accept. In a revealing passage towards the end of *The Descent of Man*, however, Darwin's argument goes further, claiming that the lower animals displayed a capacity for nobility absent in primitive human tribes:

> For my own part I would as soon be descended from that heroic little monkey, who braved his dreaded enemy in order to save the life of his keeper, or from that old baboon, who descending from the mountains, carried away in triumph his young comrade from a crowd of astonished dogs – as from a savage who delights to torture his enemies, offers up bloody sacrifices, practises infanticide without remorse, treats his wives like slaves, knows no decency, and is haunted by the grossest superstitions.[26]

Here Darwin transfers qualities of civilisation, heroism and magnanimity, from the human to the animal and qualities of savagery from the animal to the human. This is done in order to downplay the deanthropocentricism of his evolutionary theory but at the cost of asserting the 'savage' nature of primitive human society. Thus Darwin's attempt to circumscribe the most radical consequence of his findings, the savage basis of human civilisation, merely emphasises the impossibility of maintaining a primary separation between barbarism and civility within the context of biological determinism.[27]

The form of Darwin's logic in this instance is analogous to O'Grady's. Darwin brings nobility and savagery together in his image of the 'heroic little monkey' just as, more broadly, O'Grady's genealogical tree brings science and myth together. In so doing, Darwin is compelled to open the gap between heroism and savagery in the contrast he draws between man and beast in the passage above, just as O'Grady is forced to open the gap between science and myth in his treatment of the Gadelian and Atticottic legends. This indicates that a dialectic of barbarism and civilisation structures the discourse of genealogy in Darwin's scientific form and in O'Grady's mythic form during the 1870s and 1880s. The major importance of Darwin for O'Grady was that he provided a framework within which race would be granted scientific respectablity and mythical status. The dialectic of barbarism and civilisation latent within that framework reveals an inescapable contradiction running through the three volumes of *History of Ireland*. O'Grady's attempt to create a unity of science and myth or history and imagination fails because the first term in both pairs is defined in opposition to the second term. The second term functions as a form of absence necessary to the constitution of the primary term as a form of presence. It also follows from this, however, that the relationship O'Grady establishes between science and myth or history and imagination is one of interdependence, in which both terms inversely mirror each other.

Because race lies at the interface between science and myth in *History of Ireland: Critical and Philosophical*, it provides the space where the tension between the opposition and interdependence of the terms becomes most apparent. This lends credence to the view of race as a supplement to nationalism that Christoper Morash adopts from Jacques Derrida and Etienne Balibar in interpreting discourses of Celticism in late nineteenth-century Ireland.[28] Edward Hagan also identifies the potential for stability and instability that this 'supplementary' view of race involves: he suggests that O'Grady used the Aryan myth to reconcile Protestant and Catholic culture in Ireland but that the myth was popular in Anglo-Irish thought partly because of its anti-Catholic undertones.[29] In the light of this, it is not coincidental that the Irish aristocracy would lead in the united Ireland O'Grady envisaged: 'The Aryan Myth could be a new, Anglo-Irish "will to power"'.[30]

The importance of this relationship between race and nation in *History of Ireland* generally cannot be underestimated and it is highly pertinent to an understanding of O'Grady's politics and its subsequent influence, examined in the following chapters. However, O'Grady's treatment of race brings to the surface a historiographic problem that cannot be explained exclusively in terms of the relationship between race and nation but suggests *why* that relationship can be viewed as supplementary. This problem is focused on the question of the relationship between science and ideology.

Some of Marx's most important comments on the relationship between science and ideology were made in opening sections of *The German Ideology* written in 1845, the year that Louis Althusser locates for the transition in Marx from a Feuerbachian to a properly Marxist understanding of ideology.[31] The work of Althusser has been instrumental in exploring the science–ideology relationship in Marx in a manner that challenged the economistic reductionism of the Soviet period. In *The German Ideology* Marx stated that '[i]f in all ideology men and their circumstances appear upside-down as in a *camera obscura*, this phenomenon arises just as much from their historical life-process as the inversion of objects on the retina does from their physical life-process'.[32] Athough Althusser believed that this work was still influenced by a Hegelian and Feuerbachian understanding of ideology, this statement expresses a claim that Althusser develops expansively in 'Ideology and Ideological State Apparatuses', that the relationship of ideology to science shows that the form of ideology is eternal.[33]

In order to illustrate how race functions as a moment in the revelation of history as a dialectic of necessity and contingency in *History of Ireland: Critical and Philosophical*, it is worth observing Marx's understanding of science in *The German Ideology* as a pretext to Althusser's view of ideology as eternal. Scientific knowledge for Marx is primarily dialectical. In the Marxist method of description 'history ceases to be a collection of dead facts as it is with the empiricists (themselves still abstract), or an imagined activity of imagined subjects, as with the idealists'.[34] The two sentences that follow illustrate the problem dialectics itself presents for Marx's concept of science: 'When speculation ends – in real life – there real, positive science begins: the representation of the practical activity, of the practical process of development of men. Empty talk about consciousness ceases, and real knowledge has to take its place.'[35] A shift appears to take place here from a dialectical to an empirical view of science – it is conceived by Marx as the representation of practical reality uncovered behind the veil of speculation.

This slippage in Marx's understanding of science can be attributed to the fact that *The German Ideology* is written during the period of what Althusser defines as the epistemological break in Marx. Norman Geras interprets Althusser's concept as an assertion that 'a science is founded only at the cost of a complete rupture with the ideological problematic which precedes it, a thorough-going mutation of its basic structure'.[36] This transition, however, is not immediately total; *The German Ideology* remains indebted to concepts alien to the form of critique it is instigating, such as the empirical view of science; for Althusser, 'it offers us precisely a thought in a state of rupture with its past'.[37]

For Althusser, science is not the description of reality independent of ideology but the description of the ideological construction of reality.[38] The difference between the empiricism he identifies with the early Marx and the dialectical–historical view of the later Marx resides precisely in this. The former remains ideological in its empiricism, in which the opposition between fact and ideology is rendered absolute; the latter is properly scientific because it identifies the *necessary* role of contradiction, in which ideology is revealed as such, in the establishment of fact. Althusser defines the relationship between the subject and his/her real conditions of existence (R1) in terms of the relationship (R2) between this relationship and an imaginary relationship between the subject and his/her real conditions of existence (R3).[39] Therefore, his view of science incorporates ideology in its structure, but only when it reveals itself *as* ideology and not as fact.

71

To return to O'Grady's concept of race in *History of Ireland: Critical and Philosophical*, the reason why it can be interpreted as a supplement derives from its relationship to science. O'Grady's racialism is both mythic and scientific; he remains within ideology as defined by Althusser to the degree that both mythic and scientific treatments of history in racial terms are treated by O'Grady in opposition to each other, as in the Gadelian and Atticottic legends. In recognising the complicity between the mythic and the empirical, however, their ideological surplus (supplementarity) is illuminated, thereby unveiling the force of a conditioning history subduing claims to total explanation. From this perspective, the failure of O'Grady's genealogical method to produce a total integration of myth and science unconsciously anticipates the view of science that Althusser identifies in the later Marx.

The importance of *History of Ireland: Critical and Philosophical* is that not only does it bring to a point of highest intensity the force of contradiction governing the entire *History of Ireland*, it implicates the scientific method in the process, thereby undermining empirical historical criticism of O'Grady's approach as unrigorous. The force of this contradiction is indicated by the fact that subsequent to *History of Ireland: Critical and Philosophical* O'Grady felt obliged to develop his literary and historical work in different spheres. Therefore, his own work repeats the pattern identified in Figure 2 which O'Grady offers as one of the reasons why Irish bardic material came to be regarded as purely imaginative. Implicit in his philosophy of the epic was the belief that his failure to convey his *History of Ireland* as historical, rested on his inability to shape his source material into a harmonious epic form; just as in his argument that the accumulation of mythology became so dense in ancient history that a point was reached when mythology itself separated from history, so the weight of the legendary material he works from proves too dense to be toned down into the epic proportions he envisages. In the light of this failure of his epic project, it is unsurprising that O'Grady moves to the novel form in his literary work and that his treatment of history becomes more empirical as his writings on the Elizabethan period in Ireland illustrates. However, this division is not absolute; his novels, even when given a contemporary setting, are concerned with the theme of history, while he treats the Elizabethan period in Ireland in imaginatively colourful accounts, concerned as much with literary narrative as with conveying historical information.[40] This suggests that even after the failure of *History of Ireland* O'Grady still harboured sentiments for the unity of history and the imagination he envisaged in that work. However, it also suggests O'Grady's increased cognisance of the dialectical structure underwriting this vision of unity. In consequence, his subsequent writing acquires an oxymoronic quality, whereby the conservatism of his unitary vision is signified in its feudal patriarchal form while the concession of its unrealisability foregrounds its dialectical structure. It remains to consider his novels and his historical treatment of the Elizabethan period in this context.

The content of O'Grady's bardic novels show little change from that in *History of Ireland*. Much of the material is taken directly from it and although Edward Hagan makes much of the fact that his notion of the heroic expanded in these novels, the aspects fundamental to *History of Ireland* remain firmly in place. One vitally important change comes with the novels however – the pressure to render the narratives historically rooted is absent. In his preface to *The Coming of Cuculain*, published in 1894, O'Grady writes:

> I will therefore ask the reader, remembering the large manner of the antique literature from which our tale is drawn, to forget for a while that there is such a thing as scientific history, to give his imagination a holiday, and follow with kindly interest the singular story of the boyhood of Cuculain . . . [41]

The full title of this work, *The Coming of Cuculain: A Romance of the Heroic Age of Ireland* indicates an important shift in O'Grady's attitude since so much of what he wrote in his introduction to *History of Ireland: Cuculain and His Contemporaries* and in *History of Ireland: Critical and Philosophical* when he argued against regarding his bardic works as historical romances. *The Coming of Cuculain*, however, does not signal a decisive break with historiography on O'Grady's part; its style suggests that it was written for a young audience and certainly for a popular readership; the academic issues of *History of Ireland: Critical and Philosophical* are left aside. Furthermore, its romanticism does not permeate the range of O'Grady's subsequent bardic writings. Clear evidence of this lies in the fact that the concern for history reappears in what was apparently meant to be a sequel to *The Coming of Cuculain*, *In The Gates of the North*, published in 1901. The cyclic notion of history, evident in both volumes of *History of Ireland* when considered organically is once more re-asserted:

> Our heroic literature is bound to repeat itself in action and within the constraining laws of time and space and the physical world. For that prophecy has been always, and will be always fulfilled. The heroes are coming, of that you may be sure; their advent is as certain as time. [42]

Nevertheless, O'Grady's self-acknowledged romantic treatment of the legend of Cuchulainn in *The Coming of Cuculain* is significant. It admits to the possibility of regarding the legend as purely imaginative, one consequence of which is to render any subsequent claim for its historicity suspect. The examination of *History of Ireland* in this chapter reveals that this claim was always laden with contradiction, thus making inevitable O'Grady's move to a literary form like that of the novel, abandoning his own aspirations to the epic. The fact that certain sections of *The Coming of Cuculain* are taken untouched from *History of Ireland: The Heroic Period* renders much of the historiographic argument in *History of Ireland: Critical and Philosophical* untenable. If the reader is expected to regard the same material in the earlier context as historical and in the later context as fanciful, then the force of contradiction governing O'Grady's historiographic claims becomes evident.

Given this, it might be assumed that O'Grady's attempts to intervene in Irish intellectual life with his bardic literature ended in failure. Certainly, if success is regarded as the historiographic deduction of the empirical basis of Irish bardic literature, then his endeavours were abysmally unsuccessful. On the other hand, if we understand his final pronouncement on historiography as an affirmation of the symbiosis of history and the imagination, then his intervention in the intellectual discourse of his generation is immense. However, O'Grady never overcame his vacillation between his affirmation of the centrality of the imagination in comprehending history and his anxiety over the empirical historical validity of his work; thus, his movement away from the high-serious form of the epic to the popular one of the novel is highly predictable.[43]

O'Grady's *Lost on Du-Corrig* and *The Chain of Gold* are two novels where the fictionality of the narrative is not obscured by authorial attempts to render them historical. They are unique in his literary corpus in that they are given a contemporary setting. Written, along with *The Coming of Cuculain*, in the mid-1890s, they represent a period in which O'Grady's concern for history in his literary work was surpassed by his concern for fictional narrative. It would be tempting to dismiss the significance of this attitude by claiming that these novels were written for a juvenile audience primarily; while this may be true, the narrative strategies O'Grady employs suggests that this question of readership is not so simple as it at first appears. These narrative strategies indicate O'Grady's changed attitude to history reflect an even more significant development, initiated in *History of Ireland: Critical and Philosophical*; a new concept of myth.

Roland Barthes's essay 'Myth Today' is a significant treatise on the function of myth in the light of Saussurian linguistics. One of Barthes's most telling insights is that 'myth cannot possibly be an object, a concept or an idea; it is a mode of signification, a form'.[44] This view of myth continues to act as a radical challenge to criticism that assumes a simple binary opposition between myth and history, an assumption pervasive in criticism of the Literary Revival. In 'The Literary Myths of the Revival', for example, Seamus Deane heavily criticises what he sees as Yeats's blurring of the distinction between the terms 'aristocracy' and 'ascendancy' in the latter's version of eighteenth-century literary and intellectual history which Deane regards as 'manifestly absurd.' Assessing this strategy, he writes:

> Yeats was so eager to discover an aristocratic element within the Protestant tradition and to associate this with the spiritual aristocracy of the Catholic and Celtic peasantry – defining aristocracy in each case as a mark of Irishness and Irishness as a mark of anti-modernism – that he distorted history in the service of myth.[45]

Deane poses the myth in this case, Yeats's 'idea' of an Irish Protestant antimodern tradition, against history, conceived as the 'real' conditions that obtained outside it.[46] According to Barthes's formula, this move effaces the ubiquity of myth by reducing it to the level of an 'idea' defined by its diametric opposition to history. The form of O'Grady's narrative in *Lost on Du-Corrig* and *The Chain of Gold* suggests a structural development towards a Barthesian concept of myth. This can be seen in O'Grady's development, through the form of the novel, of Carlyle's notion of the past informing the present. On the one hand the supernatural events and characters of a Gaelic past continue to assume a central place within O'Grady's narrative. On the other hand, interaction of past and present is not one in which a static idea of the past intervenes in the complexity of the present, but rather one in which there is a reciprocal effect of one upon the other, in which the complexity of the present is elucidated rather than simplified by the past, a dynamic at variance with Bakhtin's notion of epic distance informing O'Grady's *History of Ireland*.

Lost on Du-Corrig illustrates this development. In the novel, John Freeman, the son of a Protestant clergyman, is lost while fishing somewhere along the west coast of Ireland. In trying to find his brother, Edward Freeman repeats the actions of his brother the day the latter disappeared and he vanishes also. The rock upon which both brothers disappear is called Du-Corrig, a name that carries significance for an interpretation of the narrative. The boys spend their time in a cave called Curry's Window until they eventually manage to get off the rock.

The central mythic element of the story is sourced in Curry's Window but the manner of its elucidation displays O'Grady's increased amenability to the narrativity of myth. The myth in this case is that of the *Piast*, a water-serpent who lived, according to local folklore, in Curry's Window and who had come out from the cave, a large part of which formed an underwater tunnel, to devour local fishermen at sea. O'Grady takes various narrative approaches to this myth. First, an account of the boys' disappearance and the search for them is given by a character named Samuel Watkins. Watkins is presented as the figure of officialdom whose rational attitude fails to decipher the mystery of the disappearance. This rational attitude manifests itself in a passage from a letter Watkins sends to newspapers in his region, giving a description of the missing boys, in which he refers to a dispute between himself and the boys' father on a question of scripture:

> It is unfortunate that the Rev. Mr. Freeman and myself are not on the best of terms. I once flung out the suggestion that the days mentioned in the first chapter of Genesis were ages or long intervals of time. Some meddler told him of this, since when he has regarded me coldly and askance as a dangerous Freethinker. Moreover, I am not a very regular attendant at Church. In short, our relations are cold and strained, though I like and respect him very much.[47]

Watkins's rationality here is presented to reveal the value and the limitation of his narrative. As a rationalist he is astute enough to realise that knowledge of the Gaelic language will prove useful to him in his search for the boys in a region where Gaelic is spoken by the natives. On the other hand, his rational nature entertains a scepticism which precludes a belief in providence, a concept central to the dynamic of the *Piast* myth, and one which Rev. Freeman, 'whose principles and practices were of the Low Church or Evangelical School', held to strongly.

A second and more central narrative approach is found in John Freeman's own account of events following his disappearance. He records his various failed attempts at escape and his battle to survive in the cave. At one point, when he is at his lowest ebb, a ghost appears to him. At first he believes it to be the ghost of the smuggler Curry (after whom the cave 'Curry's Window', was named) but then informs the reader that the decorum of the ghost was too antiquated for the nineteenth century. On reflection, he believes the ghost to be an ocular delusion brought on by hunger, as it disappears once John obtains some food.[48] After John and his brother Edward arrive safely home, they return to the cave in the hope of discovering a treasure-trove believed to have been hidden there by the smuggler Curry. They find gold and show some of the more interesting metalwork to an antiquarian scholar who informs them that it relates to an antique Irish warrior. On learning that the correct pronunciation of the cave was 'Cooree' and not Curry, he informs them that this was the name of the sea-god of the southern and western Irish in the pre-Christian ages which, during Christian times, began to be regarded as an evil thing, a *piast* or great water-serpent.

The relation Barthes draws between language and myth can be applied to the story in order to reveal the change in O'Grady's understanding of the relationship between myth and history. According to Barthes, the linguistic system, as first conceived by Saussure, constitutes the signifier within a greater, metalinguistic system, which he defines as myth. He illustrates this relation as follows:

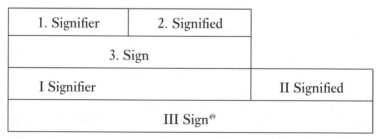

1. Signifier	2. Signified	
3. Sign		
I Signifier		II Signified
III Sign[49]		

Source: Roland Barthes, *Mythologies*, p.115.

Figure 2

If the story of the boys' disappearance is conceived provisionally in isolation from the novel's folklore elements, then it may be interpreted as the signifier of the myth and the *Piast* folktale as the signified, the sign being their narrative coalescence. This reveals the ambiguity O'Grady creates by giving the novel a contemporary setting. The contemporary context, the story of the boys' disappearance, is simultaneously *meaning* and *form* (as defined by Barthes) in the narrative. As meaning, the contemporary context displays its own narrative richness; the intricacies of the process by which the boys' whereabouts are discovered, and the ideological differences between the contemporary voice of rationalistic officialdom (Samuel Watkins) and Protestant evangelicalism (the Freeman family). As form, however, the richness of these narrative vicissitudes is concealed. Barthes comments: 'When it becomes form, the meaning leaves its contingency behind; it empties itself, it becomes impoverished, history evaporates, only the letter remains.'[50] The contemporary context of the story, in other words, is reduced to the monomialism of a pure signifier. In terms of Barthes's understanding of form, the *Piast* myth reveals the concept of providence governing the entire narrative. The process by which the boys come to escape from Du-Corrig involves the process by which Watkins discovers their whereabouts, and both these processes are bound up with the manner in which the mythological significance of Du-Corrig is revealed. So the various narrative tracks lead to the same mythic source where they coalesce under the sign of providence.

Barthes, however, claims that this impoverishment of meaning is not the same as its suppression. In relation to O'Grady's novel, this claim implies that the historicity of the contemporary narrative, fossilised during its formalisation as the signifier of the *Piast* myth, re-emerges in the myth's concept, in this case providence. Providence re-opens the historicity of the narrative at the point where it appears to close it; as a Calvinist concept, it points to O'Grady's Protestantism. In addition, given the historical relationship Max Weber draws between Protestantism and capitalism (in which the doctrine of predestinarianism functions as a central conceptual element), providence opens up the complex problem of O'Grady's relationship to the capitalism he criticises throughout his political writing.[51] The narrator makes a telling comment in this regard about the crowd who had gathered at the rectory to greet the safely returned boys:

> Most of them were Roman Catholics, but this was in the pre-Disestablishment days, when the relations between Protestant clergymen and their Roman Catholic parishioners were less strained and strange than I have been informed they are now.[52]

Barthes states:

> In actual fact, the knowledge contained in a mythical concept is confused, made of yielding, shapeless associations. One must firmly stress this open

character of the concept; it is not at all an abstract, purified essence; it is a formless, unstable, nebulous condensation, whose unity and coherence are above all due to its function.[53]

The function of providence as the concept of the *Piast* myth corroborates this only when Barthes's view of the concept is recognised in its dialectical moment as simultaneously fractured and coherent. As the *telos* of the narrative, the concept of the myth invests it with coherence while also revealing its multifariousness; therefore, it is split, simultaneously positing a narrative unity and multiplicity that mutually define each other. This indicates the continuing importance of history to O'Grady's literary endeavours; the novel form might suggest a retreat from a concern for an empirical historical credibility, but its subject-matter prevents him from retreating into pure imaginative free-play, an undertaking he regarded as decadent, as his criticism of Yeats's drama would later reveal.[54] O'Grady continually looked to history to intervene in the social life of his day, unlike Samuel Ferguson, who, in order to elide the social contradictions of his day, conceived of myth as radically anterior. However, so long as he insisted on the empirical historicity of his narratives, the influence O'Grady aimed at remained thwarted. On the other hand, by re-constituting myth and history in the novel form of narrative, as in *Lost on Du-Corrig*, it became possible for him to direct Celtic folklore in a manner that would establish his influence more widely.

O'Grady's other contemporary novel, *The Chain of Gold* contains virtually the same story as *Lost on Du-Corrig*, the differences being the introduction of a new character, Frank Furbisher, and alterations to contingent aspects of the story. The notion of providence continues to act as the narrative's organising concept but a feature hinted at in the first novel becomes more pronounced here, i.e. the dialectic of barbarity and civilisation. The novel is reminiscent of the work of Edgar Allan Poe and Frank Furbisher remarks early on in the book that he would love to be a participant in one of Poe's stories.[55] In its anxiety over barbarism the novel can be situated in the context of a general *fin-de-siècle* concern for human value undermined in particular by the advent of Darwinism, thereby recalling O'Grady's preoccupations in *History of Ireland: Critical and Philosophical*. More specifically, it can also be situated in the context of the Irish gothic genre, in which a crisis of identity specific to Irish Protestantism, related to the erosion of the political ascendancy of the Irish landed gentry during the latter-half of the nineteenth century, is given literary expression in grotesque form.[56]

Thus the novel is more explicitly marked by anxiety than *Lost on Du-Corrig*. In chapter one O'Grady writes that one of the novel's narrators, Frank Furbisher, is suffering from insomnia and he has been brought to Brittany for rest. While there, Furbisher finds a jar washed in from the sea that contains a message which ultimately leads him to locate the two brothers, John and Edward Freeman, who, as in *Lost on Du-Corrig*, are stranded in a cave on a rock off the west coast of Ireland, in this novel called Demon's Rock. Later in the novel, the reader is informed that the message Furbisher found was written by one of the brothers, John, with his own blood. O'Grady writes that John has observed how their struggle to survive in the cave was turning them more barbarous yet making their spiritual awareness more acute:

> I think, in supreme crises of the kind which we were now experiencing, the soul retires into herself, and becomes more and more solitary.[57]

While this anxiety reflects a concern generally felt in the 1890s regarding barbarism, it can also be read in terms of the development of O'Grady's treatment of myth and history from the volumes of *History of Ireland* to his novels.[58] The adoption of the novel form suggests a development in the structure of O'Grady's literature away from the conception of myth in epic terms, standing above engagement with contemporaneity, to a mode in which past and present are structurally bound to one another. In O'Grady's move to the novel form, the hitherto necessary status of the absolute epic past becomes split by the contingencies of the present. I have suggested that this development takes place because the novel form was more likely to extend O'Grady's influence than his attempts at epic, since this mode of treating the past entertained a lesser risk of history being considered as fossilised and since it freed him from the empirical historical imperative that acted as a constraint on his literary treatment of Gaelic legend in *History of Ireland*. However, by turning to contemporary fiction, O'Grady's quest for authority, both in terms of his own work and the literary revival it helped to instigate, becomes no longer tenable.

This crisis of authority, first evident in *History of Ireland: The Heroic Period*, reaches a critical stage in *The Chain of Gold*. During the novel, while commenting on his brother's attempts to make a small garden on the rock on which they were stranded, John Freeman recalls the following:

> I once met in some book a sentiment which pleased me so much that I committed it to memory: 'Man is here to make rule out of the ruleless. By his living energy, he will cause the absurd itself to become less absurd.' Ned, I think, was formed to make ugly things beautiful, and disorderly things orderly.[59]

This instance in the narrative brings the contradictions informing O'Grady's literary career to the foreground with striking ironic intensity. Edward Freeman's attempt to make a garden on the rock reflects the anxiety-ridden effort by O'Grady to bring order to the chaos he felt he was confronted with, in literary terms, in the fragmented nature of the Gaelic legends he used in *History of Ireland*, and in political terms, in the fragmentation he associated with the capitalist social structure. It suggests the sense of alienation that drives O'Grady's quest for order; Freeman's effort at gardening represents an attempt to domesticate the unfamiliar.

Interestingly, Samuel Weber observes a similar anxiety in Fredric Jameson's view of history as necessity expressed in *The Political Unconscious*. Weber suggests that the view of history as necessity may be a motive for critics who 'desired to be "hurt"…rather than to court the risks of being left beside themselves, "beside the point", by desires they no longer controlled'.[60] In a type of analysis that might be described as Nietzschean, Weber identifies in Jameson's view of history a desire not to be left stranded in the kind of formless wilderness the boys in O'Grady's story find themselves in. Thus Jameson's assertion that history is 'what hurts' is not unlike Freeman's attempt at gardening – an attempt to create formal clarity in the wilderness of postmodern desire. However, Weber implies that because this desire for the certainty of necessity is no less a desire than the desire for freedom, wilderness and spontaneity, necessity collapses into desire, shipwrecking Jameson's argument no less forcefully than the shipwrecking of the boys. Jameson's argument survives the storm, however, because the wilderness Weber invokes in postmodern fashion is not just a place of imaginative freedom, but also of survival. John and Edward Freeman may be lost and thereby made conscious of their contingency – but while the experience may be one of imaginative liberation, it is also one in which the material necessities determining their existence is starkly revealed.

The passage above also suggests that O'Grady's anxiety arises from a struggle of gender identity; beauty is presented as domestic and ordered, and ugliness as alien and chaotic, recalling Fergus's attack on Maeve in the first volume of *History of Ireland*. However, the attempt to create order occurs in a 'barbarous' context – Edward's effort at making the garden and John's recollection of the adage take place when they are stranded, implying that the 'masculine' quest for order is borne out of the 'feminine' chaos it seeks to control.[61] It is symptomatic of how the dialectical form structuring O'Grady's treatment of the imagination and history has become more pronounced as his work progresses. Furthermore, it indicates where O'Grady's crisis of authorship (as authority) has taken him – to a fictional novel form and to a contemporary world he views as barbaric. The crisis is one in which authorial intent is crippled; unable to sustain the historicity of his epic project, O'Grady collapses history into narrative in the form of the novel, producing a contemporary form of myth where the archetype (providence) is elucidated not through a suppression of but a negotiation with the contingencies of the contemporary, formally reflected in the multiple narrative voices in these novels.

In making these observations, the aesthetic quality of O'Grady's novels is neither being defended nor criticised. It is important to understand that the narrative strategies O'Grady employs in these novels constitute a radical gesture within the terms of his thought and are therefore relevant in assessing his influence on the Irish Literary Revival. This fiction has been critically ignored, but whatever about its literary value, it is important in illustrating the varieties of fictional approaches O'Grady took to the question of history. It forms the literary side of the split that emerged in O'Grady's working out of the contradictions of *History of Ireland*. O'Grady's treatment of the

Elizabethan period in Ireland represents the more conventionally historical side of this split.

Consideration of O'Grady's literary works indicates how the problems arising from his treatment of history frustrate his ambitions to create an epic of Gaelic legend and direct him towards the novel form. This development is evidence of the force of contradiction impacting ever more emphatically on his treatment of history, rendering more stark the division between its imaginative and empirical components. The result is that a certain schizophrenia, discreetly evident in *History of Ireland*, becomes increasingly manifest as O'Grady's work moves into the 1890s. On the one hand, history collapses into fictional narrative, and on the other hand, the positivistic attitude to history re-emerges as the dominant motif (if not always the method) in O'Grady's treatment of the Elizabethan period. This is not to underplay the fact that he treats this period in a highly narrativised form but to indicate that its subject-matter is empirically historical. As noted earlier, when O'Grady makes empirical historiographic claims in *History of Ireland: Critical and Philosophical* the political ideology informing his literary work is revealed. This also occurs in his treatment of the Elizabethan period but in this case the closer proximity of that period to his own indicates that the focus of his intellectual life is becoming more obviously centred on contemporary politics.

In the collection of stories *The Bog of Stars* and the preface to his edition of *Pacata Hibernia*, a late sixteenth-century work written by lieutenant Thomas Stafford, O'Grady outlines his interpretation of the characters and events of a period that witnessed the final destruction of the old Gaelic order in Ireland which, for traditional Irish nationalism, was a simple and brutal case of colonial oppression. O'Grady exercises his historiographic skills in arguing against this interpretation. However, in so doing, he is careful to avoid any racial denigration of the native Gaelic population. His succinct employment of historical data negotiates a path between two extremes that reflect the cultural nationalist/political unionist position O'Grady takes in relation to the events of his own time. The style of his argument anticipates that of contemporary historical revisionism, in which beliefs that have gained widespread acceptance are interrogated with reference to historical material either ignored completely or strategically downplayed.[62]

O'Grady's treatment of Sir Richard Bingham in *The Bog of Stars* contains an example of this strategy. He records how, when out on a raid, one of Bingham's captains, John Gilson, killed a woman and her baby in a brutal manner. The government, based in Dublin Castle, ordered Gilson's arrest but Bingham resisted and placed him instead on the Council of Connaught, an important body he had sent to quell rebellion in that province. As a passing remark, O'Grady writes: 'By the way this Gilson was an Irishman – nearly all Bingham's people were Irish.'[63] With this single statement he undercuts the emotional impact generated by the image of the child-murdering English soldier within Irish nationalist tradition.[64]

O'Grady supplements this strategy with a broad reading of the period that belies a nationalist argument for the universal antipathy of the Gael to all things English, especially the throne. He claims that 'The Crown, in all its struggles with the great dynastic houses, always had the majority of the Irish nation on its side. For the controversy was not at all England *versus* Ireland, but the Crown, plus the majority of the nation, *versus* the great lords.'[65] He backs up this claim by observing that at the outbreak of the Nine Years War, the queen's army in Ireland was less than a thousand men. Every Irish chieftain was assessed as to the number of his soldiers and was obliged to have them ready for battle upon receiving the queen's summons. O'Grady takes this as proof that the queen's government pre-supposed the loyalty of the Irish. Furthermore, the middle-class merchants and traders were never, according to him, in rebellion, because it was never in their interests to be disloyal.[66] These arguments are supplemented by the claim that the Irish and English nobility shared much the same culture and moved in the same circles. In *Red Hugh's Captivity*, a story that deals with the imprisonment and escape of one of O'Grady's favourite heroes of the Elizabethan period, we learn that Brian Ogue O'Rourke, a cousin of Red Hugh's, has been educated at Oxford. Some remarks in *The Bog of Stars* re-iterate this argument:

> I would have the reader remember that there was little or no difference between great people in Ireland and great people in England and elsewhere at this time. They were essentially the same class. So we find that while Brian of the Ramparts married one sister of Ulrick the Earl, Sir Henry Malby, the Queen's President of Connaught, married another.[67]

These arguments are put forward to prevent O'Grady's central thesis in his Elizabethan writings from appearing anti-nationalist in the cultural sense, namely, his belief that the decline of Gaelic independence was historically inevitable. In fact, far from being anti-nationalist, he elucidates this thesis on the grounds that the nation-state was the *telos* of events in the Elizabethan period; the political homogenisation that the nation-state embodied necessitated the destruction of autonomous regional government. Therefore, the Irish chieftains would inevitably be stripped of their power by force of historical necessity:

> The Elizabethan conquest of Ireland was, in my opinion, as inevitable as salutary, and the terrors and horrors which accompanied it, to a considerable extent, a necessary condition of its achievement. These petty kings and princes had to be broken once and for all. In blood and flame and horror of great darkness it was fated that Ireland should pass from barbarism to civilisation, from the wild rule of the 'monocracies' to the reign of universal law.[68]

This attitude bears all the hallmarks of a Calvinistic sense of providence seen in O'Grady's novels in its teleological conception of history. It also reveals the fear of barbarism that pervades *The Chain of Gold*. Nevertheless, the attitude expressed reveals a contradiction between O'Grady's Elizabethan writings and the rest of his literary works. Flying in the face of his aversion to instrumental and self-motivated rationality expressed so often throughout his bardic literature, O'Grady now views history as teleologically directed towards this intellectual condition, politically embodied in the emergence of the bourgeois nation-state and the capitalist economic and social structure. The relationship Max Weber draws between the Calvinist doctrine of predestinarianism and the entrepreneurial ethos of capitalism is relevant to this anomaly, yet given the extent to which O'Grady's efforts at integrating the imagination and history were motivated by an aversion to what he saw as the social fragmentation resulting from the rise of the bourgeoisie, Weber's analysis is not sufficient for resolving it. Furthermore, in spite of the fact that he still displays a great admiration for the heroic and selfless gesture as his treatment of Red Hugh illustrates, presenting the old Gaelic order as barbaric is hardly congruent with O'Grady's view of contemporary mercantilism as barbaric when set against the heroism of antiquity.

How is this central anomaly in O'Grady's work to be accounted for? First, while the incongruities between his bardic literature and his Elizabethan writing are startling, certain attitudes are common to both. Cuchulainn embodied a patriarchal order whose unity was disrupted by rebellion. In the Elizabethan period, O'Grady argues that the only group holding back the unity expressed in the idea of the nation-state were the *rebel* Irish chieftains, an observation acquiring moral force when O'Grady's view of revolt as satanic, expressed in *History of Ireland: Critical and Philosophical*, is recalled. Second, it is possible to read the barbarity attributed by O'Grady to the Irish clan system as synonymous with the barbarity John and Edward Freeman feared when on the Demon's Rock in *The Chain of Gold*. While the supernatural element of the tale, sourced in Gaelic legend, may have helped the boys escape from the rock back to civilisation, it could also be argued that they discovered the Gaelic manuscript that helped them to safety in the 'barbarous' environment of the Demon's Rock.

Despite these considerations, the anomaly remains. O'Grady's view of history in the Elizabethan writing contradicts his support of Carlyle's idea of myth as the keeper of authentic history and his aversion to positivistic historiography often expressed in his bardic literature. He not only regards history in empirical terms in *Pacata Hibernia* and his Elizabethan stories, he also views it in terms of a progression towards bureaucracy and utilitarian rationality. The values of feudal heroism that reputedly dominated the politics of the old Gaelic order are replaced by a politics of strategy, diplomacy and self-interest. In *Red Hugh's Captivity* the author's account of Hugh O'Neill conveys this. O'Neill is the Earl of Tyrone and brother-in-law to Red Hugh. O'Grady continually refers to him as 'the inferior person' because he brooked disloyalty among the O'Neill clan towards the queen's viceroy. O'Grady's narrative records that by gaining a patent of lands from the queen, Hugh O'Neill achieves a status clashing with Turlough Lynagh who, until then, had been chivalrously loyal to the queen. The intervention of the viceroy Perrott serves to accommodate the conflict of interests but Hugh comes out very well in the end, gaining a foothold in Ulster.

This strategic practice of politics is also borne out in O'Grady's account of Red Hugh's capture. Perrott recognised the loyalty the Irish chieftains showed to him but he did not regard this as sufficient were a Spanish invasion to materialise, Ireland being a predominantly Catholic country. Therefore, he demanded that all the chieftains provide him with hostages as a security bond. All agreed except Red Hugh's father, Sir Hugh O'Donnell of Tir-Connaill, husband to lady O'Donnell, otherwise referred to by O'Grady as the Dark Daughter. Red Hugh was then taken into the protection of Owen Ogue McSweeney. Perrott sent a boat of wines to Lough Swilly with the aim of capturing Red Hugh. The proprietor of the ship, Captain Birmingham, lured Owen Ogue and Red Hugh on board under the pretence of an offer to taste wines. They were taken back to Dublin where they were imprisoned. While O'Grady adopts a tone of admonition towards the tactics employed by Perrott in the narrative, he nevertheless regarded his actions as inevitable so long as they weakened the independence of the Irish clans.

If we look at this anomaly in O'Grady's treatment of history in terms of the intellectual schizophrenia becoming evident during his 1890s writing, then a direct link between his attitude to history in the Elizabethan stories and his political ideology can be drawn. A precedent for this already exists in *History of Ireland: Critical and Philosophical*; as has been noted already, when O'Grady made appeals to empirical scientific objectivity in that work, the nature of the political ideology underlying his aspirations to the epic became apparent. Now, in works that are governed by the same appeals, the ideology partly effaced by an aesthetic of feudal heroism is once more revealed. For example, O'Grady continues to express an aversion to mercantilism characteristic of this aesthetic in his Elizabethan stories but now it only serves to highlight its poignancy, rendering it anterior. A story from *The Bog of Stars*, 'Brian-of-the-ramparts O'Rourke', is one example of this. In O'Grady's account O'Rourke revolted against Bingham when the latter invaded the land of Breffni. He went to Scotland seeking support, where he was captured by James VI who handed him over to the queen. He was charged with high treason but refused to plead on the grounds of his high standing. He would only plead if certain conditions were met, including the queen personally presiding over his trial, demands which were inevitably refused. Regarding this stand taken by O'Rourke, O'Grady comments:

> There is surely something very refreshing in this proud refusal of the O'Rourke to plead his cause before a hired brehon and a parcel of money-grabbing London shopkeepers.[69]

This merely underlies the fact, however, that full integration into the English monarchy, a keystone idea in O'Grady's politics, would render an indigenous Gaelic aristocracy obsolete if it continued to pre-suppose that a feudal heroic code was universally regarded.

This curious ambivalence pervades O'Grady's attitude to the landlords of his own day; repudiating them for their servility to England, unlike O'Rourke, yet further admonishing them for their lack of friends at Westminster. Implicit in O'Grady's comment is the suggestion that while O'Rourke's gesture is politically empty in the context of a bourgeois nation-state, it is a powerfully imaginative gesture that contributes to strengthening the aristocracy within that context. This indicates the meaning of O'Grady's incongruous applications of history in the 1890s. The coalescence of history and myth upon which his bardic *History of Ireland* was based has inevitably fragmented, with history mutating into narrative in the aesthetic realm (*Lost on Du-Corrig, The Chain of Gold*) and aesthetics becoming anachronistic, superfluous to the progress of 'real' history in the historical realm (the Elizabethan stories). As feudal heroism becomes divorced from teleological history, its imaginative power becomes magnified. When this imaginative power is redirected at contemporary history, the dialectical form structuring O'Grady's work transforms the contradiction between barbarism and civilisation into a paradox, a process that establishes the mode by which his work will exert its influence on the Irish Literary Revival. Before tracing that influence in the political writing of George Russell and the early work of W.B. Yeats, it is necessary to examine O'Grady's political ideology more directly. His most important work in this regard is *Toryism and the Tory Democracy*, examined in the following chapter.

Towards a politics of paradox:
Toryism and the Tory Democracy

O'GRADY'S POLITICAL WRITING spanned over thirty years, commencing with *The Crisis in Ireland* in 1882. The development of his political outlook over that period was immense and he displayed an extraordinary capacity for adapting his fundamental political principles to the rapidly changing conditions of the period. The importance he attributes to history, his desire to erase class division and his disdain for bourgeois materialism are crucial aspects of his political thought. In order to illustrate the form by which the contradictions informing O'Grady's literary work manifest themselves in his political thought this chapter will focus on *Toryism and the Tory Democracy* as the seminal expression of O'Grady's political ideology.

Toryism and the Tory Democracy was written in 1886 as a response to the Tory Democracy movement within the Conservative Party. This faction, led by Lord Randolph Churchill, was perceived by O'Grady in an over-idealistic fashion as it was essentially a vote-winning tactic created in response to the second Reform Act of 1867 which expanded the franchise.[1] Nevertheless, the movement suggested to him a reconciliation of the landed gentry (traditionally the conservative power-base), with the increasingly threatening British proletariat. O'Grady saw in this an opportunity for a polemical rebuttal of a Toryism that was couched in the smug pre-supposition of its political security and of a radicalism that sought to break up the landed interest. Lord Randolph Churchill's Tory Democracy provided O'Grady with an attractive phrase and an immediate context for the elucidation of a political philosophy inspired by John Ruskin: 'But for Mr. Ruskin and his books, I should probably not have written this work'.[2] In the second part of the book he applies his political ideas in criticism of the Irish landlords, admonishing what he sees as their political ineptitude during the Land War and the popular struggle for Home Rule of the 1880s.

The political *credo* of *Toryism and the Tory Democracy* essentially consisted of appealing to a traditional sense of loyalty O'Grady perceived among the peasant and proletarian classes in Ireland and Britain: such an appeal, he believed, might prevent their acquiescence to radicalism and popular revolt. O'Grady felt that because of the franchise reforms of the nineteenth century, the Conservative Party could not hold power if it remained exclusively tied to the landed aristocracy. But he also believed that if it abandoned the landed aristocracy, Britain would eventually descend into anarchy.

In view of the fact that O'Grady was himself a member of the landed gentry in Ireland, it would seem obvious to read his espousal of this idea of Tory Democracy as primarily a polemic aimed at securing the interests of his class. This may be the case but the manner in which O'Grady elucidates his political philosophy indicates that his political ideology is more complicated than a conventional aristocratic conservatism. As an example of this, the following consideration of *Toryism and the Tory Democracy* shows how the most dominant motif of the Irish Literary Revival, that of the noble peasant, arises partly from a political strategy directed against the captains of industry in the rapidly expanding manufacturing sector of the British economy during the nineteenth century.

The key question that emerges in reading this work is whether O'Grady's argument is primarily utilitarian (aimed at securing the interests of his class) or whether it is primarily moral, criticising a society in which personal interest is replacing ethical responsibility. O'Grady is certainly concerned about the interests of his class both in Ireland and England but because he conceives those interests in terms of an ethical position opposed to utilitarian values, an interpretation of his argument as utilitarian is problematical. O'Grady shared Marx's belief that the conditions of English society were more ripe than any other for revolution; he examines this in *Toryism and the Tory Democracy* in terms of religion and economics. Echoing an argument made by many Victorian thinkers,[3] he identifies the root of contemporary social fragmentation with the decline of religion as a vital social institution:

> In all past times religion has been the deep centripetal force which has held societies together, compacting them into coherence and solidity. But religion, to act so, to bind together men and classes, the upper with the lower, the rich with the poor, the governors with the governed, must be vital and sincere, vital in the strong, the clear-headed, the well-informed, as among the rude and unthinking many. The strenuously organised hypocrisy of the present day, though never so generously supported, will not do.[4]

This attack on the Established Church shows that O'Grady attributed its success in attracting members during a period of immense social change not to their sense of moral propriety but to their concern for personal status. He believed that values of charity and moral rectitude propounded by the Church were no longer internalised in its members but had become mere emblems of social propriety – social relations based on authentically shared values were being replaced by purely pecuniary ones. He saw this leading to the interests of the individual retracting away from the social whole towards those with whom the individual shared an immediate common interest; with this class solidarity and, in consequence, class conflict emerged.

O'Grady read the amoralism of a pecuniary-based society in two ways. On the one hand, the factory manager, lacking all sense of responsibility to his employees other than that of maximising their labour-value, would stop at nothing to increase profit, an attitude that O'Grady recognised as leading to class antagonism and the eventual acquiescence of the proletariat to doctrines of political radicalism.[5] On the other hand, traditional respect for authority (characteristic of pre-modern social relations) could no longer be relied upon as a defence against plebeian revolt. He argued that if sentiment could no longer be appealed to (either in the moral sense of duty or in the affective sense of spontaneous loyalty), then no justification of the disequilibrium of wealth distribution could be made forthwith to the peasantry and industrial working class. Ostensibly tenuous in the circumstances of the latter half of the nineteenth century in Britain, O'Grady nevertheless regarded this sentiment as 'the only really powerful defence of the Throne'.[6]

Given this transition from a sentimental to a utilitarian mode of social relations during the British Industrial Revolution, O'Grady argued that democratic Toryism was the only credible political doctrine that protected the United Kingdom. He proposed that radicalism should be tackled by appealing both to the interests of the peasantry and the industrial working class and to the loyalty he believed to be innate to them. To illustrate how such an appeal could be successful, O'Grady began by citing the economic radicalism of Henry George as an example of the radical outcome of liberalism. George argued that the break-up of the landed interest was a pre-requisite to the development of a truly *laissez-faire* society regulated by the rights and duties attaching to the Enlightenment idea of citizenship.[7] Beneath the apparent egalitarianism of this aspiration O'Grady identified a determination upon the part of the Whigs to divert proletarian animosity away from the industrial bourgeoisie onto the landed aristocracy.[8] Believing, however, that the 'wealth which has been acquired in trade, commerce, and manufacture, is actually regarded with more unfriendly eyes by the working-men than that which consists in the ownership of land', O'Grady saw an opportunity for aligning the landed aristocracy and subaltern classes, based on a shared hostility to the economic parallel of George's bourgeois liberalism, industrial capitalism.[9]

To convince his readership of the necessity and the efficacy of such an alignment, O'Grady first alludes to the negative consequences that he believed would follow from the break-up of the great estates. Following this he proposes that his idea of the nation-state would simultaneously awaken the sentiment of loyalty he associated with the peasantry/urban working class and undercut the conditions fertilising proletarian radicalism. In the first part of this argument, he states that to break up the great estates on the basis of a bill put forward by the MP Henry Broadhurst would be an absurdity from a national perspective.[10]

> The normal economic tendencies continuing unchanged, the small fee-simple estates would forthwith begin rapidly to aggregate themselves into larger and ever larger estates. It would be no more than baling out a boat whose bottom is pierced. Meantime, in mere idleness, without any public duties or responsibilities, the evicted aristocracy would be consuming, without any return, a gigantic proportion of the national wealth.[11]

This argument is used by O'Grady to dissuade Tories such as Randolph Churchill from following radical lines, indicated in Churchill's determination to break up the 'bloated estates'.[12] Besides contending that the break-up of the estates offered no real economic advantages to the country as a whole, O'Grady warns Churchill that to pursue a radical line would henceforth preclude any appeal to notions such as 'the sacredness of Property, the wickedness of public plunder, the great deeds of the barons, Magna Charta, etc., and appeal to strong human sentiments of sympathy and admiration so commonly felt towards ancient and noble families'.[13] He believed that the abandonment of such sentiments would inevitably result in the long-term victory of Whig radicals. In other words, O'Grady linked the break-up of the great estates directly to the break-up of the Tory Party, the inevitable result of which, he believed, would be wholescale revolution in England.

Having thus illustrated that the break-up of the landed aristocracy would serve neither the interests of the Tory Party nor those of the rural/urban working class, O'Grady introduces the concept of the nation-state as the foundation upon which an alignment of the gentry and the proletariat could be realised. With his warning against the abandonment of the aristocracy still fresh in mind, he nevertheless insists that conservatism must grapple with the labour problem in industrial England. He believed that state-employed labour provided the solution: 'The State, the Nation, will get better work out of its employees than any private individual will get out of his.'[14] Elucidating this assertion, he writes:

> If Conservatism does not intend to keep stumbling along the same line of advance [as the Whigs], and is really in earnest in its intention of appealing to the masses for support, it must adopt that other alternative, and enunciate just as distinctly, and with just as fierce an emphasis, as the cardinal principle in its policy, the natural and indefeasible right of labour to employment and maintenance at the hands of the State.[15]

The form of the state that O'Grady has in mind is organic, a state structured as a totality whose component parts are interdependent, each part a microcosm of that totality: 'Not alone to hold society together but to bind and compact it into a vital whole, is the task towards which democratic Toryism, by the law of its existence, ceaselessly and inevitably tends.'[16] This organic concept of the state is best exemplified in the support O'Grady offers to a scheme for the re-afforestation of Ireland. The scheme proposed that thirty thousand men would be employed by the state in the project. O'Grady argued that the food, clothing, tools, etc. that these men would require would stimulate the flagging industries of the country and the value of the wages invested in them by the state would be reflected in national forests, in his opinion a growing source of national wealth: 'Thirty thousand men of the class most dangerous to the State would be converted into loyal citizens, inasmuch as average human nature is generally true to its salt.'[17] This last comment reveals the two-pronged motive behind his deployment of the nation-state idea. On the one hand he wished to strengthen the foundations of society by subjugating individualism to the organicism of the state, thereby re-instituting the commonality of interests that was perceived to be the social condition of feudalism; on the other hand, he identified the nationalisation of industry as the most effective means by which the 'only real danger to society and the State ... the unemployed or underpaid masses of men', would be neutralised politically.[18]

This neutralising function of the nation-state idea points to its ideological specificity, a specificity re-inforced by the fact that though O'Grady supported the nationalisation of wealth in the industrial sector, agriculture was to remain the private domain of the aristocracy. In attempting to justify this inconsistency, O'Grady argued that if land was nationalised, then the amount of rent paid to landlords (Henry George claimed that the sum was £200 million per annum) would be diverted into different channels of employment, dislocating not just those dependant on rental income but also industrial firms affected by the diversion into new modes of expenditure money previously used for rental payment.[19] It is significant that O'Grady turns to a monetarist argument here in arguing against the nationalisation of land, given the opposition of his general argument to bourgeois *laissez-faire* individualism. It recalls his need to employ an empirical historical argument in denying the historical plausibility of the 'plebeian' Atticottic revolt in *History of Ireland: Critical and Philosophical* in a general argument that rejects an empirical approach to history, considered in the previous chapter. Both instances illustrate the contradiction in O'Grady's work, of a specific interest – the authority of the aristocracy – motivating his articulation of an ethos asserting the primacy of communal over individual interest.

Given this desire to prevent the emergence of a radical proletariat that lay behind O'Grady's recruitment of the nation-state concept in his argument and given his exemption of agriculture from his proposal to nationalise industries, to conclude that this address to Randolph Churchill and the Tory Democrats was anything other than a polemic aimed at securing the economic interests of the aristocracy in the light of an expanded franchise would appear to invest it with a sophistication it scarcely deserves. Two considerations, however, present difficulties for such a conclusion. First, while O'Grady introduced the nation-state idea within the context of a defence of the economic interests of the landed aristocracy, there is no necessary reason for the exclusive reduction of that idea to those interests. Second, O'Grady wrote as a member of the *Irish* landed interest and this necessarily coloured his general perspective of nationality and its relationship to economics. This points to the problematic gap between state and nation in his work (O'Grady's understanding of the Irish nation is set in the context of the British state) that becomes evident in his attitude to Parnell considered below. These considerations must be examined in order to arrive at a more informed assessment of his political writing.

It is worth observing that the idea of the nation-state as an antidote to the problems of late nineteenth-century Britain was shared by leading Victorian thinkers. Matthew Arnold saw in the state, defined as 'the representative acting-power of the nation', an alternative to aristocracy and a solution to the problems created by the increased democratisation of the British electoral system.[20] In proposing a paternalistic model of social relations, Ruskin propounded the view that state intervention ought to take precedence over doctrines of *laissez-faire* with regard to the question of the freedom and responsibilities of individuals within society, thus implying that the state ought to be the new basis of affective social relations:

> ... because the real type of a well-organised nation must be presented, not by a farm cultivated by servants who wrought for hire, and might be turned away if they refused to labour, but by a farm in which the master was a father, and in which all the servants were sons; which implied, therefore, in all its regulations, not merely the order of expediency, but the bond of affection and responsibilities of relationship, and in which all acts and services were not only to be sweetened by brotherly concord, but to be enforced by fatherly authority.[21]

Ruskin's paternalistic state differed from Arnold's political philosophy in that it prolonged the notion of social hierarchy. Arnold regarded class hierarchy as anachronistic and, particularly in *Culture and Anarchy*, sought to rid English society of the tendency to ape the mores of the superordinate class.[22] It is significant, however, that both men articulated their response to the changing political environment of nineteenth-century Britain in terms of an organic concept of the state. It was a concept that became extremely pervasive during the latter half of the nineteenth century both on the right and the left.[23] O'Grady's intervention in the political discourse of the late nineteenth century, therefore, carries no stamp of originality but is merely a variation on a theme already predominant.

To reduce O'Grady's idea of the nation-state as expressed in *Toryism and the Tory Democracy* to the single role of articulating the interests of the landed aristocracy would be to commit, therefore, what Chantal Mouffe terms the economistic fallacy associated with vulgar Marxism, in which the superstructure is interpreted simply as a mechanical reflection of the economic base.[24] This is not, however, to imply that O'Grady's nation-state concept must be read in terms of ethics rather than interests on his part; the interests of his class remain paramount to his political discourse.[25] The use he makes of the nation-state concept, however, in formulating a doctrine that would secure those interests, goes beyond this objective to a point where O'Grady must check his own application of the concept so as not to contravene those interests: his need to exempt agriculture from his vision of a nationalised economy is evidence of this.

If this idea of the nation-state as expressed by O'Grady cannot be explained exclusively in terms of interests or ethics, then how is it to be accounted for? Firstly, it must be acknowledged that nationhood is an infamously nebulous concept that has proven to be extraordinarily resilient in the field of contemporary intellectual discourse, in spite of certain postmodernist attempts to render it obsolete along with all other metanarrative offshoots of the Enlightenment.[26] The extent of left criticism over the past twenty-five years that has attempted to disengage from 'hard' determinist readings of nationalism without falling into the trap of reifying it bears witness to this resilience. Etienne Balibar's 'The Nation Form: History and Ideology' exemplifies such criticism. In rejecting the idea that the nation form can be deduced from capitalist relations of production, Balibar breaks with the determinist teleology within traditional Marxist thought.[27] He contends that the pre-history of the nation–state is represented *as* a pre-history by the ideology of nationalism in order to confer a necessary and eternal status upon itself. This conceals the fact, he claims, that the structures that made the nation–state possible belong to other rival forms such as that of imperialism, and that the events leading to the emergence of the nation–state were spread out over time with no single event necessarily implying a subsequent one.[28] Nevertheless, he argues, political forms with non-national objectives, such as the dynastic form, did provide for the nationalisation of society and at some point a threshold of irreversibility had to be reached; a threshold he locates in 'the development of market structures and class relations specific to modern capitalism...'[29] This suggests that Balibar shares the classical Marxist idea of the nation–state as a bourgeois project: he rejects this, however, as a historical myth and turns instead to Immanuel Wallerstein's thesis of 'world-economy' in which Wallerstein argues that the forces of exchange are structured in a manner that secures the domination of the 'periphery' by the 'core', a structure that necessitates the refraction of the world-economy into core and peripheral elements. A necessary consequence of Wallerstein's thesis is that the modern nation–state is inextricably bound up with colonisation.[30] The efficacy of the nation–state in ensuring this economic domination of the periphery by the core lies, according to Balibar, in providing for the control of class struggle and the emergence of a bourgeois hegemony out of that struggle that would in turn produce a dominant bourgeoisie, in a scenario where both the hegemony and its dominant group act upon one another reciprocally.[31] However, Balibar stresses that the nation–state form relies upon the production of a *social community* in order to achieve this class control and this hegemony; he does not accept that these objectives are spontaneous offshoots of the form of the nation–state: 'The fundamental problem is therefore to produce the people. More exactly, it is to make the people produce itself continually as national community.'[32] Balibar identifies ethnicity as the product of this nationalisation of social formations, not a pre-given entity taken up and transformed in that nationalisation process. Therefore, he differs from one of the most important theorists of nationalism, A.D. Smith, who claims that ethnic communities and sentiments have existed throughout recorded history.[33] Smith's views concord with Balibar's insofar as he identifies 'territorial' nationalism as the ideology of 'nation-building' by which the leaders of a political community attempt, mainly through 'the coercive and administrative apparatus of the state', to create a culturally homogeneous population. However, he also delineates ethnic nationalism as a form whereby a recognisable cultural community embarks on a political process the aim of which is to transform itself into a nation.[34]

Antonio Gramsci's theory of hegemony represents one of the most important theoretical contributions to the understanding of nationalism this century. The broad range of areas within which the theory of hegemony has been applied has contributed to obscuring the fact that Gramsci developed this specifically as a means of understanding the relationship between the nation and the state. Chantal Mouffe argues that the most important aspect of this theory was its break with the economistic theory of ideology that marked the discourse of the Second International, while Nikos Poulantzas criticises it as a Hegelianised Marxism.[35] Mouffe and Ernesto Laclau argue that economism in Marxist theory is most evident in the dogmatic priority it gives to the working class:

> The centrality attributed to the working class is not a practical but an ontological centrality, which is, at the same time, the seat of an epistemological privilege: as the 'universal' class, the proletariat – or rather its party – is the depository of science.[36]

They identify in Gramsci's concept of hegemony a break from this epistemology because it makes symbolism the basis upon which power struggles are enacted in class, gender or ethnic terms. In their view, the priority given to the symbolic in this theory not only breaks from the pursuit of objectivity that provided the scientific basis of classical Marxism, but also re-conceptualises the terrain within which the struggle for domination among competing groups takes place, a re-conceptualisation that ultimately leads Laclau/Mouffe to abandon the concept of society itself.[37] They identify in Gramsci's concept the replacement of relationships of identity necessary to the concept of class unity with relationships of equivalence, so that instead of literal class conflict, hegemonic conditions provide for conflicts between popular and dominant, often involving alliances of disparate class elements, e.g. the urban working class and the peasantry.

In Gramsci's theory, certain revolutionary moments of history bear the hallmarks of real historical development yet have been disregarded as manifestations of false consciousness by Marxists because their revolutionary form is not explicit proletarian. In expressing this view Gramsci was reacting to the social realism advocated by Zhandov *et al.* to the French Revolution and the Italian *Risorgimento*. Gramsci believed that the French Revolution was a real moment of historical transformation because it emerged from a process in which the Jacobins established a hegemony that they successfully extended from Paris to the country, thereby igniting a national-popular movement in which they were in the vanguard. Real historical development took place, according to Gramsci, because the Jacobins offered real political leadership and had an 'inflexible will to become the "leading" party'.[38] Gramsci identified the historically revolutionary form of this in their creation of a bourgeois state, a synthesis of classes in which the bourgeoisie became 'the leading, hegemonic class of the nation'.[39] The French Revolution was, in Gramsci's terminology, a case of 'expansive' hegemony, whereby the revolutionary class, the bourgeoisie in this case, extended itself beyond its own particular interests to forge a relationship of dominance with the rural peasantry, thus producing a synthesis that crystallised into the form of a national-popular movement. Gramsci distinguishes this from the 'transformist' hegemony of the Action Party during the Italian *Risorgimento*. The *Risorgimento* was, in his view, reformist rather than revolutionary, because 'the Italian bourgeoisie was incapable of uniting the people around itself, and this was the cause of its defeats and the interruptions in its development'.[40] He takes the role of the Action Party, led by moderates such as Gioberti and Manzoni, as evidence of this: the Party figured as the leading group within the context of parliamentary alliances, but it failed to create a synthesis uniting and existing beyond the different factions in Italian politics at that time.[41] Gramsci describes this historical process as follows:

> In what forms, and by what means, did the Moderates succeed in establishing the apparatus (mechanism) of their intellectual, moral and political hegemony? In forms, and by means, which may be called 'liberal' – in other words through individual, 'molecular,' 'private' enterprise (i.e. not through a party programme worked out and constituted according to a plan, in advance of the practical and organisational action.)[42]

Deciding whether the role O'Grady designates to the nation-state in *Toryism and the Tory Democracy* is 'transformist' or 'expansive' in Gramsci's sense is crucial in assessing its ideological position. Certainly, there can by no question as to the conservative nature of O'Grady's polemics as is shown in his appeals to *Magna Carta* and 'the old catch-words and magic phrases and the old traditional policy of the party'.[43] Neither can there be any doubt that securing the interests of the landed aristocracy was paramount to his objectives. Nevertheless, he insisted that this class must confront the changing social circumstances within the United Kindgom if it was not to be destroyed. Democratic Toryism was a form of politics that O'Grady believed to be the only way by which gentry could preserve its position in the context of an historical movement towards increased democratisation of political institutions. It involved the Tories extending their appeal beyond the confines of their particular class whose interests they represented to secure a position of leadership and domination through the ideological form of the nation-state. This hegemonic project may be viewed as expansive rather than transformist, since O'Grady proposed a thorough party programme that precluded any negotiation with Whig radicalism. However, its limitations are revealed in the fact that O'Grady refused to envisage the great estates as part of a nationalised economy. Nevertheless, in proposing state intervention in the economy on a large scale, he offered the landed aristocracy a vehicle by which they could transform social relations so as to secure a position of leadership in a mass society without, he believed, retarding economic progress.

The danger that such a hegemonic project involved for O'Grady was that the potential failure of the landed interest to offer the leadership required could result in an ethnic nationalism highjacking the nation–state idea. The risk of appealing to British national loyalty, in other words, was that it could quickly ignite a more regional loyalty, a wholly uninviting prospect from O'Grady's perspective, particularly with reference to Ireland. Indeed, the whole of *Toryism and the Tory Democracy* is at heart concerned with the position of the Irish landlords, although less than half the book is directly addressed to them. O'Grady's aim in addressing the Tory Party was ultimately to ensure that they would not abdicate to the radical project of breaking up the great estates, for without a politically authoritative landed interest in England, the Irish landlords, already feeling the pressure of the Land War, would find themselves utterly cut off, both from their land of residence and the foundation of their political security at Westminster.

This prospect accounts in part for the peculiarly oxymoronic nature of O'Grady's political discourse. His attitude to Parnell is a case in point. In 'Ireland and the Hour', the address to the Irish landlords included in *Toryism and the Tory Democracy*, he implicitly attacks Parnell in his condemnation of Irish landlords who would compromise with agitators for land reform:

> Such [landlords] would placate the National League by rent reductions and rent remissions – concessions contrary to justice, and which they know to be so. Like the cowardly pre-Norman Saxons, they would pay Danegelt to their enemies. In some instances they even join the National League and contribute to its funds, an act of baseness incredible but that we know it to be done.[44]

Published in 1886, the year in which the second Home Rule Bill passed through the House of Commons and during which the land movement was exercising an immense political influence over the whole country, these remarks are startling in their irredentism. Yet in 1898 O'Grady looked back on Parnell and his achievement in terms of admiration:

> Yet Parnell, wielding only the power of a party, shook the State as he passed, compelled the two Imperial parties to approach him with competitive proposals, and despatched the greatest statesman of the day round England as a preacher of his doctrine . . . He was strong because he was a man of purpose in the midst of men of no purpose.[45]

The contradiction between these attitudes can be partly accounted for by the retrospective nature of his remarks in *All-Ireland*. However, it also indicates the anomalies within O'Grady's ideology of the nation-state which he first expresses during the 1880s. His dual perspective of Parnell is indicative of the difficulties that his circumstances bring to bear upon his political position and of the anomalous nature of the object of his reproach and admiration – Parnellism.

Interpretations of Parnell's relationship to the movement he led are various and his legacy has divided historians in a particularly marked fashion. Conor Cruise O'Brien concludes that Parnell undoubtedly desired 'a united self-governing Ireland' that would be 'a willing partner in the British Empire': 'He sought not to break the connexion with England, but to make it more flexible, more efficient, and more acceptable'.[46] However, O'Brien argues that to achieve this, he had to enlist the 'residues' of Irish revolutionary tradition in the service of his parliamentary political project. He proceeds to claim that this could only be effected through a cult of the leader:

> But the driving force of the 'residues' could be successfully directed in the sense of the 'combinations' [parliamentary strategies] only under one condition. This was that *the ambiguity of the system must be crystallized in terms of personality*. The leader, in short, had to become a mysterious and awe-inspiring figure.[47]

R.F. Foster casts Parnellism in a similar light when he points out that even after the land movement had been 'clericalized and radicalized' under Parnell's direction, his most frequent guests at his shooting-lodge at Aughavannagh, Thomas Esmonde, John Redmond, W.J. Corbet, belonged to the conservative element in the Home Rule movement.[48] 'Schizophrenia,' writes Foster, 'as a concept if not a word, recurs in contemporary descriptions of Parnell's position. But he certainly makes sense as a pragmatic, Tory-inclined landlord, just as much a figure in the tradition of Lord Edward Fitzgerald, Erskine Childers, Maud Gonne or Bridget Rose Dugdale; the zeal of the convert is not appropriate. Carson is nearer the type, or Bismarck (whom he admired).'[49]

It is not one of the purposes of this book to decide upon the nature of Parnell's role in the land movement. I refer to these views of that role solely to illustrate the fact that it is possible to fit Parnell into the role O'Grady advocated for the Irish landlords in *Toryism and the Tory Democracy*, or to read it as confirmation of O'Grady's belief in the destructive consequences if conservatives adopt radical policies in an attempt to win votes after the expansion of the franchise. This suggests that no adequate assessment of the hegemony advocated in *Toryism and the Tory Democracy* can be arrived at without consideration being given to two mutually dependent poles of O'Grady's political thought; his concept of nationality with reference to Ireland and his concept of nationality with reference to the United Kingdom. From this perspective the question of ethnicity and its relation to nation-statehood is relevant to the form of hegemony articulated by O'Grady in *Toryism and the Tory Democracy*. For O'Grady, ethnic nationalism, particularly in Ireland, presented a threat to the mode of nationhood he offered as a response to the changing political conditions of the United Kingdom in the latter half of the nineteenth century. There are strong grounds for contending that he never envisaged ethnic nationalism (as defined by A.D. Smith) in his politics. This view may seem curious in view of the extent to which community and tradition feature in his writing; it is based on reading the use of these concepts in terms of a discursive project of 'producing a people' (Gramsci, Balibar) rather than pre-supposing the existence of homogeneous ethnic groups.

The complexity of this question of ethnicity creates immense difficulties for a thesis that would separate cultural from political nationalism, as John Hutchinson does in *The Dynamics of Cultural Nationalism*. In outlining the terms of his argument, Hutchinson writes:

> I intend to show...that cultural nationalism is a movement quite independent of political nationalism. It has its own distinctive aims – the moral regeneration of the national community rather than the achievement of an autonomous state – and a distinctive politics. In this enterprise, I will argue, historical memory rather than language as such serves to define the national community.[50]

'Regeneration of the national community', suggesting both an intrinsic connection between nation and community, *and* a national community that has had an unbroken, if currently inert, existence, is a phrase emblematic of the complexity, indeed of the confusion, of Hutchinson's basic proposition. This points to a need for a clarification of the meaning of ethnicity and its relationship to nationalism.

Ernest Gellner offers a definition of nationalism that, as with Balibar though not in the same manner, makes ethnicity and nationality inseparable:

> In brief, nationalism is a theory of political legitimacy, which requires that ethnic boundaries should not cut across political ones, and, in particular, that ethnic boundaries within a given state – a contingency already formally excluded by the principle in its general formulation – should not separate the power-holders from the rest.[51]

Gellner acknowledges that this definition rests on concepts that are extremely difficult to define precisely, state and nation. Yet even if we allow for the looseness of the definition, objection can be made immediately to the binding of ethnic boundaries to political ones. What, for a start, constitutes an ethnic group? A.D. Smith offers a response when he remarks that ethnic separatism 'is based upon the reality or myth of unique cultural ties, which serve to demarcate a population from neighbours and rulers'.[52] The difficulty with this is, once more, a perhaps unavoidable lack of precision. A plausible ethnic group in Smith's sense could be that expressed by Pan-Celticism, a movement based on the notion of a shared cultural heritage between people separated by national boundaries. This illustrates that ethnicity is a highly elastic term that, depending on the circumstances within which it is being applied, may or may not correspond to an aspiration towards or a realisation of political autonomy.

E.J. Hobsbawm derives an interpretation of ethnicity from the classical Greek historian, Herodotus, who believed that in spite of their geographical and political fragmentation, the Greeks were one people because they had a common origin, a common language, common gods, festivals, customs and social mores. Hobsbawm argues that 'such ethnicity has no historic relation to what is the crux of the modern nation, namely the formation of a nation–state, or for that matter any state...'[53] Invoking examples of pluri–ethnic nations such as Switzerland, he contends that ethnicity in itself rarely provides the basis for territorial nationalisation. Its main relevance, he argues, lies in the manner in which physical traits can be used to 'reinforce distinctions between "us" and "them", including national ones'.[54] It is interesting to observe here the speed at which he slips from a purely cultural sense of ethnicity (the Herodotean sense) when arguing for its marginal importance to the production of a nation–state, to a purely biological sense when illustrating its relevance to modern nationalism. This is yet another indication of the confusion that the use of the term produces, a confusion underlined by the fact that elsewhere in the book Hobsbawm argues that a genetic approach to ethnicity is irrelevant.[55]

Nevertheless, Hobsbawm's separation of ethnicity from nationalism is useful because at least it offers the possibility of the latter escaping the ambiguities surrounding the former. As he indicates, ethnicity, in either the cultural–linguistic or the physical sense, is rarely homogeneous within a national territory, so that, if an ethnic group is interpreted as the *primum mobile* of nationalism, then the number of politically disempowered 'nations' (Basque, Catalonian, Breton, Flemish, etc.) would be immense to the point of absurdity.[56] If ethnicity and nationality are separated, however, then Balibar's argument that nation-formation involves a process of ethnicisation is not valid. Certainly, some process of 'people-making' is involved in the constitution of a nation, but as the example of Switzerland indicates, it has no necessary connection with the ethnic group(s) within the national territory. Confusion can be avoided if this process is thought of not as one of ethnicisation but of the production of an imagined community as outlined by Benedict Anderson. One of the values of Anderson's thesis is that it does not get embroiled in the nebulosity of ethnicity because it concerns itself only with the type of communities produced by nation-formation. Furthermore, Anderson treats nationalism not as a specific ideology like liberalism or Marxism, but as something akin to religion in the broadest sense.[57] This allows him to historicise nationalism without reifying it, as happens with A.D. Smith's treatment of ethnicity.

The broad tenets of Anderson's argument run along similar lines to

Balibar's, recognising the importance of capitalism (particularly print-capitalism), colonisation and language to the formation of nations. One of his most telling insights is that the initial crystallisations of nationalism in the French and American revolutions were bourgeois but also popular, in that they produced a discourse of citizenship, rights, sovereignty and emblems such as national flags and anthems that would act as the ideological framework of popular consciousness.[58] This roughly corresponds to Gramsci's hegemonic reading of the French Revolution but Anderson follows it up by illustrating how a second crystallisation of nationalism took place from the middle of the nineteenth century with the 'naturalisations' of Europe's dynasties, the best example of which is Czarist Russification.[59] This later movement began largely in reaction to the earlier populist one yet it also signified a realisation on the part of the dynasties of the need to adapt to the new political conditions created by nationalism. This general context sheds light on the paradox that O'Grady advocates the idea of a nation-state in *Toryism and the Tory Democracy* on the basis of an appeal to monarchical sentiment – according to Anderson, such a position would have been absurd before 1815. It reveals the discrepancy between nation and empire, a discrepancy concealed in an imperial ideology that has, as Anderson puts it, 'the character of a conjuring trick'.[60]

O'Grady's tract *All-Ireland* (1898) could be interpreted in this way. Written opportunistically in response to the publication of a report of a Royal Commission on the financial relations between Britain and Ireland which revealed that Ireland had been seriously overtaxed since the Act of Union, O'Grady made a strong rallying cry for the expression of a united national protest over the findings of the report in order that Ireland might take what he saw as its position of rightful authority within the British Empire. Implied in the rhetoric of the tract is the belief that Irish citizenship could be truly realised only by recognising that the basis of Irish nationhood resided within a British context, its constitutional integrity being underwritten by the Crown. In one sense this appears to correspond to Anderson's concept of 'official nationalism' through which 'Slovaks were to be Magyarized, Indians Anglicized, and Koreans Japanified, but they would not be permitted to join pilgrimages which would permit them to administer Magyars, Englishmen, or Japanese'.[61] However, this concept fails to account for the fact that O'Grady writes as an Irishman insisting that the members of his class, the landed gentry, affiliate themselves more thoroughly to Irish history and culture. Constitutional monarchy is appealed to by O'Grady in a call for the strengthening rather than the weakening of Irish identity as *national*.

This raises the question of the concept of nationality advocated by O'Grady in *Toryism and the Tory Democracy* once more. Nationhood in both the British and Irish sense are inextricably linked in this work; his polemic on Tory Democracy can only be read in terms of his appeal to the landlords of Ireland to integrate more profoundly into Irish culture and tradition, and vice versa. Ethnicity, therefore, cannot form the basis of his ideology of nationhood. Were it to do so, then it would be impossible to marshal both poles of his political thought.[62] His concept of the nation-state requires the integration of both Irish and English landed classes into their respective countries in a manner that makes their political authority answerable to national sentiment. He believed that the English landed interest should, through the Conservative Party, assimilate themselves into a broad national movement on the pretext that the imaginative currency of that movement would embody sentiments of tradition and loyalty that would secure them as a class against radical egalitarianism. O'Grady implores the Irish landed interest to pursue a similar line also on the pretext that Irish history and culture were replete with sentiments of tradition and loyalty, sentiments whose presence he sought to illustrate through the production of a Victorian discourse of Irish history and legend in his *History of Ireland*. Therefore, during the 1880s O'Grady saw nationality primarily as an ideological mode by which proletarian radicalism, which he believed originated in bourgeois liberalism, could be curbed. This partly explains why the Literary Revival so utterly sentimentalised the peasant as the organic prototype of Irishness – it bears witness to the influence exercised by O'Grady through his adaptation of Victorian political discourse to late nineteenth-century Ireland, an influence felt strongly even by those who would wish to distance themselves from what they regarded as O'Grady's pro-monarchical philosophy.[63]

However, it is also the case that O'Grady's use of the nation-state idea in *Toryism and the Tory Democracy* is evidence of a dialectic of necessity and contingency structuring his political ideology and consequently subverting his intentions. The nation functions as the imaginative force in his political ideology, expressing sentiments of magnanimity, community and idealism, in direct contrast to the historical force in his political ideology, securing the economic interests of his class. As observed in this chapter, however, both aspects of his political ideology are interdependent: in order to secure the economic interests of his class, he must appeal to the concept of the nation. The form of this contradiction is structurally analogous with that in *History of Ireland: Critical and Philosophical*. O'Grady's need to revert to empirical historical argument in the context of a work that puts forward a view of history transformed by the force of myth corresponds to his refusal to include agriculture in his vision of a nationalised economy in an argument against *laissez-faire* economics in *Toryism and the Tory Democracy*: both are evidence of the specific interests of his class motivating his work, signs of the force of historical necessity breaking through the desire for imaginative freedom inscribed in his concept of nation. Nevertheless, the leap O'Grady makes beyond empirical history in *History of Ireland*, corresponding to the leap he makes in *Toryism and the Tory Democracy* beyond the specific interests of his class to one of national community, transforms the historical and political landscape, setting in train a concept of history released from empirical certainty and a political discourse of revolutionary potential. The prospect of O'Grady's political discourse subverting his original intentions was as certain as the prospect of his imaginative transformation of history subverting his original intentions in *History of Ireland*.

This instance of the radicalising potency of a political discourse so ostensibly conservative would appear to justify Ernesto Laclau and Chantal Mouffe's claim that Gramsci's theory of hegemony justifies the abandonment of the concept of working class identity as the basis for Marxism's analysis of historical development, replacing it with the concept of equivalence. They describe a relation of equivalence as follows:

> A relation of equivalence is not a relation of identity among objects. Equivalence is never tautological, as the substitutability it establishes among certain objects is only valid for determinate positions within a given structural context. In this sense, equivalence displaces the identity which makes it possible, from the objects themselves to the contexts of their appearance or presence. This, however, means that in the relation of equivalence the identity of the object is split: on the one hand, it maintains its own 'literal' sense; on the other, it symbolizes the contextual position for which it is a substitutable element.[64]

This definition can be viewed as an attack upon the view of history as necessity articulated by Jameson in *The Political Unconscious*, for the shift from identity to equivalence ensures that there can be no inexorable logic of historical self-unfolding through the dialectical emergence of new modes of production from the contradictions of those superseding them. Moreover, the category of necessity itself is interrogated in the definition, for if context determines identity, then identity is always contingent. Laclau and Mouffe take the emergence of the 'people' in Communist thought (particularly Gramsci's) as an example of equivalence in action, whereby the relation of equivalence splits the identity of classes. In citing this example, they advance their definition of a relation of equivalence to that of a general equivalent:

> ... given its internal logic, the relation of equivalence cannot display its presence simply through the incidental substitutability of its terms; it must give rise to a general equivalent in which the relation as such crystallizes symbolically. It is at this point in the political case we are examining, that national-popular or popular-democratic symbols emerge to constitute subject positions different from those of class: the hegemonic relation then definitively loses its factual and episodic character, becoming instead a stable part of every politico-discursive formation.[65]

A relation of equivalence, therefore, does not simply reduce the identity of its terms to that of their context within which they are articulated, it manifests itself as the dominant form through which identities are articulated and struggled over in the broad field of political discourse. O'Grady's vision of an aristocracy united with the peasantry and proletariat in opposition to the middle classes might be a case in point, particularly when the cultural influence of this idea in the Literary Revival is considered.

Central to accepting the tenability of this post-Marxist argument is the question of necessity, for necessity permeates *Toryism and the Tory Democracy*, in that O'Grady felt he *had* to write the book, believing that the aristocracy *must* act immediately to avoid their own demise if they were not to become contingent to the political landscape emerging at the end of the nineteenth century in Ireland and Britain. In addition, the work is concerned to re-establish a sense of historical necessity, given O'Grady's belief that the bourgeois destruction of feudal relations had led society into a form of collective hysteria, in which the forms of historical reality had become indiscernible. Necessity, then, is both something O'Grady is responding to and something he is arguing for in *Toryism and the Tory Democracy*.

While post-Marxism suceeds in liberating itself from the reductive determinism of a vulgar Marxist reading of history, it runs into difficulty in its attempt to abandon the concept of necessity itself, a concept identified with such determinism. This is evident in the fact that although the move Laclau and Mouffe make away from identity to equivalence is anti-necessitarian in motive, they cannot abandon the concept of necessity outright. They argue that Gramsci's concept of hegemony, conceived in terms of this move to equivalence, is only intelligble beyond the necessity/contingency opposition, for neither category is exclusively adequate to expressing the operation of hegemony as they conceive it.[66] However, they are incapable of articulating this position beyond the necessity/contingency binary opposition. Therefore, necessity remains as an oblique yet indispensable concept in a theoretical argument designed to get rid of it.[67] As a work that is conservative in political motivation yet radical in its political consequences, *Toryism and the Tory Democracy* justifies the post-Marxist view that radical politics is not exclusive to a discourse of working-class liberation. Equally, however, it illustrates that such politics cannot be divorced from the force of history – if an ostensibly conservative political doctrine contains radical potency, it is because it is subject to that force, conceived as a dialectic of necessity and contingency. The extent to which *Toryism and the Tory Democracy* subverts old social scientific views of political revolution, in other words, offers a pretext for a new assertion of genuinely dialectical consciousness rather than a denigration of it.

It remains to consider the legacy of O'Grady's politics in terms of this contradiction. The trace of his political ideology is most deeply inscribed in that of the Irish Co-operative Movement as articulated by George William Russell. Russell saw in the movement the basis for the articulation of the feudal, organic communalism expressed by O'Grady in his literary and political writing. The contradictions informing O'Grady's *Toryism and the Tory Democracy* continue to be felt in Russell's writing on co-operation, in the tension between its practical and idealistic elements and in its treatment of the question of individualism and communalism. Furthermore, as in O'Grady's politics, the question of class and national interest is central to understanding the political status of the Irish Co-operative Movement. The following chapter considers Russell's involvement with the movement in these terms.

A matter of ideals: George Russell's ideology of co-operation

<small>I</small>N *APPRECIATIONS AND DEPRECIATIONS*, Ernest Boyd saw George Russell as the natural successor of Standish O'Grady, as someone who directed the criticism once directed by the latter at the landed aristocracy against the new landowning classes in Ireland after the Wyndham Land Act of 1903, and who directed this new class towards an ancient civilisation through the Co-operative Movement.[1] Certainly, Russell never veiled the influence O'Grady had on him. In his introduction to the 1919 edition of O'Grady's *The Coming of Cuculain*, Russell described him as an artist of grandeur rather than subtlety, a type upon which he placed greater importance:

> Standish O'Grady had in his best moments that epic wholeness and simplicity, and the figure of Cuculain amid his companions of the Red Branch which he discovered and refashioned for us is I think the greatest spiritual gift any Irishman for centuries has given to Ireland.[2]

Russell went on to acknowledge his personal indebtedness to this legacy:

> For my own part I can only point back to him and say whatever is Irish in me he kindled to life, and I am humble when I read his epic tale, feeling how much greater a thing it is for the soul of a writer to have been the habitation of a demigod than to have had the subtlest intellections.[3]

The fact that Russell chose to express his admiration of the epic form in deferring to O'Grady is relevant to assessing his relationship with the most skilled practitioner of the lyric form in the Revival, W.B. Yeats.[4] The concern in this chapter, however, is with Æ's socio-economic discourse and the relationship it bears, both personal and ideological, to O'Grady's politics.

Under the pseudonym Æ, Russell became most famous for his involvement with Yeats in the theosophical movements popular at the turn of the century. However, literary scholars have paid less attention to his involvement with the Co-operative Movement and the philosophy of nationality he developed through it; when they do so, this philosophy is usually seen in terms of his theosophical beliefs. Darrell Figgis, for example, writing when Russell was still expounding his co-operative philosophy, considered his involvement in the Co-operative Movement as a means by which his spiritual beliefs could be practically articulated.[5] Russell's co-operative ideal took a large amount of its inspiration from the doctrine of feudal communalism that O'Grady portrayed through his characterisation of Cuchulainn. Furthermore, O'Grady became personally concerned with the Co-operative Movement initiated by Sir Horace Plunkett, entering into dialogue through his newspaper, *The All-Ireland Review*, with the journal of the Co-operative Movement, *The Irish Homestead*, on the subject of co-operation.

Interpretations of the history of the Co-operative Movement in Ireland during the late nineteenth/early twentieth century are sharply divided. The movement began in humble surroundings and was slow to develop initially. Sir Horace Plunkett started his first co-operative society at Doneraile, Co. Waterford in 1889, but it was to be another six years before a national body governing co-ops was established, namely, the Irish Agricultural Organisation Society. F.S.L. Lyons reads the movement as a mode of constructive unionism, part of a strategy, however benevolent, deployed to stall what he regards as the inevitable movement of Irish nationalism towards political independence after the Famine.[6] It comes as no surprise, therefore, that Lyons sees the movement as a failure, and identifies the source of this failure in what he regards as Plunkett's error of subordinating politics to economics:[7]

> Plunkett made one miscalculation more fundamental than any that have yet been mentioned. Because Home Rule was moribund when he entered public life he assumed that politics had become less urgent and vital for Irishmen than economics. But here he was profoundly mistaken. In the very years when he was launching his movement the whole political situation was in ferment and out of that ferment would come a mood and temper sharply inimical to the well-meant efforts of Protestant landlords to lead their fellow-countrymen through co-operative paths to quiet pastures.[8]

Paul Bew accepts that Plunkett was politically unionist and that he prioritised economics over politics. However, Bew also notes that 'Plunkett was still a difficult man to pigeonhole: he did after all support some rather unconventional causes (for a Unionist MP for South Dublin) – the G.A.A., the Gaelic League and the campaign for a Catholic University.'[9] This ambivalent persona reflected in many ways the movement Plunkett initiated. Lyons's assumption, for example, that the Co-operative Movement was landlord led is undermined by the fact that one of its strongest campaigners during the 1890s was a Jesuit priest, Fr Finlay, who often joined his voice to those of Plunkett, H.F. Norman and Æ in criticism of those who opposed the movement both politically and economically.[10]

More important than this question of leadership, however, is the issue of the movement's relationship to Irish nationalism in the aftermath of the Parnellite split. Paul Bew's examination of Redmondite politics during the period 1890 to 1910 reveals the cleavages within Irish nationalism that Lyons plays down with his idea of nationalism as an essentially homogeneous bloc. Bew argues that these cleavages arose out of a tension between agrarian radicalism and constitutionalism that informed nationalist politics in Ireland since the New Departure of 1879–1882. He regards as erroneous the view that the emergence of an anti-Parnellite wing in the Home Rule movement after the split was evidence of a re-emergent agrarian radicalism moving beyond constitutional strategies to a position that would reach its zenith in Easter 1916. He supports the view by focusing on the political alienation fom the United Irish League of potentially the most radical group in rural Ireland, the landless labourers, and on the fact that the interests of the graziers and middlemen (a powerful bloc) who supported the League very often clashed with those of their subordinates, the small tillage farmers and landless labourers.[11]

> It is clear that as the U.I.L. expanded across the country it made its way as an electoral and political organisation. It ceased to have any pretensions as an organisation of grassroots agrarian radicalism. The police reports harp on this point time and time again. It was a pressure group for land reform and national independence. It was not a semi-revolutionary challenge to the British state in Ireland; it was not, in other words, the Irish Land League re-born.[12]

Bew's analysis of the political landscape in Ireland after the Parnellite split helps to contextualise the arguments fought out in the pages of *The Irish Homestead* over many years, most significantly between the Co-operative Movement and the Dillon/Healy wing of the Home Rule movement. The intensity of the conflict between these two groups is reflected in the fact that in February 1899, *The Freeman's Journal*, effectively Dillon's mouthpiece, decided not to print any letters defending the Co-operative Movement.[13] Russell was particularly vociferous in defending the Co-operative Movement and read *The Freeman's Journal* attacks as arising from the threat it posed to the power of the middlemen in rural Ireland.[14] His tone was often venomous:

> The gombeen men, jobbers, commission men, and all that lot, add their voice in council meetings and in the Press to help Mr Dillon in the House. They realise the farmers are escaping from their clutches, and hence this obscurantist cry is heard out of the stupid old Ireland which lost its trade and its industries while it listened to long speeches, promises, and sentimentalities.[15]

This criticism of Dillon might be read as a continuation of the strategy initially proposed by Standish O'Grady in *Toryism and the Tory Democracy*: accommodating the interests of the landed aristocracy in Ireland's changing circumstances by proposing an alliance between them and the rural peasantry in opposition to the politically dominant group in the country – the Catholic rural middle-class. This interpretation lends credence to Lyons's view that the Co-operative Movement was primarily concerned with the interests of the landed gentry. However, the extension of O'Grady's strategy could contrariwise be seen in the Gramscian sense of transforming the political environment in such a way that the particular interests of the landed aristocracy melt into a national-popular movement ignited initially by the pursuit of those interests.[16] In order to ascertain the more accurate interpretation it is necessary to consider the nature of the ideological battles that the Co-operative Movement had to fight. The most important of these were its battles with a nationalist group represented by *The Freeman's Journal* and with the Co-operative Wholesale Society, a Manchester-based organisation established in 1863 to provide a structure through which English co-operative societies could trade products with each other.[17]

The conflicts between *The Freeman's Journal* and *The Irish Homestead* lasted many years, fuelled primarily by John Dillon's animosity towards Sir Horace Plunkett whom he described at one stage in parliament as 'a subtle and dangerous Unionist politician'.[18] One of Dillon's constant demands was that since Plunkett lost his parliamentary seat in 1900, the government should insist on his resignation from the Department of Agriculture and Technical Instruction, which Plunkett himself had been instrumental in establishing. Because of Dillon's pressure Plunkett eventually resigned from this post in May 1907. Dillon continually claimed that Plunkett's involvement with DATI and the IAOS was part of an anti-Home Rule strategy. This conflict came to a head over the controversy surrounding a letter written by T.W. Rolleston published by *The Freeman's Journal* on 21st January 1908. The letter was written by Rolleston as a cover note to a report of a speech given by Plunkett at the IAOS conference which he sent to a prominent Irish American. The letter ended up in the hands of John Redmond who then wrote to *The Freeman's Journal* quoting the letter in full and referring to it as evidence of a conspiracy against the Irish Parliamentary Party. Russell immediately identified Dillon as the person behind Redmond's attack:

> It seems that Mr. Rolleston's letter is a complete justification of all the charges ever brought against the I.A.O.S., so it was used as dynamite, stuffed into a torpedo, Mr. Redmond being the blunt nose, while the driving force in the rapidly revolving tail was, as we believe, Mr. John Dillon.[19]

In view of the fact that Redmond's accusation was aimed ultimately at Plunkett, the latter felt obliged to respond. In a letter published in *The Irish Homestead* on 1 February 1908, he repudiated the suggestion of conspiracy, stating that he carried no responsibility for Rolleston's letter and knew of it only when he saw it in *The Freeman's Journal*.

The effect of the Rolleston letter incident was detrimental to the IAOS. The letter was referred to at a meeting of the Agricultural Board, an advisory body largely elected by the Council of Agriculture and entrusted with the power of veto over the department's expenditure. Consideration of the angered reaction to the letter in *The Freeman's Journal* resulted in a decision to alter an agreement previously held between the IAOS and DATI in which the subsidy to the work of the former was to cease at the end of three years. It was decided at the meeting that the subsidy would end after one year. Furthermore, the department took the decision to take over the work of the IAOS which, for Russell, represented an attempt by the state to kill off an active voluntary body.[20] The Co-operative Movement continued to be active long after this incident but the rapid expansion which it had experienced between 1889 and 1898, in which the number of societies increased from 1 to 243, was halted once and for all.

The incident reveals the fact that the failure of the Co-operative Movement to realise its ideals could not simply be explained in terms of its internal contradictions – forces were at work that lay beyond the control of the movement, forces that aimed at breaking it. Furthermore, these forces moved under the guise of a nationalist discourse that was designed to obscure the clash of interests between rural/urban proletarian and middle-class elements within the United Irish League and the Irish Parliamentary Party. Thus Redmond's attack on the Co-operative Movement cannot simply be read as part of a united nationalist front against unionism.

Paul Bew views Redmond as the carrier of the Parnellite torch illuminating a land settlement in which the landlords and the peasantry would be reconciled: 'Redmond's tactics of co-operation with moderate Unionists on the financial relations question and above all, the policy of toleration following the democratisation of local government (1898) revealed this clearly.'[21] However, he also recognises the necessity, from 1899 onwards, for Redmond to keep a united front in the Irish Parliamentary Party, a front that was threatened with division by the increased influence of the United Irish League.[22] So the grounds are solid for interpreting his response to the Rolleston letter as motivated primarily by a need to pacify the anti-Parnellite wing of his party, chiefly represented by Dillon, rather than as an expression of a united nationalist opposition to unionism.

Keeping this political context in mind, it is necessary to consider the objectives of the Irish Co-operative Movement in order to evaluate its political status. Certainly, Russell and Plunkett hoped that the movement would accommodate the interests of the landed gentry within circumstances altered by dual ownership and peasant proprietorship in rural Ireland. Russell was keenly aware of their dwindling political status in the new conditions prevailing since the advent of Parnell: 'The position of Irish landlords and of ex-landlords, the latter class growing rapidly now, and almost outnumbering the former, is one which they themselves are always discussing... They [the landed gentry] see no place for themselves in Ireland.'[23] He argued that they could find such a place through the stance taken by Plunkett and others like him. He claimed that the apparent vindictiveness towards the landlords as a class was largely confined to the public realm: 'The platform and the Press and the clubs are the safety valves letting off most of our national share of vindictiveness, and our people have continued, thanks to these safety valves, to preserve the kindliest manners in private.'[24]

Considering the extent to which Plunkett and Russell subordinated party politics to economics in their co-operative ideology, these observations on the landed gentry suggest the validity of an argument made by Thomas Boylan and Timothy Foley in relation to the Co-operative Movement. They situate it within the tradition of political economy in Ireland, whereby the latter marketed itself as a doctrine deployed to maintain the status quo:

> Political economy was especially well qualified as a bonding agency in society as it seemed to provide consensus both at the discursive and at the 'material' economic levels. Interestingly, with the eventual failure of the project, and the fall of Parnell, which ended many hopes of a political (seen as the quintessential arena of division) solution to Irish problems, consensus was sought at the 'material' level of agricultural co-operation (the foundation of the Irish Agricultural Organisation Society), 'below' the divisiveness of politics, as it were, and at the cultural level, 'above' politics, in the revival of the Irish language (the Gaelic League) and the Literary Revival.[25]

They give weight to their argument by considering the role education played in nineteenth-century Ireland. Boylan and Foley read the promulgation of political economy in the non-denominational national school system, established in 1831, through Archbishop Richard Whateley's *Easy Lessons on Money Matters: For the use of Young People*, a simplified version of his *Introductory Lectures on Political Economy* in terms of a strategy of pacification in Ireland.

> Education, formal and informal, set out not only to augment the meagre store of Irish knowledge and to deplete the impressively abundant holdings of Irish ignorance and error, but, in effect, to change what was perceived as the Irish 'character', to substitute order, rational discourse (hence the teaching of logic in the national schools) for rhetorical excess, thereby promoting affection for England and the established Church.[26]

One finds this idea of changing Irish character in Russell's *The National Being*. Here, he continually insists on the need to create a spirit of independence in Irish people through the Co-operative system. He perceived a mentality of dependence among the small farmers and landless labourers in rural Ireland, fashioned largely out of a lack of education, and a stultifying myopia among traders and middlemen, in which their pursuit of personal profit thwarted any magnanimous concern they might have felt for the interests of their immediate community or the nation. Russell hoped the Co-operative Movement would free these most vulnerable elements of rural Irish society (the small farmers and landless labourers) from financial enslavement to the traders and middlemen:

> That a ring of traders should dictate to the farmers of a country who produce nearly all the wealth of the country, where and from whom they

are to buy, and where and to whom they are to sell, is a pretension not to be tolerated. And the pretension is all the more ridiculous that they make their money out of the soil, while all the others make money out of them. They are independent in a sense in which the term is not applicable to any other section of the community; to command them to manage their business in the interests of a class which is wholly dependent on them argues a profound belief in their stupidity or servility.[27]

Russell envisaged the creation of a new, independent Irish character by, ironically, co-operative *inter* dependence that would crystallise at the national level in the form of an economically viable and spiritually unified state. This indicates that the tradition of political economists such as Whateley, who were primarily concerned with the production of Enlightenment *homus ratio* in Ireland, may have influenced Russell, though he was not content to remain exclusively at the level of material concerns; though influenced by this tradition, his philosophy of co-operation was not entirely reducible to it.

In contradistinction to political economists such as Whateley, neither Æ nor Plunkett ever envisaged Anglicisation as part of the co-operative project. As evidence of this, one of the most important battles the IAOS fought centred on its clash with the Co-operative Wholesale Society on the subject of control of distribution. The CWS was a powerful organisation governing trade between English co-operative societies and was concerned with protecting the interests of those societies when conceived as consumers as much as producers. It intervened initially in the Irish co-operative scene when an internal dispute between Catholic and Protestant members of the Castlemahon Co-operative Creamery in 1894 threatened to close the creamery down. In order to keep the creamery in production the CWS agreed to rent it but eventually it bought the establishment outright. Following this, the CWS brought forward plans to build two creameries of its own in Ireland.[28] Plunkett saw this as potentially stifling to the native co-operative movement he sought to develop. In his view, the CWS plans would create the circumstances whereby Irish rural producers would become slaves of the English consumers.[29] More generally, he argued that the source of conflict between Irish and English co-ops rested on the Wholesale co-ops and those directly controlled by the farmers themselves. He saw problems arising when the manufacture of foodstuffs, particularly butter, moved from the homestead to the factory. The Wholesale co-ops governed the distribution of the product but the IAOS sought to counter this monopoly by establishing the Irish Co-operative Agency Society: 'The Wholesale policy, backed by millions sterling, and the principles we are preaching in support of which we have always appealed to the highest English Co-operative authority, will inevitably come into collision.'[30] A representative of the English Co-operative movement, Mr Cochrane, was unconvinced by the distinction Plunkett drew between the Irish and English Co-operative movements and gave air to his belief that free trade had made the English workingman wealthier. Plunkett responded, however, that, ironically, Cochrane's attitude revealed the heart of the problem:

> Free trade, which has made the English workingman rich, has made the Irish farmer poor. There has been no more disastrous policy for the farmers of Ireland, there has been none which has done more to throw them into that position of helplessness in the face of foreign competition from which the I.A.O.S. is endeavouring to rescue them, than that very policy on the fruits of which the co-operative workingmen of the English Wholesale Society are flourishing today.[31]

This view reflects Plunkett's belief that the sudden imposition in the seventeenth century of a land system in Ireland alien to the tribal system of 'open fields and common tillage', lay at the heart of Ireland's rural economic problems. Its negative effect was seen in the manner in which the sense of communal ownership 'did not perish like a piece of outworn tissue pushed off by a new growth from within: on the contrary, it was arbitrarily cut away while yet fresh and vital, with the result that where a bud should have been there was a scar'.[32] It is somewhat ironic that the social class from which Dillonite nationalism drew most of its support, the traders and middlemen, aligned themselves to the position of the English Co-operative Wholesale Society in opposition to the IAOS. Their opposition even reached a point where local traders refused credit to members of the IAOS to whom it had previously been custom to accord.[33] Evidence of the extent of this opposition is revealed in the fact that *The Independent* newspaper, precursor of *The Irish Independent*, took a defensive position in favour of the traders within a year of the IAOS's foundation.[34]

To argue, therefore, as Boylan and Foley do, that movements initiated and/or led by 'enlightened' unionists such as Plunkett and Æ, were at heart part of a British colonial strategy of pacifying Ireland, is a problematical claim. Certain observations included in their analysis are borne out in the pages of *The Irish Homestead*, for example, the production of the notion of Irish character and a desire to accommodate the interests of a landed gentry looking increasingly isolated, but Boylan and Foley give insufficient attention to the effect of changed political circumstances after the fall of Parnell on the discourse and political status of constructive unionism in Ireland.[35] The social and parliamentary attacks on the Co-operative Movement arose primarily from a concern to protect the interests of the rural Catholic middle-class that emerged in Ireland after the Famine, not from an attempt to launch a national-popular offensive against spokespersons of colonial ideology.[36]

To fully assess the ideology of the Irish Co-operative Movement as articulated by Russell, attention must be given to *The National Being* and *Co-operation and Nationality*, his most comprehensive explications of the movement's ideology. These works display evidence of the contradictions informing O'Grady's literary and political writing; in examining them, a critique of co-operative ideology can be formulated in terms of its hegemonic or counter-hegemonic status, keeping in mind the context, considered above, within which that ideology was practised.

In *The National Being*, Æ makes a number of direct acknowledgements of O'Grady's influence on his thought as, for example, when he writes that the heroic literature of ancient Ireland 'is, as our Standish O'Grady declared, rather prophecy than history'.[37] This influence is not selective but constitutes the ideological deep structure of Russell's work. In it the ideology of co-operation acts as the means by which Russell's concept of nationality is made manifest. This concept is informed by the philosophy of communalism that dominates O'Grady's treatment of the Cuchulainnite sagas. Significantly, the Victorian form of that treatment is made explicit in the following passage, worth quoting at length for the extent to which it reflects Carlyle's philosophy of heroism emerging in Russell's thought via O'Grady:

> It appears almost as if in some of those ancient famous communities [the city states of ancient Greece] the national ideal became a kind of tribal deity, that began first with some great hero who died and was immortalised by the poets, and whose character, continually glorified by them, grew at last so great in song that he could not be regarded as less than a demi-god. We can see in ancient Ireland that Cuchulain, the dark sad man of the earlier tales, was rapidly becoming a divinity, a being who summed up in himself all that the bards thought noblest in the spirit of their race; and if Ireland had a happier history no doubt one generation of bardic chroniclers after another would have moulded that half-mythical figure into the Irish ideal of all that was chivalrous, tender, heroic, and magnanimous, and it would have been a star to youth, and the thought of it a staff to the very noblest. Even as Cuchulain alone at the ford held it against a host, so the ideal would have upheld the national soul in the darkest hours, and stood in many a lonely place in the heart.[38]

To the extent that this passage reiterates the doctrine of mythological historiography that functioned as the intellectual basis of O'Grady's treatment of Cuchulainn, it suggests that Russell was also opposed to the empirical approach to history. This being the case, it is inevitable that the tensions in O'Grady's work would emerge also in Russell's writing under a different guise. They can certainly be identified in the problem of individualism and communalism in *The National Being*.

As noted, Plunkett and Russell aimed at creating an independent Irish character through the Co-operative Movement. This independence would be achieved, they believed, by freeing the most disadvantaged elements in Irish society from their enslavement (maintained, in their view, primarily through lack of education) to traders and middlemen. This ideal of self-reliance was the shaping force of their understanding of nationality. This is exemplified in the value placed by Russell on the decision of the IAOS to adopt a national brand for butter in January 1901, a decision, he believed, that had national significance since it affirmed the uniquely Irish nature of IAOS products.[39] Given this affirmation of independence of character at both the personal and the national level, the attack on individualism that is made explicit in *The National Being* may seem curious. It re-introduces the complexity of the question of individualism informing O'Grady's *History of Ireland: Cuculain and His Contemporaries* considered in Chapter 2.

The nature of Russell's thought rules out any facile mode of distinguishing between communalism and individualism. In the following passage, for example, he considers citizenship, with its double connotation of duty and autonomy, to be absent in the most advanced nations:

> Our big countries, our big empires, and republics, for all their military strength and science, and the wealth which science has made it possible for man to win, do not create citizenship because of the loose organisation of society; because individualism is rampant, and men, failing to understand the intricacies of the vast and complex life of their country, fall back on private life and private ambitions...[40]

This statement constitutes not just a detour from the Enlightenment concept of citizenship as the ground of duties and rights attaching to individual membership of the nation-state, a concept generally allied with the privatisation of commerce and affective human relations; it is also a remarkably lucid statement of the epistemological crisis of modernity more contemporaneously identified by Fredric Jameson.[41] Russell's co-operative ideology was communalist, but he conceived of this as the basis for the realisation of rather than the denial of individual autonomy. This becomes evident in his description of the circumstances of a hypothetical small farmer in rural Ireland, Patrick Maloney:

> He might be described almost as the primitive economic cave-man, the darkness of his cave unillumined by any ray of general principles. As he is obstructed by the traders in a general vision of production other than his own, so he is obstructed by these dealers in a general vision of the final markets for his produce.[42]

Russell presents Maloney in this way to argue that his autonomy can only be realised through a consciousness of economic horizons broader than his own; the Co-operative Movement, in providing for that emancipation through its educational and economic strategies, was the vehicle by which such a transformation could be achieved.

Russell insisted, however, that this autonomy must not be confused with individualism; he believed that independence of character could only be realised when the interests of the individual were understood to be identical with the interests of the community.[43] Without this identification being made, Russell believed that the purely self-interested individualism of free-market economics would perpetuate what he regarded as the erosion of rural civilisation in Ireland, eventually leading to a situation whereby it would not matter whether Ireland was governed from Westminster or from Dublin, such would be the decrepitude of its cultural and economic life. Russell's understanding of individualism in this context is close to that of Plunkett's. Plunkett was concerned that the transfer of land from landlord to peasant that was taking place in Ireland during the last decades of the nineteenth century would create social atomisation and economic fragility without the organisational influence of the Co-operative Movement:

> Without this agency of social and economic progress, small landholders in Ireland will be but a body of isolated units, having all the drawbacks of individualism, and none of its virtues, unorganised and singularly ill-equipped for that great international struggle of our time, which we know as agricultural competition.[44]

This distinction that Russell drew between individualism and independence of character (what Plunkett termed 'virtuous' individualism) relates directly to his understanding of the state: it corresponds directly to the distinction he makes between mechanistic and organic forms of statehood. Therefore, it locates his thought within the German Enlightenment tradition, particularly with reference to the ideas of statehood found in the work of Hegel and Herder. Adrian Oldfield's interpretation of the role of the state in Hegel's philosophy reflects the unifying impulse of O'Grady's feudal communalism and of Russell's co-operative ideology: 'Hegel sees the coming together of freedom/necessity, the particular/universal, subjective/objective in the state.'[45] F.M. Barnard's description of the idea of the *Volk*-state in the writing of Herder distinguishes it from the notion of the state as an administrative bureaucratic apparatus: 'The *Volk*-State is conceived as a territorial community with its own language, laws and customs. It is the "natural" social framework within which various sectional bodies and associations operate and co-operate, and not an administrative machine.'[46] According to Barnard, Herder was intent on promoting co-operation between individuals within the state as the basis upon which the regulation of society would emerge naturally from the people rather than being artificially imposed from above by monarchical despots or bureaucratic apparatus.[47] His *Volk*-state had no need for a sovereign authority wielding supreme political power. It embodied a pattern of communal life that was rooted in tradition, where each citizen identified his interests naturally with that of the community, conscious as they were of their interdependence.[48]

Hegel and Herder's philosophies of the state were articulated within broader philosophical frameworks and within the immensely complex context of the German Enlightenment, neither of which is the concern of this book. Nevertheless, it is not implausible to claim an influence of Hegel's view of the state as a locus of unity and Herder's organic concept of the *Volk*-State on *The*

National Being. In this work Russell writes of the state as a physical body prepared for the incarnation of the soul of a race.[49] Furthermore, he rejects the bourgeois structuring of the state as a bureaucratic apparatus, regarding the elimination of the power of interest groups controlling state bureaucracy as part of the project of the Co-operative Movement. Rural organisation, according to Russell, should not be the work of state bureaucracy but of the farmers themselves and those genuinely concerned for their welfare, *not* those content to exploit the farming community for their personal financial gain:

> To ask the State or a State Department to undertake this work is to ask a body influenced and often controlled by powerful capitalists, and middle agencies which it should be the aim of the organisation to eliminate.[50]

Russell conceives of the state as the natural emanation of the national community and his commitment to co-operation is born out of the desire to bring this spiritual form of community into the fullness of being. He hoped that co-operation would realise the interests of the rural population through the creation of a sense of communal identity that would act as the foundation stone of a new, dynamic civilisation in Ireland. He believed that these interests could never be realised, however, until a genuine sense of interdependence was fostered in the indigenous rural population of Ireland. From Russell's perspective, rural Ireland was in a state of perennial decay.[51] He believed that this arose from a general discontent with rural life that was felt both in Europe and America during the latter half of the nineteenth century.[52] He argued that this discontent had its origins in the break-up of the clan or communal system by the bureaucratic form of the state that emerged during the Enlightenment, resulting in the small farmer becoming isolated in the modern world. He believed that co-operation was instinctive in ancient rural communities and that a revitalisation of the Irish national community could only be realised through a reawakening of that instinct.[53]

Evidence suggests, therefore, that when Russell referred to the state in a positive sense, he had the idea of a national community in mind, an idea corresponding to Herder's concept of the *Volk*-State, although the latter is expressed as a tradition whereas the former is articulated through the institution of the Co-operative Movement. There are occasions when Russell admitted the need for state assistance and in particular he placed great value on the work of the Department of Agriculture and Technical Instruction.[54] For the most part, however, he was critical of state intervention and viewed the expansion of state bureaucracy as a form of 'despotic government' threatening democracy.[55] This re-conceptualisation of the state in organic terms by Russell suggests a distinction between cultural and political nationalism in his writing on co-operation. John Hutchinson focuses on this distinction, arguing that 'whereas cultural nationalists aspired to revive a distinctive Irish *community*, the goal of political nationalists was Ireland's normalisation among the nations of the world by regaining her independent *statehood*'.[56] Hutchinson argues that political nationalists had no sense of Ireland as a civilisation separate from Britain but that they aspired to an Ireland modelled on English liberal lines that would acquire status as a partner in British Imperialism. On the other hand, he claims, cultural nationalists proclaimed Ireland as an organic entity personified in many forms but particularly in the forms of Cuchulain and Cathleen Ní Houlihan:

> Revivalism took on the characteristics of a religious movement in which Irish names, language, literature, sports and manufactures were to be adopted and their English equivalents renounced. Its goal was the 'inner' regeneration of a spontaneously evolving decentralized community led by an elite of public spirited men and women... For membership of the nation was defined not by birth, religious or political affiliation but by an active participation in the nation's cultural, economic, social and political development.[57]

The distinction Hutchinson draws between cultural and political nationalism is ostensibly borne out in Russell's rejection of administrative bureaucracy in favour of an organic concept of statehood. The weakness of his argument, however, lies in the lack of consideration he gives to the strategic discursive aspect of the deployment of cultural nationalist motifs.

The specific context in which the Herderian concept of organic community is deployed by Russell highlights this weakness. It has been noted already that Plunkett and Russell's co-operative philosophy was in part designed to facilitate the landlord class in social conditions that were eroding their political ascendancy. In *Ireland and the Death of Kindness* Andrew Gailey sets this aspect of the ideology of co-operation in the context of constructive unionism as practised by A.J. Balfour, who was appointed by Lord Salisbury as Irish chief secretary in July 1895 and with whom Plunkett closely associated. Gailey interprets Balfour's thought and policies in remarkably similar ways to Russell's thinking on co-operation. Balfour was anti-interventionist, believing that the state should not be involved in the direct alleviation of social impoverishment through legislation, but that it ought to work towards the re-establishment of economic conditions that would encourage self-help:

> If there was a central theme to Gerald Balfour's policies in Ireland, it was education and the development of 'character'. D.A.T.I. would breed the economic and agricultural skills which would lay the foundations of a stable and prosperous society; in turn these conditions, together with the experience of participation in local administration, would encourage individual responsibility and a wider understanding of the country's problems and position.[58]

Balfour's policies have traditionally been interpreted in terms of a perceived Tory policy of killing Home Rule with kindness. But Gailey argues that regardless of what events of the period suggested, no set agenda of killing

Home Rule with kindness actually existed: 'A phrase that was too striking to be forgotten only ensured that a rather limited policy of economic reconstruction was lost and confused amid the glamour of a rhetorical myth.'[59]

Whatever the validity of this contention, Plunkett and Russell's co-operative endeavours were significantly in line with Balfour's policy of aiding the creation of new social conditions in Ireland through agricultural and economic education in order to bring about an independent and better-informed Irish character, even if the emergence of a Victorian individualist ethos was the fundamental motive of the Chief Secretary whereas, at least for Russell, an aspiration towards a feudal communalist ethos lay at the heart of his co-operative activities. This suggests that the opposition between cultural and political nationalism that John Hutchinson argues for in *The Dynamics of Cultural Nationalism* fails to account for the degree to which cultural activities were to some extent in sympathy (even if not always intentionally so) with aspects of Tory government policy on the Irish question in the 1890–1910 period.

The organic concept of the state that Æ advocates in *The National Being*, a concept influenced by the German Enlightenment tradition, can at least partly be seen in terms of a compliance with Balfour's constructive unionist policies in relation to Ireland. This interpretation allows one to read Russell's critique of the technocratic administrative apparatus in Ireland, increasingly assimilated to the broadly Catholic bourgeoisie that emerged after the Great Famine, as a guise for the promotion of a unionist agenda, however liberally that agenda might be construed. Such a view implies that while its defence of small farmers against the interests of a conservative rural bourgeoisie in Ireland suggests that the movement was genuinely radical, the truth was otherwise: the objectives of the movement were significantly consonant with some of the means by which the Conservative Party attempted to neutralise the drive for constitutional independence for Ireland, particularly after the Parnellite split. Convincing as this interpretation might seem, it is nevertheless undermined by two considerations. Given the tenuous evidence for the existence of a coherent Tory policy of killing Home Rule with kindness, the likelihood of Plunkett and Russell simply deferring to such a policy through their co-operative project is wholly untenable. Furthermore, as with the 'killing Home Rule with kindness' thesis, no blueprint for consolidating the Union could be directly related to the IAOS even though aspects of co-operative ideology, such as a desire to accommodate the interests of the Irish gentry, might be construed as evidence of such a blueprint as, indeed, politicians like John Dillon claimed.

Russell's distinction between an organic and a mechanistic concept of the state, therefore, cannot *simply* be interpreted in terms of a distinction between cultural and political nationalism in Ireland after the Parnellite split. The historical context in which he makes this distinction was informed by an ideological struggle between constructive unionism as advocated by Balfour and the party political bourgeois nationalism advocated by Dillon. This implies that the notion of a national community underlying his organic concept of the state, presenting itself as a natural and spontaneous phenomenon, cannot be understood without reference to the relations of antagonism and alliance that constitute the matrix of political discourse in Ireland after the Parnellite split.[60]

Aside from the question of the proximity of the Co-operative Movement's ideology to constructive unionism, the question of its rural orientation is also relevant to assessing its political status. Consideration of the role of the concept of *Volk* in Russell's thought is indispensable to understanding this question. The association of rurality with this concept, originating in the work of Herder, became so close as to be virtually synonymous in the folk element of German and British Romanticism during the nineteenth century. In *The Country and the City* Raymond Williams traces the development of this association in English literature in pastoral poetry. He argues that Goldsmith's 'The Deserted Village' (1769) represents a change in pastoral poetry that would subsequently be developed into a Romantic structure of feeling. Williams argues that the precision of observation that Goldsmith brought to the decline of a bucolic society distinguishes it from the tradition of general complaint characteristic of sixteenth and seventeenth century pastoral poetry. This precision, he argues, is concomitant with an identification of the poet's personal suffering with the decline of the rural village but he argues that this empathy refracted rather than reflected the real social transformations taking place, for it implied that the destruction of the village was bound up with the destruction of poetry: 'And then the village itself becomes a pastoral and a poetic mode: its expropriation is assigned to the general vices of wealth and luxury.'[61] Williams points out that the break-up of feudal social relations resulted in the increased productivity of the land, which, in 'The Deserted Village' is represented as 'stinted' and 'choked'. In his view this indicates that Goldsmith responded to the social transformation of rural life that he witnessed by extricating from that life an idea of it that would be consigned to memory and imagination, producing both the idea of an idyllic past and a utopian/dystopian future: 'Here, with unusual precision, what we can later call a Romantic structure of feeling – the assertion of nature against industry and of poetry against trade; the isolation of humanity and community into the idea of culture, against the real social pressures of the time – is projected.'[62]

Williams's examination of representations of urban and rural life in English literature, particularly from the eighteenth century, suggests that nineteenth and twentieth-century adaptations of organicist thought were mediated through a structure of feeling that arose from the emergence of industrial society in Europe. If we accept his contention that this structure of feeling involved an idealisation of rural life that removed it from the historical processes that were transforming it, then the connotations surrounding Herder's concept of *Volk* – naturalness, simplicity, spontaneity – belong to an aesthetic response to industrialisation rather than to a descriptive account of a living society. This implies that where organicist thought is applied with a

118

bias towards the rural, actual historical conditions are addressed through an imaginative rather than a descriptive medium. As in O'Grady's depiction of Gaelic heroes in his stories of Elizabethan Ireland, the concept of *Volk* becomes an aesthetic motif designed to intervene in social conditions that have rendered it materially obsolete, in order to materially re-establish that which it embodies aesthetically.

Russell's application of organicism in his philosophy of co-operation is certainly biased towards the rural. The peasant rather than the industrial worker was to be the foundation upon which a national community would be articulated; his emancipation from poverty through education and co-operation would, Russell believed, form the basis upon which Ireland as a whole would become economically independent and culturally articulate. This belief runs implicitly throughout Russell's writings on co-operation in *The Irish Homestead* and is made explicit in his analysis of the condition of a fictional small farmer in *The National Being*.[63] However, Russell also saw in the resistance of the Dublin proletariat to the despotism of William Martin Murphy during the 1913 lockout, the sentiments of brotherhood and self-sacrifice that he desired to promote in his philosophy of co-operation.[64] The admiration that he expressed towards these people must be considered in the light of the fact that Russell was not an advocate of socialism as a solution to the chronic unemployment and forced migration that large-scale industrialisation had produced; though he admired the sentiments of the proletariat he did not subscribe to their socialist goals.[65] Although noble gestures could be found in urban politics, urban politics, whether socialist or capitalist, could not form the basis upon which 'the soul of the race' would be incarnated, from Russell's perspective.

Consideration must be given to the fact, however, that Æ argued for the primacy of rural over urban civilisation on *economic* as well as cultural grounds, sharing Plunkett's belief in 'the never-to-be-forgotten inter-dependence of the sentimental and the practical in Ireland'.[66] The economic case is made in chapter four of *Co-operation and Nationality* where Russell argues that town life in Ireland ought to be considered subordinate to rural life since the latter was involved in production and the former in distribution: 'A country must first of all safeguard its producers. It depends absolutely on them to create wealth, and they must be allowed to create it under the best possible conditions they can devise.'[67] He believed that town life had become stagnant and burdensome on the rural economy, as production was concentrated almost exclusively on the land in Ireland. If Irish towns continued to be exclusively distributive, he claimed, their decline will be inevitable and in the long term, their disappearance would be of no loss to the national community as a whole: 'Anyhow some rows of licensed premises, with a few men spitting at the corners, do not constitute a civilisation whose lapsing Ireland need not lament over with too exquisite a pain.'[68] The target here is, once again, the middleman who exerted a tight grip on the small farmer. Russell's claims that because the dependence of structures of distribution on production forces was the sign of an economically healthy environment, this grip was detrimental to the economy as a whole since it inverted this relationship of dependence, thus creating a false economy.[69] An insidious aspect of this economic climate was the mass migration of rural populations to urban centres, the effect of which was to stagnate rural life and to increase food prices (as a consequence of increased production costs and increased demand).[70] The fundamentally Romantic perspective (predominant in Russell's poetry) underlying what, on the surface, appear to be convincing economic arguments, is revealed in his prophecy that this rise in food prices would lead to a repopulation of the countryside, 'and the reflushing of the veins of humanity with the old divine vigour got from sun and air, and the smell of the earth and rural labour'.[71] Furthermore, Williams's 'Romantic structure of feeling' is exemplified in the final sentences of the chapter, where, instead of coming to terms realistically with prevailing social conditions, Russell ponders an idyllic past in which a utopian future is signified:

> Nature has no intention of allowing her divine brood, made in the image of Deity, to dwindle away into a crew of little, feeble, feverish city folk. She has other and more grandiose futures before humanity if *ancient prophecy* and our deepest, most spiritual intuitions have any truth in them.[72]

Despite the economic arguments, therefore, the rural bias informing Russell's concept of *Volk* within his organicist philosophy reveals the extent to which Romantic idealism conditions his thought. Nevertheless, this does not take away from the efficacy of co-operative ideology as a critique of the forms of social and economic relations that prevailed in Ireland at the turn of the century. Many aspects of Russell's analysis are verified, for example, in Hugh Brody's anthropological study of west of Ireland communities during the 1930s. Brody examines how the erosion of a sense of community ran in tandem with the decline of rural life in the west. By the 1930s, the communalisation of rural work practices was indelibly replaced by the privatisation of farm work.[73] Brody points out, however, that traditional communal work practices were just as conditioned by economic considerations as those practices that replaced them. He sees the changes wrought by emigration on rural Ireland re-inforcing the traditional independence of the family farm but also signifying the decline of rural Ireland as a vibrant residue of tradition and local interaction. The emergence of the entrepreneurial family in rural Ireland was, argues Brody, the clearest sign of this erosion, describing it as 'part of a country's final acquiescence in urban capitalist culture'.[74] His analysis supports Russell's claim that the effect of the individualism concomitant with free-market economics and industrial capitalism was detrimental to the cohesion of rural Irish society. However, whereas Russell viewed the communalism of traditional rural Ireland as the embodiment of heroic and magnanimous character traits, Brody recognises that securing individual interests was just as important a factor in the mutual aid schemes characteristic of that society as in the more ostensibly capitalist form of society that replaced it. Brody is at one with Russell, however, in his belief that self-reliance was fundamental to peasant society in Ireland as elsewhere.[75] This suggests that while a Romantic idealist version of Germanic organicism governed Russell's thinking on traditional rural Irish society, the peasant way of life that he wished to preserve *did* contain values of co-operation and self-reliance: the 'idea' of the people in Russell's thought was not entirely at variance with the reality of rural life in Ireland.[76]

Through the concept of *Volk* articulated in *The National Being* and *Co-operation and Nationality*, therefore, Russell tries to combine pragmatism and idealism in pursuit of a vision of an Irish society capable of asserting its national identity on economic and cultural grounds rather than purely on the basis of parliamentary independence from Westminster. This develops O'Grady's attempt to integrate a concern for the practical economic conditions of society with an appeal to sentiments of loyalty, magnanimity and idealism in *Toryism and the Tory Democracy*. The contradictions informing that aspiration continue to be felt in Russell's work, to the extent to which a dialectic of necessity and desire structures his vision of a pragmatism integrated with idealism: his idealism is structurally Other to his economic thought, even though he viewed his economic thought as merely a means to idealistic ends, since it imagines a form of society free from economic necessity.

This failure to integrate idealism into economics anticipates the problem of reconciling the economic and the utopian in Marxist theory throughout the twentieth century. Louis Althusser's concept of relative autonomy was, perhaps, the closest Marxist theory has ever come to achieving such a reconciliation. Althusser attempted to reconcile the anti-determinist view of language, proposed first in structuralism and later in Derrida's post-structuralist theory of language and Foucault's theory of discourse, with Marxism's belief in the relationship between forces and relations of production as the key to understanding the totality of human experience. For some Marxists, the effort was ultimately unconvincing, leading them to abandon precepts fundamental to the Marxist tradition and enter an orbit they define as post-Marxist. One such theorist, Nicos Mouzelis, disputes the belief that the concept of relative autonomy in Althusser's structural causality can actually resolve the problem of economic reductionism. Mouzelis argues that the conceptual tools necessary for 'the relatively autonomous study of political and cultural phenomena', do not currently exist in Marxist theory: 'When Marxists analyse the non-economic spheres. . . they do so in terms of concepts derived from the economy, that is, in terms of class or the reproductive requirements of the mode of production.'[77]

Another post-Marxist theorist, Tony Bennett, criticises the work of Fredric Jameson, someone whose theory of literature is indebted to Althusser's concept of relative autonomy, in a similar fashion. Bennett views Jameson's theory of history in *The Political Unconscious* as an attempt to resolve the contradiction between constructivist and empiricist conceptions of history, quoting John Frow in interpreting it as a case 'of having one's referent and eating it too'.[78] While it would be stretching things too far to equate Bennett's notion of constructivism with Russell's idealism, both notions share the view of history as something imaginatively created, in the discursive sense in Bennett's case, and in the Platonic sense in Russell's. Bennett's argument against Jameson is an updated statement of the problem faced by Russell – how to reconcile non-empirical idealism with empirical economics. His criticism reflects Samuel Weber's view that Jameson is attempting to outflank poststructuralism, particularly in its challenge to history, by incorporating it into a Marxist analysis that offers a causal explanation for the instability of language and indeterminacy of meaning celebrated in poststructuralism.[79] The end result of this, in Bennett's view, is the collapse of history into an idealism of form: '"Always historicise!" is the opening injunction of *The Political Unconscious*, yet almost every step Jameson subsequently takes prevents him from doing so.'[80]

However one judges the validity of these post-Marxist objections, their pertinence to the problem of idealism and pragmatism in Russell highlight the error in judging this problem as no longer relevant. Furthermore, they are not a basis for justifying the belief that Russell's idealism weakened the credibility of his analysis of Ireland's economic problems, nor for the view that his concern for practical necessity rendered his idealism disingenuous. The integrity of Russell's pragmatism and idealism can be weighed by considering his communalism in relation to O'Grady's. We have seen from *Toryism and the Tory Democracy* that the dominant motif in O'Grady's political doctrine was to awaken the landlord class to their sense of identity with the indigenous Irish population; how he argued in favour of a practical economic strategy of nationalisation of industries such as forestry in Ireland, combined with a sense of cultural identity. However, the pressure of historical circumstances rendered O'Grady's communalism increasingly utopian, finally resulting in his promotion of the idea of abandoning society totally in favour of an almost pre-lapsarian communal lifestyle. In an article in *The All-Ireland Review* of November 1905 he wrote of contemporary civilisation that 'I hold it to be doomed past recall, and that the only course left for our adoption, if we would save ourselves and others, is to come out of it and found and build up a new life outside its doleful precincts; that the world *cannot* be reforged from within'.[81] The nature of O'Grady's utopia involves a remarkable transformation in his political and cultural thought. In the 'New Order' that he envisages replacing civilisation, for example, he believes that women would take positions of social leadership and, in consequence, replace the militaristic heroism that was so important to O'Grady's treatment of Cuchulainn, with a feminine sentimentality that O'Grady previously regarded with disdain: 'Men will lose that power which they exercise today, to such ill results, over the lives of women, and all our able-minded and able-bodied masculine ruffians reduced to their proper place.'[82] While Russell was critical of the impractical nature of this 'New Order', he nevertheless defends O'Grady against advocates of political economy who judge O'Grady's proposals exclusively on the basis of economic rationality:

> Political economy is not logic – a mistake, made by Mill and others of the *laissez-faire* school – but it is, or rather ought to be, the science of how to live to the best advantage. I admit that that is not the definition usually accepted, but I am assured, and my conceit must be pardoned, that it is a definition that will in the near future, be universally assented to. Logic relies on the sequence of steps of reasoning; political economy relies on the truth, or otherwise, of its general ideas. When Mr O'Grady makes a mistake in regard to the yield per cent of potatoes, his teaching as to the wonderful fruitfulness of the earth, and the consequent favourableness of agriculture as an investment, is not thereby invalidated.[83]

Arguments such as this suggest that the vacillation experienced in interpreting Russell's ideology of co-operation in either a radical or conservative political form is due to the fact that it embodied an alternative form of political discourse deconstructing unionist–nationalist paradigms, a form best exemplified in Lady Gregory's description of Standish O'Grady, perhaps the writer who most influenced Russell, as a 'Fenian Unionist'.[84] Furthermore, the combination of pragmatism and idealism in Æ's philosophy of co-operation ensures that to argue against it on the idealist grounds that it was too concerned for practical economics, as O'Grady did, is to deny the cultural dimension that is inseparable from those economic considerations.[85] On the other hand, to argue that it was uneconomic, as some commentators contend, is to ignore the cogency of Russell's description of the economic conditions of rural Ireland at the turn of the century and particularly the pertinence of his assertion that the trading classes and middlemen had created a false economy that produced the general economic stagnation of rural Ireland.[86] While a dialectic of necessity and desire structures his holistic world-view, it is nevertheless the case that it eludes exclusively pragmatist or idealist criticism, offering a paradoxical political discourse that tends to foreground rather than efface its dialectical form.

Liam O'Dowd argues that the tendency to regard the Co-operative Movement as either marginal to the cultural task of forming a national identity or the economic task of integrating Ireland's economy into global capitalism, arises from the fact that intellectual activity in Ireland has traditionally failed to integrate materialistic concerns into cultural ones. Because Ireland's national boundaries continue to be contested, according to O'Dowd, the role of traditional intellectuals, in Michel Foucault's sense, continues to predominate. This has reached a point where these traditional intellectuals' pre-occupation with Irish identity threatens to become a speciality in its own right. In this scenario, he argues, the material element is neglected and a false holism is created by these intellectuals. On the other hand, specialist intellectuals see no need to locate their activity in a wider social context (by specialist intellectuals, O'Dowd has in mind those class of economists, administrators and business people who, particularly since the economic revolution enacted by Sean Lemass during the 1960s in the Irish Republic, have been at the forefront in promoting free-market strategies sympathetic to the demands of international capitalism):[87] 'In an attempt to undermine the politics of emotional abstraction in the early 1920s, George Russell was among the few to insist on the material underpinning of both politics and culture (including intellectual activity).'[88] In his view, Russell tried to link the Literary Revival to the Co-operative Movement; the Revival would draw people together regardless of class or creed and the Co-operative Movement 'would form the democratic economic base of the new cultural order'.[89]

O'Dowd's analysis of Russell's thought is revealing to the extent to which it reveals the pre-suppositions underlying the dismissal of the Co-operative Movement as uneconomic. However, his claim that Russell's position was materialist is flawed. While we have noted the fact that he was critical of utopian projects with no chance of practical survival (as in the case of O'Grady's communes), the assumption that this attitude was materialist overstresses the economic aspects of Æ's thought and underplays his intrinsic idealism. O'Dowd's inability to avoid implication in that of which he is critical in others, a lack of holism, is revealed in his dismissal of the spiritual/theosophical aspects of his writing as 'shortcomings'.[90] Contrary to this, Alan Denson claims that Russell's theosophical beliefs inspired him to become involved in the Co-operative Movement.[91] Darrell Figgis, writing at a time when Russell was still expounding his co-operative ideals, recognised a spiritual aspiration at the heart of his involvement in co-operation.[92] Robert Davis also claims that Russell's mysticism was the ground of his economic theory.[93] Furthermore, the extent of O'Grady's influence on Æ indicates the degree to which the mythic heroism of the former permeated his cultural and economic aspirations. These considerations emphasise the fact that a definitive judgement on Æ's co-operative ideology depends upon the manner in which one interprets the relationship between his mystical and literary endeavours and his political and economic writings. In the case of O'Dowd, the latter are given precedent and the former are considered as 'shortcomings'; for commentators such as Figgis, Denson and Davis, the former are viewed as the foundation stones of the latter.

In conclusion, Russell's co-operative ideology must be considered not just on its own terms but also in terms of the discourses of political economy, romanticism and organicism that informed it. Furthermore, the extent to which one can attribute to it the status of a counter-hegemonic discourse depends on the context within which Russell articulates his ideology. As has been noted, elements within that ideology approximate closely to A.J.

Balfour's policies on Ireland and more generally the philosophy of constructive unionism promoted by Horace Plunkett and enacted by Balfour and George Wyndham.[94] Furthermore, the bias towards the rural that informs Æ's writing, particularly in *Co-operation and Nationality*, indicates that Raymond Williams's concept of a romantic structure of feeling, whereby actual historical processes are mediated through an idealisation of the past and/or a millenarian/utopian view of the future, informed Russell's co-operative philosophy.[95] On the other hand, the extent to which Dillonite nationalism mobilised press and parliament to isolate the Co-operative Movement in the interests of securing a stranglehold by the middlemen in rural Ireland over the small farming communities, indicates the degree to which the movement threatened the forces of conservative bourgeois nationalism that sought to establish a position of hegemony in Ireland after the Parnellite split. Russell's opposition to middle-class interest groups in Ireland during this period was not a replication of the aristocratic dimension of Standish O'Grady's aversion to bourgeois mercantilism; it was, rather, a transcendence of the conservative motivation of *Toryism and the Tory Democracy*. O'Grady's primary concern for the landed gentry became, in Russell's co-operative writing, just one aspect of the articulation of an organicist philosophy of nationhood. Thus, Russell realised the counter-hegemonic potential of O'Grady's *Toryism and the Tory Democracy*, transcending the political conservatism originally motivating that work.

CHAPTER SIX

'A sea-covered stone': O'Grady's influence on the young W.B. Yeats

THE PRECEDING EXAMINATION OF THE PHILOSOPHY of co-operation developed by George Russell reveals the enormity of O'Grady's influence upon him. Russell's determination to integrate practical economic necessity and imaginative idealism in his organic concept of nationhood was clearly inspired by O'Grady's efforts to integrate history and the imagination in the two volumes of *History of Ireland* and science and myth in *History of Ireland: Critical and Philosophical*. The forms of contradiction that arise in the course of Russell's co-operative writing are clearly traceable to those forms located in O'Grady's work. The split in Russell's public persona, between the co-operative economist George Russell and the mystical poet Æ, formally repeats the split that develops in O'Grady's work subsequent to the volumes of *History of Ireland* between the historian of Elizabethan Ireland and the romantic novelist. However, O'Grady's influence on Russell emerges primarily in his co-operative writing; little evidence of a concern for practical economic necessity (parallel to O'Grady's concern for historical fact) can be found in Æ's mystical poetry.

If O'Grady's influence on Russell emerges in the latter's determination to transform the practical with idealism, his influence on Yeats emerges in the opposite direction. This may seem absurd in view of the dandyist persona associated with the early Yeats and his lifelong condemnation of bourgeois materialist values. The assertion is made on the basis that O'Grady's influence on Yeats has been grossly underestimated and that Yeats's treatment of history is central to understanding his literary development. Before arguing these claims it is worth viewing Yeats's relationship to Russell in terms of the split that emerges in O'Grady's work out of the contradiction in the volumes of *History of Ireland*. It has been shown that the relationship between both sides of the divide is one of dominance and residuality rather than absolute difference: the concern in O'Grady's novels is primarily imaginative but the importance of history remains in these works; obversely, history dominates in his Elizabethan stories but the importance of the imagination is communicated in their imagery and narrative vibrancy.

The relationship between Russell and Yeats in terms of O'Grady's influence can be conceived in an analogous way. Russell's co-operative writings are primarily concerned with practical economic questions but these cannot be abstracted from the imaginative element that becomes dominant in his mystical poetry. Yeats's literary work is, of course, primarily concerned with aesthetic problems but these cannot be abstracted from a concern with history that runs right through his literary career. In focusing on the manifestation of O'Grady's influence in Yeats's work, therefore, one is not simply concentrating on the imaginative side of the imagination-history dialectic structuring O'Grady's work. The contradiction that runs through *History of Ireland* and that becomes explicit in the split emerging in O'Grady's output during the 1890s is manifested in Yeats with a force equal if not greater than that in Russell's co-operative writing.

Like Russell, Yeats acknowledged the profundity of O'Grady's influence on the Irish Literary Revival.[1] Claiming that his *History of Ireland* 'started us all', Yeats asserted that 'here was a man whose rage was a swan-song over all that he held most dear, and to whom for that very reason every Irish imaginative writer owed a portion of his soul'.[2] To a much greater extent than Russell, however, Yeats subordinated O'Grady's writing to his own and was careful to distance himself occasionally from a tendency he detected in his elder towards poor artistic or political judgement. In his second essay on Irish National Literature in the *Bookman* journal of 1895, for example, Yeats made the following comments on O'Grady's *The Story of Ireland*:

> I disagree with his conclusions too constantly, and see the armed hand of nationality in too many places where he but sees the clash of ancient with modern institutions, to believe that he has written altogether the true history of Ireland; but I am confident that, despite his generalisations, his slipshod style, his ungovernable likings and dislikings, he is the first man to have tried to write it, for he is the first to have written not of battles and enactments, but of changing institutions and changing beliefs, of the pride of the wealthy and the long endurance of the servile tribes of ignoble countenance.[3]

This criticism is typical of the interpersonal rivalries of the Irish Literary Revival most vividly captured in George Moore's *Hail and Farewell*. As Estella Ruth Taylor remarks: 'Nowhere has comment been more profusely personal than in the writings of the modern Irish whose fiction and criticism are tinged with personal prejudice, and whose accusations and recriminations give zest to their letters and memoirs.'[4] However, the importance of Yeats's relationship with O'Grady extends beyond this question of personal rivalry. Yeats became intimately engaged with an intellectual tradition mediated in O'Grady's work in which the relationship between history and the imagination was paramount. Consequently, in this chapter O'Grady's influence on Yeats will not be examined in biographical terms but as a trace of the structure of contradiction in Yeats's dramaturgy, given that the relationship between history and the imagination receives its most thorough philosophical treatment in this aspect of Yeats's writing. Following this, I will consider 'The Wanderings of Oisin' as a representative instance of Yeats's preoccupation with the relationship between history and the imagination in his early work and, consequently, as evidence of O'Grady's influence on him early in his career. Finally, the *Daily Express* controversy that Yeats was involved with at the end of the 1890s will be considered as evidence of how Yeats's attitude to the relationship of history to the imagination had developed beyond O'Grady's by this period.

The conflict that ensued between O'Grady and Yeats/Russell over the dramatisation of the Irish heroic legends forms the point of departure for understanding the relationship between them on the subject of history and the imagination. O'Grady was opposed to any dramatisation of legends centring around the Táin Bo Cuailgne and levelled severe criticism at Æ's play *Deirdre* on this basis in 1902. He was not opposed to the dramatisation of Irish history *per se*, as is borne out by his own drama based on the life of Hugh Roe O'Donnell performed in August 1902; it was the dramatisation of the heroic cycles that offended him: 'Dramatise Irish history... as much as you like, and with as much freedom and abandon as you like, but leave the heroic cycles alone and don't bring them down to the crowd, not, at least, through drama and the stage.'[5]

The criticism inevitably drew a hostile response from Russell and Yeats. Russell complained of the elitism implicit in O'Grady's remarks, responding that the legends of Ireland 'had no special message to the aristocrat more than to the man of the people'.[6] He went on to express astonishment at O'Grady's fear that salacious elements of Irish legend would be dramatically staged for the titillation of a contemporary audience, thus vulgarising the heroic figures of Maeve, Cuchulainn, Ferdia and Concobhar MacNessa. For Russell, the danger of art lay not in its subject matter but the attitude of the artist in treating that subject-matter: 'The nobler influences of art arise, not because heroes are the theme, but because of noble treatment and the intuition which perceives the inflexible working out of great moral laws.'[7]

Yeats's response, published in the 1902 edition of *Samhain* and in the *All-Ireland Review* of 1 November 1902, defended the dramatisation of the heroic cycles on two interrelated points; first, the primacy of aesthetic sensibility to the task of literary activity and second, the generic inadequacy of O'Grady's own treatment of the cycles. With regard to the first of these, Yeats held that books of literary propaganda and literary history were merely preparations for a literature concerned with 'the creation of an emotion of beauty'.[8] The reference he makes to literary history here is an initial signal of Yeats's awareness of the historical imperatives governing O'Grady's *History of Ireland*, in which O'Grady refutes with venom the suggestion that the heroic legends of the Red Branch cycle were purely imaginative. Yeats's position in this instance appears to dismiss this historical imperative; this has consequences for the gender and formal aspects of Yeats's treatment of the material of the Red Branch cycle, given the interrelatedness of history, gender and form in O'Grady's *History of Ireland*.

In relation to Yeats's second point of defence, the generic treatment of the legends, his pronouncement on O'Grady's efforts is generous even if typically authoritative:

> Mr O'Grady in his youth had the epic imagination, and I think few people realise how great and heroic that inspiration was; but the net that is spread for Leviathan will not capture all the creatures of the deep, and neither epic nor romance will manifest fully the power of the mythical ancestors of the modern Gael who now seek incarnation anew in the minds of their children.[9]

Yeats locates this formal shortcoming of O'Grady's in the incapacity of the written word to recapture the power within speech that, he believed, marked the bardic renditions of the heroic narratives:

> The Literary man, has gone into strange byways through long contemplation of books and he writes with elaboration what could never be spoken, and he loses that power of the bards on whom tongues of fire had descended, who were masters of the magic of utterance, whose thoughts were not meant to be silently read from the lifeless page.[10]

Expressed here is a central aspect of Yeats's dramaturgy – his belief in theatre as a spiritual medium, a place of ritual and incantation summoning primeval and transcendental forces obscured by the dominance of a rationalist *Weltanshauung* in modern society (reflected in the pervasiveness of realism in drama). He claims that through drama alone a writer could summon the power inherent in speech, believing that 'it is possible we yet may hear on the stage, not merely the mimicry of human speech, but the old forgotten music which was heard in the duns of kings, which made the revellers grow silent and great warriors to bow their low faces in their hands'.[11]

Both Russell and Yeats's refutation of O'Grady's criticism represents an important modification of the principles governing the latter's treatment of the heroic cycle in *History of Ireland*. In recognising this, however, it must not be forgotten that the idea of history culminating in art was one to which O'Grady subscribed in *History of Ireland: Critical and Philosophical*, an idea derived from Carlyle's view of history as biography. As has been shown, however, O'Grady's vacillation between his aspiration for a suitably epic rendition of the Red Branch cycle and his insistence on the historical veracity of the legends was never resolved because of the unavoidable necessity of falling back on the empirical method of historical analysis in *History of Ireland: Critical and Philosophical*. With Yeats, however, the primacy of the imagination becomes all-pervasive and he attempts to incorporate history itself into the mythic structure he develops in his poetic and dramatic treatment of the Gaelic legend.

Yeats frees himself from any reliance upon empirical historiography partly because in the early 1900s his view of nationality was subordinate to concerns he regarded as universal; primarily, the conflict between the Apollonian and Dionysiac impulses in human history and the importance of drama in fuelling the re-emergence of 'the simplicity of the first ages, with knowledge of good and evil added to it'.[12] However, this did not amount to a rejection of provincialism in favour of cosmopolitanism, as O'Grady believed it did.[13] Yeats wrote that although he was excited by the symbolist drama of Verhaeren and Maeterlinck emerging from Paris in the early 1890s, he could not stand 'an international art, picking stories and symbols where it pleased . . . Have not all races had their first unity from a mythology that marries them to rock and hill?'[14] He recognised, however, the dangers implicit in producing a mythology exclusively for regional and national aims, reducing as it did universal and transcendental motifs to political propaganda. From this perspective, he shared more with O'Grady than the latter was willing to admit, given O'Grady's concern to posit a nationality grounded on the notion of a national community free from sectarian division. Yeats insisted on countering the movement from aesthetics to propaganda in the Literary Revival:

> It is easy for us to hate England in this country, and we give that hatred something of nobility if we turn it now and again into hatred of the vulgarity of commercial syndicates, of all that commercial finish and pseudo art she has done so much to cherish. Mr Standish O'Grady has quoted somebody as saying 'the passions must be held in reverence, they must not, they cannot be excited at will', and the noble using of that old hatred will win for us sympathy and attention from all artists and people of good taste, and from those of England more than anywhere, for there is the need greatest.[15]

Significantly, Yeats relies here on O'Grady in his attempt to counter ethnic nationalism with an idea of nationality based primarily on an aversion to bourgeois mercantilism and the empiricist, individualist and rationalist ethos associated with it, an idea promoted most forcefully in O'Grady's *Toryism and the Tory Democracy*, itself rooted in Carlyle's communalist and anti-dilettantist philosophy.

Two interrelated motifs lie at the centre of Yeats's treatment of ancient Irish legend during the 1890s and 1900s: that of magic, associated distinctly with Gaelic folk culture and expressed primarily through the lyric form; that of articulating a relationship between community and individualism, expressed primarily in the dramatic form. These concerns were intertwined in Yeats's enduring preoccupation with the occult, in which he aspired to transform through the nominalist esotericism of his dramatic persona that simplicity and imaginative freedom he associated with Gaelic folk culture into a symbolism bespeaking a re-emergent paganism.

Walter Benjamin's insights in *On the Origins of German Tragic Drama*, offer a passage into an understanding of the occult form of Yeats's dramaturgy. Benjamin's thesis argues that the German baroque *Trauerspiel* was radically different from *Tragodie*, a claim running counter to the classicising orientation of German literary theory and scholarship in his own day, according to George

Steiner. In his introduction to Benjamin's work, Steiner takes Benjamin's assertion that *Trauerspiel* was, unlike tragedy, rooted not in myth but in history as the departure point of Benjamin's thesis.[16] In developing this argument, Benjamin refers to the story of the veiled image of Saïs, whose unveiling destroyed whomsoever sought to thereby learn the truth, interpreting this as a revelation of the nature of truth itself:

> Truth is not an intent which realizes itself in empirical reality; it is the power which determines the essence of this empirical reality. The state of being, beyond all phenomenality, to which this power belongs is that of the name.[17]

Benjamin believed that the task of the philosopher was to restore the primacy of the symbolic character of the word, in which the use to which language was put in empirical thought was abandoned in the process of acknowledging its self-reflexive structure.[18] This task, however, has historically taken classical and modern paths; that of Platonism and neo-Platonism, where the autonomy of the word is comprehended in the ideality of form, and that of post-Nietzschean linguistic relativism, particularly contemporary poststructuralism, where this autonomy is invoked to signify the death of metaphysics and the arbitrariness of the sign.[19]

Yeats's involvement from 1890 with the Hermetic Students of the Golden Dawn indicates that, as with the early Benjamin, he understood linguistic autonomy in mystical terms.[20] For Benjamin, the sacredness of the hieroglyph, underlying the Jewish Kabbalah, governed his analysis of the baroque *Trauerspiel*, and, as Richard Wolin indicates, the twin myths of Kabbalistic origin, that of the Tree of Life and of the Tree of Knowledge, were the foundation stones upon which his doctrines of fall and redemption, of messianic time and empty, homogeneous time, were based.[21] Yeats's dramaturgy was one influence on Benjamin's Kabbalistic interpretation of *Trauerspiel*, as George Steiner notes.[22] This is clear in the theory of tragic theatre Yeats put forward in 1910, when he argued that tragic moments were those where lyrical intensity drew one away from character and the real world, into the condition of a trance:

> Certainly we have here the Tree of Life and that of the knowledge of Good and Evil which is rooted in our interests, and if we have forgotten their differing virtues it is surely because we have taken delight in a confusion of crossing branches. Tragic art, passionate art, the drowner of dykes, the confounder of understanding, moves us by setting us to reverie, by alluring us almost to the intensity of trance. The persons upon the stage, let us say, greaten till they are humanity itself.[23]

As with Benjamin's understanding of tragedy, Yeats sets truth beyond the grasp of rational classification constitutive of empiricism; he identifies emergent insight in the traversal of the gap between experience and thought (life and knowledge), disrupting the mental regulation of sensory experience in the process – tragic knowledge is portrayed as phenomenal but not empirical. In 'setting us to reverie', tragic art is a 'confounder of understanding', for which revelation is possible only through a moment of catharsis when experience and thought compenetrate.

This form of dramaturgy is indebted to Nietzsche's *The Birth of Tragedy from the Spirit of Music*. Nietzsche agreed with Schiller that tragic art originated in the satyr chorus of the ancient Greeks. His thought is manifestly anti-empiricist, empiricism being, for him, a latter-day offspring of a detested Socratism:

> Poetry does not lie outside the world as a fantastic impossibility begotten of the poet's brain; it seeks to be the exact opposite, *an unvarnished expression of truth*, and for this reason must cast away the trumpery garments worn by the supposed reality of civilized man. The contrast between this truth of nature and the pretentious lie of civilization is quite similar to that between the eternal core of things and the entire phenomenal world. Even as tragedy, with its metaphysical solace, points to the eternity of true being surviving every phenomenal change, so does the symbolism of the satyr chorus express analogically *the primordial relation between the thing in itself and appearance*.[24]

Two movements in Nietzsche's argument can be observed here that illustrate the profundity of his influence on Yeats's understanding of drama. Truth is conceived by Nietzsche neither as purely imaginative nor purely objective but as something that confounds the opposition between subjective imagination and objective reality, just as revelation emerges in Yeats in the 'confusion of crossing branches'. He goes even further to claim that the way to truth is not outside but through the world of sense experience, just as for Yeats the visionary moment is realised not through a transcendence but a disruption of the senses.

Music exemplifies this relation of truth to appearance most strikingly for Nietzsche. He conceives the music of satyr chorus, the marriage of autonomous figuration to pure sound, as the origin of tragic vision, a belief that is also found in Yeats's determination to express the original power of bardic redaction of heroic Gaelic sagas in symbolic form.[25] Nietzsche's mode of expression echoes O'Grady's assertion of the power of utterance in the invocation in *History of Ireland: the Heroic Period* and in Yeats's belief in the magical power of rhythmic speech:

> In the Dionysiac dithyramb man is incited to strain his symbolic faculties to the utmost; something quite unheard of is now clamouring to be heard: the desire to tear asunder the veil of Maya, to sink back into the original oneness of nature; the desire to express the very essence of nature symbolically.[26]

This notion of sinking back to original oneness suggests that Nietzsche understood the impulse of Dionysiac music as anti-individualist, in the sense that it ran counter to the subject–object split presumed in scientific rationality and in the ethical and economic individualism of the bourgeois liberal tradition. This form of anti-individualism pervades *The Birth of Tragedy From the Spirit of Music*. Nietzsche presents Dionysius as the tragic hero whose suffering emerges out of his hybrid condition as half-god, half-man – Apollo's intervention causes Dionysius to take on an individual appearance, but Nietzsche argues that since his suffering arises from his divided condition, individuation ought to be elegised as the source of all suffering.[27] This perspective is repeated in Yeats's assertion that individual character diminishes to a point of extinction with the imaginative liberation characteristic of tragic art.[28]

In Chapter 1 of this volume, I argued that O'Grady employs Carlyle's notion of myth as the keeper of authentic history in order to counter the view that Gaelic legends were purely imaginative. Benjamin's concept of tragedy closely approximates to what can be described as Carlyle's proto-existential or utopian history, itself a powerful prefigurement of Nietzsche's 'Dionysian' reality.[29] As with Carlyle's (and subsequently O'Grady's) insistence on the historicity of myth, Benjamin's interpretation of tragedy as a tendentious reworking of legend rather than a reinvention of it, indicates the extent to which the concept of redemptive history underlying his analysis implies a mutual relation of both history and myth.[30] To nuance Yeats's Kabbalistic imagery quoted above, the branches of the Tree of Life are *necessarily* entwined in those of the Tree of Knowledge in Benjamin's dramaturgy. So while history remains alien to empirical phenomenality in Yeats's dramaturgy, *The Origins of German Tragic Drama* analogically reveals that the form of Yeats's dramaturgy is such that the vision Yeats pursues is only possible when the power of truth is realised *within* history. In the light of this, the concept of tragic sacrifice informing Yeats's drama may be considered in terms of the power of the hieroglyph; it bears witness to the force of redemption momentarily visible in the fallen condition of empirical phenomenality, when the word foregrounds its self-reflexivity, and thereby reveals its divided 'tragic' nature; as a progeny of pre-Babel utopia caught in the phenomenal world of fragmented exteriority.[31]

The question of decadence (as understood by O'Grady) in Yeats's dramaturgy is raised by this Benjaminian interpretation of his understanding of tragedy. The problem arises from the potentially contradictory motives of seeking to 'create an emotion of beauty' and to unveil history as truth (in the existential rather than an empirical sense just outlined). Dilettantism was regarded by O'Grady as destructive as radical materialism. Throughout his political writing, they are portrayed as opposite sides inversely reflecting the decadence of each other; as has been observed in Chapter 4 of this volume, O'Grady believed the rise of agrarian radicalism in Ireland ran in tandem with the decay of the Irish landed gentry as a class. Although, as noted above, Yeats distanced himself from O'Grady on artistic and political grounds, a convincing argument can be made that he was closer to O'Grady's thinking on the question of decadence during the 1890s than notable decadents like Arthur Symons or Oscar Wilde.[32]

Yeats first broaches the problem of decadence discursively in his lecture 'Nationality and Literature' published in May 1893 in *United Ireland*. Here he argues that literature develops from an original simple epic form through to a dramatic and finally a complex lyric form. The writers he chooses as exemplars of the lyrical strain in English Romanticism – Blake, Byron, Shelley and Keats – suggests that he understood lyricism in a manner typical of decadent thought at this time. Yeats proceeds to affirm that such an understanding of lyricism must be cosmopolitan rather than national.[33] Claiming that Ireland was in its epic phase (having in mind the work of O'Grady, Thomas Davis and Samuel Ferguson), which he understood in terms of a preoccupation with the legends of a people and their national history, he propounds the argument that Ireland's literature could mature only by attention to a stylistic subtlety characteristic of that literature he designates as lyrical, by which he means decadent, obscure, cosmopolitan and English.[34]

Certain aspects of his argument develop into significant touchstones for Yeats's poetics and dramaturgy subsequently. Foremost among these is the demand that Irish writers learn the subtleties of lyricism as practised by canonical figures in English Romanticism. One element motivating Yeats here is that desire on his part to avoid literary propaganda.[35] Implicit in this apparently innocent wish for a more sophisticated literary practice in Ireland, however, is an affirmation of decadence that, in the light of O'Grady's work, could be read as a literary corollary of the decadence and myopia of the Irish landed gentry O'Grady described in *Toryism and the Tory Democracy*. O'Grady criticised Yeats directly in December 1900 on this point, arguing that Yeats's criticism of the anglocentrism of Ireland's wealthy classes disguised the fact that his preoccupation with subtlety of argument indicated that Yeats was addressing a cosmopolitan London audience rather than a 'provincial' Irish one. Furthermore, O'Grady treats the integrity of Yeats's concern for Gaelic legendary material with extreme scepticism:

> You are at one with me about the iniquity of the tourist movement and the exploitation for commercial purposes of the beauty of our country. Yet holding such opinions you bring us all – we who in some poor way stand for Ireland – over to London and trot us round for the delectation of your clever London friends whose favourable opinion we don't want and can very well do without.[36]

The criticism is sharp in objecting that Yeats's concern for Celtic legend was motivated by a desire to escape from historical reality in a manner typical of the dilettantism criticised by Carlyle. There certainly was a *tendency* towards decadence in this sense in much of Yeats's poetry and prose of the

1890s. In 'Nationality and Literature', Yeats subscribed to Matthew Arnold's view of the Celt as one 'who cares much for ideas which have no immediate practical bearing'.[37] Despite modifying this deference in later years, this support for Arnold's views was, from O'Grady's perspective, tantamount to accepting the perception of the Celt as anarchic and feminine, thereby usurping all claims to historical veracity on the part of Irish legend and instead presenting it as a subject for the curiosities of a cosmopolitan, decadent, London coterie typified by the Rhymers' Club. Such a critical view of Yeats's position during the 1890s could only be reinforced by essays such as Andrew Lang's 'The Celtic Renascence' which brought the historical basis of Arnold's views into question and the Celtic Movement it spawned.[38] It is ironic in this context that Yeats invoked O'Grady as Ireland's 'one historian who is anything of an artist' immediately after a passage in which he argues that everything 'that can be seen, touched, measured, explained, understood, argued over, is to the imaginative artist nothing more than a means, for he belongs to the invisible life, and delivers its ever new and ever ancient revelation'.[39] O'Grady himself came under the influence of 'decadent' Celticism to some extent during the 1890s as his relative indifference to history in his fiction of this period suggests: *Lost on Du-Corrig* (1894) and *The Chain of Gold* (1895) are O'Grady's two works least concerned with historiographic questions. Nevertheless, O'Grady's hostility to decadence, whether artistic or political, remained implacable and even when he ventured into the realm of the imaginative it was always with a view to igniting sentiments of heroism and magnanimity that might alter what had become, from his perspective, a decrepid political landscape in Ireland since the Act of Union.

Any interpretation of Yeats's attitudes as decadent at this time, however, must be qualified by the fact that at no point in his 1893 lecture did he argue for the abandonment of the epic form in favour of the lyric. Furthermore, while his attribution of simplicity to the epic form might imply a condescending attitude towards nineteenth-century Irish literature, it is worth noting that simplicity was a quality celebrated in Yeats's aesthetics, as in later years the image of his 'wise and simple man' juxtaposed against the 'clever man who cries/The catch-cries of the clown' illustrates.[40] Indeed, Yeats's earliest poetic achievement of major importance is 'The Wanderings of Oisin', a treatment of ancient Irish saga epic in its scale. Daniel Hoffman describes it as more legendary than epical, indicative of the generic ambiguity that characterises the poem.[41] Nevertheless, it remains an effort, whether successful or not, at a rendition of Gaelic saga on an epic scale.

In describing the early Yeats's attitude to writers such as Tennyson and Browning as one of Romantic anti-Victorianism, George Bornstein ignores 'The Wanderings of Oisin'.[42] Indeed, Yeats ignored it himself when in later years he criticised Tennyson for being lured from lyric intensity into failed attempts at vaster forms, rather than accept that he was 'born in a lyrical age'.[43]

Deborah Sherman argues at length for the importance of the Victorian influence on Yeats's literary activities. She cites Edward Engelberg in this regard, who argues that Yeats's imagination 'was primarily neither lyric nor dramatic but epic'.[44] Sherman notes that even if Yeats was uncertain as to the possibility of sustaining lyric intensity in an epic time-span, he was not unwilling to attempt to do so: 'Indeed, he took issue with those who would limit Tennyson, and by implication himself, simply to the lyric, arguing that "the great work" is the true "place of art"'.[45]

Significantly, this reading of Yeats echoes Russell's attitude to O'Grady, when the former associates epic literature with artistic greatness in his praise of the latter:

> There are writers who bewitch us by a magical use of words, whose lines glitter like jewels, whose effects are gained by an elaborate art and who deal with the subtlest emotions. Others again are simple as an Egyptian image and yet are more impressive and you remember them less for the sentence than for a grandiose effect. They are not so much concerned with the art of words as with the creation of great images informed with a magnificence of spirit. They are not the lesser artists but the greater, for there is a greater art in the simplification of form in the statue of Memnon than there is in the intricate detail of a bronze by Benvenuto Cellini.[46]

Here Russell praises O'Grady's epic style not just for the vastness of its vision but also for its simplicity of thought, underlining the aesthetic importance of a term that might be seen as condescending in a non-aesthetic context. Yeats applied the phrase 'simple as a fire' to Maud Gonne in 'No Second Troy' and repeated it in 'Vacillation'. He writes of Synge finding 'a race/ Passionate and simple like his heart' in 'In Memory of Major Robert Gregory' and he wants '[n]o table or chair or stool not simple enough/ For shepherd lads in Galilee' in 'A Prayer On Going Into My House'. This indicates that epic simplicity continued to absorb Yeats in his later poetry, perhaps even to the point of his interrogating lyric subtlety and obscurity as positive aesthetic values, as the phrases 'mere anarchy' in 'The Second Coming' and 'mere complexities' in 'Byzantium' tantilisingly suggest.[47]

In any case, 'The Wanderings of Oisin' clearly reveals the extent to which Yeats was influenced by Victorian literature. Sherman describes the poem as 'an Irish version of "The Lady of Shallot"'.[48] The influence of 'The Chorus-Song of The Lotus-Eaters' might equally be seen, particularly in the third book of the poem, when Oisin journeys with Niamh to the Island of Forgetfulness. 'This notion of the fatality of the dreamworld to the dreamer, commonly found in folklore, fascinated Victorian poets and painters', writes Sherman.[49] In Book III of the poem, Oisin abandons Niamh in the Island of Forgetfulness to set out in search of his old Fenian companions, an act that Elizabeth Cullingford views as evidence of the masculine nature of the epic form; 'the epic hero leaves his woman behind'.[50] We have seen already that these two elements, the fatality of the dreamworld and the primacy of masculinity, are present in the volumes of O'Grady's *History of Ireland*.[51] Additionally, O'Grady argued in *History of Ireland: Critical and Philosophical*, that the influence of women was an important factor in the break-up of the Fenian brotherhood in ancient Ireland.[52] The destructive influence of Maeve and the generally malign perspective of femininity as a political force in *History of Ireland* reinforce this specific observation. The presence in the poem of the fatality of the dreamworld, the valorisation of masculinity and the destructive influence of women on the Fenian brotherhood, suggest that the influence of *History of Ireland* on 'The Wanderings of Oisin' may be as strong as to warrant the claim that in composing it, Yeats was directly responding to O'Grady's call on Irish writers and artists to begin treating Gaelic legend in epic and dramatic forms.[53]

The question of history is vital in considering the extent of continuity or cleavage between the poem and the Victorian epic tradition in general, particularly O'Grady's *History of Ireland*. The problem of history emerges in the dialectic between memory and forgetfulness that informs the narrative throughout. Stan Smith considers the importance of forgetfulness in Yeats's poetics:

> Forgetting his authority is not a casual act for Yeats. It is a deliberate act of rebellion in which he affirms his independence of all that might restrict his narratorial freedom, reader, source and text alike, insisting instead on the self-delighting, self-creating power of the imagination to invent its own imagined world, without benefit of history. Yet at the same time, his constant nervous deferring to these authoritative presences reminds that he is not in fact 'free of the eight and six', but has to pay his taxes to the realities of a pressing and contingent history.[54]

Although it may be argued against Smith that he overstates the intentionality behind the multiple acts of forgetfulness and remembrance pervading Yeats's writing, his claims are nevertheless borne out in 'The Wanderings of Oisin' in the homology of generic and thematic tension; the manner in which it vacillates between epic grandeur and lyric subtlety, and between 'masculine' remembrance and 'feminine' forgetfulness.

If we accept Harold Bloom's claims that this 'is probably Yeats's most underrated major poem' and that 'the whole of Yeats is already in it', then its implications reach beyond the Yeats of the early 1890s.[55] The dialogic structure of the poem notably extends the paradigm established in O'Grady's *History of Ireland*; Yeats's treatment of St Patrick recalls O'Grady's disdain both for a 'realist', niggardly temperament divorced from heroism and magnanimity, and for the empiricist attitude to history that fails to recognise beyond the evident decay of antique objects (Carlyle's ruins of St Edmundsbury), their spiritual potency. It comes as no surprise, therefore, that the poem opens with a vision of decay articulated by St Patrick:

> You who are bent, and bald, and blind,
> With a heavy heart and a wandering mind,[56]

Yeats's portrayal of Oisin recalls O'Grady's general celebration of ancient heroic brotherhood, but more specifically he reflects Fergus MacRoy in *History of Ireland* in his contradictory condition of embodying heroic sentiment, grounded in patriarchy, yet also occupying a subordinate role to a powerful woman who represented the feminine destruction of the heroic brotherhood. As the threatening Other of female subjectivity, Niamh recalls the persona of Maeve presented by O'Grady in both volumes of *History of Ireland*; just as Maeve brought division to the Red Branch Knights through a combination of black magic and seduction (setting Ferdia against his lifelong companion Cuchulainn), so Niamh leads Oisin from a mythic-heroic realm of brotherhood grounded in historic conflict to the Island of Youth and then to the Island of Forgetfulness, where all sense of historical time is usurped in the anodyne predominance of pure imagination.[57] In the context of O'Grady's *History of Ireland*, then, St Patrick signifies a barren, archaeological approach to history, Oisin, a mythic-heroic form of historiography, and Niamh, a 'feminine' flight from historical fact.

Significantly, both Patrick and Niamh threaten to emasculate Oisin for opposite reasons that inversely reflect each other; the barren vision of the present that Patrick presents anticipates the Yeats of later years in fashioning Oisin as 'a paltry thing upon a stick'; equally the Island of Forgetfulness, where Oisin falls into a hundred-year slumber, induces an anaesthesia that renders him lifeless:

> Wrapt in the wave of that music, with weariness
>   more than of earth,
> The moil of my centuries filled me; and gone like a
>   sea-covered stone
> Were the memories of the whole of my sorrow and the
>   memories of the whole of my mirth,
> And a softness came from the starlight and filled me
>   full to the bone.[58]

The theme of the Lia Fáil, the stone of destiny, which O'Grady portrayed as the mystical centre of the Gaelic race, recurs here in the form of the stone as a metaphor for the constancy of memory in the flux of life, again anticipating the later Yeats of 'Easter 1916':

> Hearts with one purpose alone
> Through summer and winter seem
>   Enchanted to a stone
> To trouble the living stream[59]

In Volume 1 of *History of Ireland* O'Grady asserts that when the Milesian aristocracy first arrived in Ireland from Spain they brought the Lia Fáil

> which the Clanna Gædhil in ancient days had brought with them to Espân, and ancestral prophecies had foretold that the sovereignty of the Gæil should not cease around it, and men said that the stone was instinct with life, and that there came from it voices and lightnings and portents, and standing upon it, the kings of the Gæil were invested with sovereignty.[60]

This image of the stone, then, reveals the extent to which the reality of history that memory presupposes is associated with ideas of brotherhood and regal authority in Yeats's mind; memory is not the innocent recollection of past events for Oisin, but the assertion of a world-view grounded in patriarchal authority. This is illustrated in Book I of 'The Wanderings of Oisin' when, in the Island of Youth, Oisin finds a broken lance that awakens in him memories of 'how the Fenians stept/ Along the blood-bedabbled plains' only for Niamh to soothe his melancholia into a knowledge that 'the old was over'.[61] Once again, the later Yeats is anticipated in terms of an aspect of his later poetry that is absent in his earlier work according to certain critics – the aestheticisation of violence – thus reinforcing Bloom's claim about all of Yeats being present in the poem.[62] However, the dichotomy between active epic heroism and passive lyric lethargy that Oisin's recollection appears to confirm is qualified by the dream-like contexts in which such acts of remembrance occur. In travelling to the Island of Youth, the couple ride out 'from the human lands', and Oisin's memory of the Fianna comes back to him in a dream during his one hundred year slumber in the Island of Forgetfulness in Book III.[63] This indicates that the realm of history and that of art are dialectically intertwined in the poem; to read it as exclusively aesthetic is to treat it inadequately.

The inability to recognise the dialectical form structuring Yeats's work that this poem exemplifies has led to critical confusion in readings of Yeats. John Reed, for example, attempts to argue for the decadence of 'The Wanderings of Oisin', but is forced to admit the difficulty in thinking of it in this way without indicating why this is so.[64] More generally, Seamus Deane automatically assumes the superiority of an empirical mode of historiography over an aesthetic mode in understanding history when he asserts that 'when Yeats speaks of the greasy philistinism of the Catholic bourgeoisie and of the intellectual fragrance of the aristocratic Protestant tradition, it is still common to find him taken literally as though he had in these instances abandoned myth for sociological analysis'.[65] The different modes of treating history that the epic and lyric forms in Yeats's work involve is ignored by Deane in this instance. The epic form of 'The Wanderings of Oisin' inscribes an imaginative engagement with history beyond the normative conventions surrounding a rational acquisition of historical facts; obversely, the lyric involves an imaginative flight from history, equally anti-empirical yet qualitatively distinct from epic engagement. Furthermore, by assuming the primacy of an empirical mode of historical analysis, Deane fails to acknowledge the fact that an aesthetic treatment of history affects both the realms of history *and* aesthetics – the meaning of art is transformed just as much as the meaning of history in the process of aestheticising history. The effect of this process, in other words, is not necessarily the subordination of one realm to the other, but of a dialectical interaction between both, a dialectic characteristic of that between memory and forgetfulness in 'The Wanderings of Oisin'.

The generic ambiguity of 'The Wanderings of Oisin,' signals the precariousness of reading the early Yeats exclusively in terms of *fin-de-siècle* decadence. Far from evoking the languid indifference and amoralism of literary decadence, the overall effect of the poem is rather one of sacralised engagement, of illuminating fundamental realms of human experience through the exercise of ritual and incantation. The interweaving of epical ('masculine', historical) and lyrical ('feminine', imaginative) elements in the poem formally signifies Yeats's desire to communicate sacred time in the poem, time 'redeemed' from empty phenomenality, in Walter Benjamin's sense; Oisin's 'masculine' history is liberated from the fragmentation and decay of contemporary Ireland, represented by St Patrick, in its engagement with the imaginative realm of Niamh. Thus time ceases to be structured empirically or heroically in the poem, instead becoming sacralised by the transformation the 'feminine' realm of pure imagination brings to it.

The constitution of sacred time in this manner is important for an understanding of Yeats's engagement with esotericism in general and occultism in particular throughout his life. R.F. Foster instructively points to Yeats's background as a key to his esoteric activities: 'an insecure middle class, with a race memory of elitism and a predisposition towards seeking a refuge in the occult'.[66] However, in view of the centrality of the notion of sacred time to Yeats's esotericism, it is oversimplistic to interpret his occult leanings exclusively in terms of a refuge from pressing historical realities. The concept of sacred time, as the redemption of a history fallen into fragmentation and externality (of which the 'Dryasdust' empirical historiography that Carlyle attacks is a symptom), was not the preserve of a threatened class in late nineteenth-century Ireland, but a concept shared by writers as diverse as Johann Herder, Jakob Boehme, William Blake, William Morris and Walter Benjamin. Yeats's engagement with the concept is derived from the dialectical interplay between the epic and the lyric – he 'redeems' epic history from the externality and conventionalism of propaganda by investing it with aesthetic subtlety, just as he seeks to rescue lyric free-play from dilettantism by binding it to epic history. The result might be described as a form of literary androgyny, in which Yeats brings together epic and lyric, conceived as 'masculine' and 'feminine' forms, to replenish history with a symbolic depth characteristic of non-linear concepts of time.

The distinction that Eric Auerbach draws between the epic time he locates in Homer's *Odyssey* and the sacred time of the Old Testament, to which I referred in examining O'Grady's concept of time in *History of Ireland: The Heroic Period*, instructively suggests the degree to which the symbolism and esotericism of 'The Wanderings of Oisin' does not represent an abandonment of any sense of awareness of history on the part of Yeats in favour of literary decadence. As has been observed, Auerbach contrasts the linear, continuous time structure of the *Odyssey* with the sacred time of the Old Testament (in which all events and characters have a sacred, universal significance):

> The Old Testament...presents universal history: it begins with the beginning of time, with the creation of the world, and will end with the Last Days, the fulfilling of the Covenant, with which the world will come to an end. Everything else that happens in the world can only be conceived as an element in this sequence; into it everything that is known about the world, or at least everything that touches upon the history of the Jews, must be fitted as an ingredient of the divine plan.[67]

While the doctrinal imperatives of this biblical narrative can be seen as a constraint on its imaginative freedom, the depth-psychology of its time structure offers no self-evident meaning; the process of discovering meaning is one of decoding the symbolic significance of the words and gestures in the narrative, as Auerbach illustrates in his analysis of the story of Abraham's sacrifice.[68] Words and gestures function as forms of ritual that draw the reader into their hermeneutic density and *power*.[69] Illustrating this in his interpretation of the presence of suspense in the Abraham story (corresponding to mere digression in Homer), Auerbach comments:

> But here, in the story of Abraham's sacrifice, the overwhelming suspense is present; what Schiller makes the goal of the tragic poet – to rob us of our emotional freedom, to turn our intellectual and spiritual powers (Schiller says 'our activity') in one direction, to concentrate them there – is effected in this Biblical narrative, which certainly deserves the epithet epic.[70]

In Chapter 1 of this volume I have considered the story of Lara and Corac in *History of Ireland: The Heroic Period* as an example of Homeric style, as described by Auerbach. There are numerous other digressions in O'Grady's narrative prolonged enough to weaken the reader's suspense, an effect Auerbach associates with the *Odyssey*. In chapter XLII of *History of Ireland: The Heroic Period*, a detailed description is given of the attire Fardia puts on before an occasion that is important to the general narrative. The needless detail of this description ensures that its effect is more digressive than suspense-inducing.[71] Furthermore, O'Grady's Cuchulainn is exclusively a man of action; the number of occasions on which he speaks in both volumes of *History of Ireland* is minimal. His actions are always heroic and the level of psychological complexity he illustrates is dwarfed by Yeats's dramatic treatment of him subsequently. While the events recorded in *History of Ireland* are characteristic of the Old Testament narrative, as defined by Auerbach, in the sense that their meaning is subordinated to the articulation of a heroic, patriarchal code, the prolonged moments of narrative digression and the absence of psychological complexity indicates that the work tilts more towards the Homeric than the Old Testament form of epic. In contradistinction to O'Grady's narrative, the dialogic form of 'The Wanderings of Oisin' and shorter poems such as 'Fergus and the Druid' and 'Cuchulain's Fight with the Sea' point to the development of a depth-psychology in Yeats's treatment of ancient Gaelic legend. Furthermore, the sacralisation of time is illustrated in his concern for ritual and incantation:

> And in a wild and sudden dance
> We mocked at Time and Fate and Chance[72]

As with Auerbach's understanding of epic, Mircea Eliade's interpretation of myth suggests why a pre-occupation with sacred ritual signifies that, in contrast to view of him as dilettantist, Yeats was deeply concerned with history in 'The Wanderings of Oisin' (Auerbach argues that the sacred 'tragic' form of epic, which this poem may be described as, was more historical than the Homeric form of epic).[73] Eliade interprets myth in human culture as the language of the inbreaking of the sacred into the world: 'the myth is regarded as a sacred story, and hence a 'true history', because it always deals with realities'.[74] The practice of ritual and incantation is, according to Eliade, integral to this form of consciousness; myth is an internally experienced mode of consciousness realisable only through the symbolic re-enactment of its narrative – it is not an abstract form of knowledge.[75] Eliade defines this re-enactment as a 'religious' experience, since it lifts the subject out of the quotidien consciousness of time that Martin Heidegger describes as 'inauthentic temporality', into the realm of the sacred, what Heidegger identifies as the experience of *geworfenheit*.[76]

In tracing connections between Victorian evangelicalism and the Literary Revival, Vivian Mercier refers to the domination of evangelical revival in the Church of Ireland during the mid-nineteenth century which, by the 1860s, had solidified into the post-disestablishment Church of Ireland.[77] She argues that the interest in Theosophy and the literary activities of the Revivalists, particularly O'Grady and Hyde, who were clergymen's sons, and Yeats and Synge, who were clergymen's grandsons, were consequences of nineteenth-century evangelicalism.[78] This suggests that concepts such as reverie, or being 'out of life' which were, as Sherman notes, so much part of Victorian aesthetic discourse, were informed by the ideas of trance and visionary frenzy particular to intense religious experience characteristic of evangelical revivalism.[79]

In the light of this, it is evident that specifically religious ideas are intimated in Yeats's notion of tragic art alluring the audience to the intensity of a trance. Angela Jenkins points to Yeats's expulsion from the Theosophical movement in

1890 by Madame Blavatsky because of his experiments with symbols as evidence of an increased awareness of the power of symbol and ritual; his movement to the Order of the Golden Dawn signified in part his increasing interest in ritual as practice.[80] John Kelly considers his proposal to found a 'Castle of Heroes' according to certain Celtic rituals as the culmination of Yeats's aesthetics during the 1890s. On the basis of the manuscript evidence of the rituals Yeats proposed for this Order, Kelly argues that he was attempting to create 'liberating images' that would 're-unite the Irish nation with the Great Memory as well as give it a unified being'.[81] Ellmann hints at the specifically Protestant form of nationalism that could be detected in this project when he notes that Maud Gonne thought the Order might work for Ireland's independence in the same way that the Masonic Lodges in Ulster were, she believed, working for union.[82]

These considerations point to the presence of a religious disposition in Yeats's literary activities during the 1890s, free from the Victorian moralism that he associated, like O'Grady, with the materialism of bourgeois society. Just as O'Grady condemned what he saw as the hypocritical practices of members of the Established Church in *Toryism and the Tory Democracy*, so Yeats criticised the 'vulgarity and insincerity' of the bourgeois mentality that found its expression 'in churches which have substituted a system of morals for spiritual ardour'.[83] This recalls St Patrick in 'The Wanderings of Oisin' who tells the warrior to abandon heroism and passion in order to save his soul, to adopt, in other words, a mentality of servility and self-interest:

> But kneel and wear out the flags and pray for your
> soul that is lost
> Through the demon love of its youth and its godless
> and passionate age.[84]

Yeats's concordance with O'Grady in this instance is ironic when the relation between his criticism of the Young Ireland Movement's literature and his refutation of O'Grady's attack on his dramatic treatment of Gaelic legend is considered. The literature of the Young Ireland Movement was 'a literature full of the civic virtues and, in all but its unbounded patriotism, without inconvenient ardours'. Yeats's derogatorily saw it as 'really the poetry of the middle class...'[85] Equally bourgeois in his opinion was O'Grady's criticism of his own drama, because its moral censure disclosed an insecurity characteristic of middle-class Victorian attitudes in the face of artistic freedom, an insecurity concomitant with the assertion of civic virtue characteristic of the *bildungsroman* tradition in English fiction, and highlighted by O'Grady's refusal to include in *History of Ireland* any material from his sources that might be regarded as salacious.[86]

These criticisms indicate that Yeats recognised that the dangers inherent in an epic literature divorced from lyrical subtlety were as potent as those inherent in the lyrical obscurantism against which O'Grady warned; such literature could only be salvaged from a stultifying orthodoxy (the 'official history' Bakhtin identifies as integral to the epic form) running concomitant with the 'civic virtue' of bourgeois taste, by an injection of the imaginative free-play of lyricism. In other words, Yeats observed in O'Grady's complaint of historical indifference, levelled at his dramatic treatment of Gaelic legend, a demand for orthodoxy that belied a Victorian morality based on a civic rather than an organic view of the relationship of the individual to society.[87]

Emphasising this distinction in 'The Literary Movement in Ireland', Yeats compares favourably 'a poet or a story-writer [who] found an older dream among the common people or in his own mind, and made a personality for himself, and was forgotten', against the literature in which 'the ideal of the good citizen' was crafted, for Yeats the cultural form of middle-class society he associated with England.[88] Yeats implies that the primary distinguishing feature between both forms of literature was the principle of interiority that lyricism provided for an otherwise, externalised, orthodox historiography implicit in the Homeric (in Auerbach's sense) form of epic characteristic of O'Grady's *History of Ireland*:

> The poetry that comes out of the old wisdom must turn always to religion and to the law of the hidden world, while the poetry of the new wisdom must not forget politics and the law of the visible world; and between these poetries there cannot be any lasting peace.[89]

Yeats's claim for the ultimate inadequacy of O'Grady's epic effort implies the necessity of integrating epic and lyric forms, interiorising empirical history and externalising the pure imagination, when he writes that 'neither epic nor romance will manifest fully the power of the mythical ancestors of the modern Gael who now seek incarnation anew in the minds of their children' (quoted above). In essence, the conflicts between O'Grady and Yeats amounted to the stresses placed on one side or another of the epic-lyric dialectic forming a sacral, mythic unity in Yeats's occult *Weltanshauung*. While his praise of O'Grady as 'the one historian in Ireland who is anything of an artist' indicated his respect for him, praise which provoked a hostile response in *The New Ireland Review*, he recognised in O'Grady's quest for historical verisimilitude and moral orthodoxy an unconscious attachment to scientific realism and the rights/duties form of civic virtue characteristic of what Yeats regarded as bourgeois materialist culture.[90] In moving beyond an epic treatment of Gaelic legend during the 1890s to a mythic, Yeats was attempting to move beyond the contradiction between historical realism and imaginative free-play that beset O'Grady's *History of Ireland*, a contradiction which Yeats raised to the intensity of a 'perne in a gyre' and found its unity in the sacred.

The development in Yeats's understanding of the relationship between the imagination and history during the 1890s reaches a turning point in his contributions to a controversy that arose in the literary columns of the *Daily Express* concerning the appropriate subject-matter for a proposed national drama; the exchanges were published in book form in 1899 under the title *Literary Ideals in Ireland*. The controversy began when John Eglinton (W.K. Magee) criticised what he saw as Yeats's inattentiveness to the primacy of native life as the basis upon which a national drama should be founded: Eglinton viewed as spurious Yeats's belief that contribution to a European literary canon should form this basis, since Eglinton regarded that canon as dubiously constructed. He accused Yeats of literary decadence, of seeking in antiquity not the forms for articulating the lived experience of contemporary Ireland but rather a refuge from that experience:

> Finn and Cuculain, if they are to appear once more in literature – and I, for one, shall welcome them – must be expected to take up on their broad shoulders something of the weariness and fret of our age, if only to show how lightly it may be carried, and to affright with shadowing masses of truth, such as mortals hurl not now, the uneasy seats of error.[91]

Eglinton believed that Yeats espoused a notion of European drama not in order to realise this aspiration but in order to escape himself and his age. He regarded with ridicule the comparison Yeats drew between Wagner's music and the chorus of ancient Greece; nor could he warm to *Peer Gynt* as Yeats did, believing that Ibsen's drama was too incoherent to be called ideal. Eglinton saw in a concern for tradition characteristic of those works praised by Yeats the implication of a progression away from the Wordsworthian idea of the poet as 'seer' towards a conception of him as 'aristocratic craftsman': 'The poet looks too much away from himself and from his age, does not feel the facts of life enough, but seeks in art an escape from them.'[92]

Yeats responded forcefully to Eglinton, restating his claims for both Wagner and Ibsen and dismissing Eglinton's avowal of Wordsworthian poetry as a choice for 'the poetry of the utilitarian and the rhetorician and the sentimentalist and the popular journalist and the popular preacher' over the aesthetic school of Keats and Shelley, that was, for Yeats, 'the poetry of "the seer" the most "aristocratic" of men, who tells what he alone has tasted and touched and seen amid the exaltation of his senses'.[93] Furthermore, Yeats took issue with Eglinton's belief that it was impossible to recapture the mode of treating ancient Gaelic legend as it was treated by the ancient bards, arguing that the prevailing spirit of the age was one in which the arts would be liberated more and more from their particular historical context, 'and leave them more and more free to lose themselves in beauty, and to busy themselves, like all the great poetry of the past and like religions of all times, with "old faiths, myths, dreams", the accumulated beauty of the age'.[94]

Given Yeats's subordination of historical context to artistic autonomy here, Eglinton's accusation of literary decadence would appear to be valid. However, George Russell defended Yeats on the grounds that his position was not one in which antiquity is celebrated for its own sake. In an argument reminiscent of O'Grady's account of the emergence of divinity from heroism in ancient Irish history in *History of Ireland: Critical and Philosophical,* Russell contended that when traditions passed from sense to memory they became symbolic and as symbols they were more potent than history in the empirical sense. He believed that this symbolic understanding of Yeats's position explained his anti-*zeitgeist* theory of art in a non-decadent way. Russell argued that symbolism was consistently illuminated through qualities such as nobility in great literature, regarding individual figures in such literature in a dimmer light to the archetypes they embodied: '. . . and Deirdre is like Helen, a symbol of eternal beauty, and Cuchulain represents as much as Prometheus the heroic spirit, the redeemer in man'.[95]

While William Larminie applauded Russell's argument, he did not believe it to be wholly embraced by Yeats who 'seems to me to incline more than is quite safe to the theories of the French schools'.[96] Larminie's observation appears to be confirmed by the discrepancy that emerged between Russell and Yeats in this debate, reflected in the pro-decadent stance adopted in 'The Autumn of the Flesh' and the criticisms levelled at it by Russell in 'Nationality and Cosmopolitanism in Literature'. Russell regarded decadence as a self-delusive pursuit of spiritual beauty through sensuality, a pursuit he envisaged as 'a crimson figure undergoing a dark crucifixion'.[97] His problems with literary decadence echoed those of O'Grady – any literature wholly endorsing a flight from historical reality and unrestricted by the pursuit of an ideal could no more contribute to the maturing of a national consciousness than a purely propagandist literature could. It is unsurprising, therefore, that in outlining what he viewed as the two alternatives available to Irish literary practitioners, that of Edward Dowden, in which all nationality is obliterated from literature, and that of O'Grady, in which a national spirit is built up, Russell chooses the latter as the standard to be pursued, describing O'Grady as 'the first in our time to treat the Celtic traditions worthily'.[98]

The historical dimension that this ideal of a national spirit introduced into an otherwise cosmopolitan view of literature was indicated later in Russell's review of Eleanor Hull's *The Cuchullin Saga in Irish Literature.* Here he re-iterated the Carlylean paradigm for the relationship of myth to history that O'Grady adopted in his treatment of Cuchulainn:

> The probability is that Cuchullin was an actual chieftain to whom his own, or succeeding generations, attributed a mystical identity with Lugh, or an overshadowing by him; and, as time went on, Cuchullin became invested with the powers of the god, his dark hair becoming golden and ruddy and flamelike, his form dilating to heroic stature when it was intended to suggest the agency of the god within him. The primitive bardic minds, while much concerned with mysterious beings, dealt with them in a spirit of profound belief, and they were realists in so far that it was only their conviction of the historical actuality of their heroes which induced them to take them up at all.[99]

146

The logic of the argument repeats O'Grady's in his introduction to *History of Ireland: Cuchulainn* when arguing for the historical basis of the Tuatha De Danann legend (see Chapter 2 of this volume). This indicates why in 'Nationality and Cosmopolitanism in Literature' when Russell writes of 'a literature or art created by a number of men who have a common aim in building up an overwhelming ideal', he relates the nobility of that literature as much to its groundedness in history as to its aesthetic quality.

The importance Russell attributes to nationhood in *Literary Ideals in Ireland* as the defining feature of a genuinely spiritual literature, then, illustrates his belief in the possibility of symbolism emerging within history, something that he believed to be unrealisable in a literature that failed to look beyond itself. This partly accounts for the disputes between Yeats and Russell at the turn of the century over the latter's poetry, in which Yeats called for more precise imagery and less concern for theosophical doctrine.[100] Despite their differences on this question, however, Yeats was deeply struck by Russell's contribution to the *Daily Express* debate and in a piece written shortly after it, 'A Symbolic Artist and the Coming of Symbolic Art', he shifts away from a tendency towards decadence to a position consonant with Russell's.[101] Both writers developed in different directions after 1900, yet both remained committed throughout their careers to a mode of thought that conceptualised the relationship of history to the imagination beyond the conventions of literary realism and literary decadence.

Fundamental to Yeats's criticism of Eglinton was, as John Kelly indicates, a view of symbolism as anti-bourgeois; believing that Eglinton's argument was premised on the assumption that literature should address the middle-classes, Yeats championed symbolism as anti-realist and anti-materialist.[102] Symbolic poetry was marked by

> a casting out of descriptions of nature for the sake of nature, of the moral law for the sake of the moral law, a casting out of all anecdotes and of that brooding over scientific opinion that so often extinguished the central flame in Tennyson, and of that vehemence that would make us do or not do certain things.[103]

Yeats intimated that the rejection of the moralism, scientific realism, propaganda and, above all, externality of Victorian literature was necessary in order to create poetry of visionary force; such poetry would be realised not through conventional perception of the external world but through hermeneutic density, through a sustained evocation of new meaning. Yeats held that this was the defining feature of symbolist poetry, whether it was thought of as effeminate or heroic:

> [Symbolic Art] must have a new meaning every day, and it must have all this whether it be but a little song made out of a moment of dreamy indolence, or some great epic made out of the dreams of one poet and of

a hundred generations whose hands were never weary of the sword.[104]

Yeats displays a cognisance in this instance of the gendering of history and the imagination that dominates O'Grady's *History of Ireland*. In assuming that symbolism could emerge from either the 'feminine' realm of the lyric or the 'masculine' realm of the epic, he intimates that symbolism offered a mode of interchange between these gendered genres. Yeats's determination to pursue the path of symbolism, therefore, is situated within an intellectual tradition (of which *History of Ireland* was his most immediate source) distinguished by the attempt to integrate history and the imagination. This is the surest context for understanding Yeats's occultism rather than the view of it as the denial of history.

Yeats's contribution to the *Daily Express* controversy brings to a conclusion one phase in his intellectual struggle with the problem of history and the imagination dominating the work of O'Grady. The irreversible commitment Yeats made to symbolism at this point renders misplaced any criticism of his work after 1899 as decadent or effeminate. To this extent it reveals how Yeats's subsequent work could not hope to escape the imagination–history problem – in identifying with symbolism, history would never leave Yeats alone. This suggests that, intellectually, O'Grady acquired a paternal role for Yeats, offering him a paradigm through which Yeats might develop intellectually but one from which he could ultimately never escape. Nevertheless, the commitment Yeats made to symbolism in the *Daily Express* controversy ensured that the restrictive burden of empiricism O'Grady carried in *History of Ireland* would not be felt by Yeats and, in this sense, the controversy marks an important point of departure with his elder. As the focus of this study is on O'Grady and his influence, an examination of how the dialectic of history and the imagination structures Yeats's work from 1899 onwards is not possible here because of its magnitude. However, this consideration of Yeats's thought in the 1890s clearly reveals just how important O'Grady's work was for him in establishing a framework out of which his symbolist dramaturgy and poetics emerged.

Conclusion

I N 1900, O'GRADY PUBLISHED A FUTURISTIC FANTASY *The Queen of the World*, under the pseudonym Luke Netterville. The influence of Morris's *News From Nowhere* can be detected in the feudal and aristocratic form of the future as imagined by O'Grady in the book and it provides a precedent for Russell's futuristic works, *The Interpreters* and *The Avatars*. It is a work symptomatic of O'Grady's belief in history as prophecy, a belief shared also by Russell. It is also evidence, however, of the increasing difficulty O'Grady experienced in grounding the imaginative energy of his writing in historical reality, a result of his inability to influence the course of Irish history in the way that he first imagined.

Evidence of this failure can be seen in the newspaper he founded in 1900 and ran until January 1907, the *All-Ireland Review*. A remarkable journal that attracted contributions from T.W. Rolleston, Russell, Yeats, Gregory and others, it epitomised the energy that O'Grady brought to Ireland's cultural and political landscape and his almost reckless ambition that led eventually to a breakdown.[1] Aside from providing discussion on many crucial events of the period, including the establishment of the National University of Ireland, the dramas of the Abbey Theatre, the Landlord's Convention, the Wyndham Land Act and the Limerick pogrom of 1904, O'Grady used his newspaper for republishing much of his earlier writing, including 'The Great Enchantment', taken from *Toryism and the Tory Democracy*.

The *All-Ireland Review* is testament to the final unravelling of O'Grady's literary-historical project. The cultural and political issues dominating the paper provide evidence of forces emerging in Irish society over which O'Grady had little control. The failure of his regular attempts to reconcile the opinions of hostile antagonists illustrates the extent to which his vision of unity in Ireland had become unrealisable. His alienation from the Irish dramatic movement showed just how much the cultural revival he helped to instigate had moved beyond his authorial control. Above all, his harking back to earlier writing was proof of his belief that this cultural revival had little sense of the historical imperative that dominated his own work. However, as the publication of such a fantastical work as *The Queen of the World* suggests, O'Grady himself could no longer maintain his belief in history as the ground of the imagination, instead coming to the view that human history was itself a form of imagination. In the final issue of the *All-Ireland Review* a millenarian tone emerges as evidence of O'Grady's disillusionment:

Then I saw that the genius of Man, of Man as he is in himself, the true, the essential Man, has been through recorded time, and as far back as archeology can pierce, the suffering victim of a long and strange and evil dream; always the subject of obsession after obsession of phantasmal creations of his own dreaming soul.[2]

Here we find, at the moment when O'Grady was about to depart the arena of Ireland's cultural and political affairs, the starkest manifestation of the dialectics of necessity and contingency structuring his treatment of history and the imagination. Throughout 'The Great Enchantment' in *Toryism and the Tory Democracy* (reprinted episodically in *The All-Ireland Review*), O'Grady argued that the loss of a sense of historical reality had led Irish society into the realm of madness; he proposed that Ireland could only escape such madness by constraining the imaginative impulse of its people through attunement to the force of historical necessity (see Chapter 4 of this volume). In the above quotation, however, history itself has become a form of madness for O'Grady – the historical reality of man has been an infernal nightmare, a history without history, a reality of phantasmagoria. Thus O'Grady has arrived at a position of absolute contingency in which the destabilising force of the imagination has become all-pervasive, a condition he tried to avoid throughout his career.

This situation was highly ironical in that it resulted from historical circumstances emerging within his narratives in the form of contradiction. His *History of Ireland*, in which he tried to harmonise empirical history and the imagination, became the inspiration of Yeats who nevertheless abandoned any concern for empirical history. His *Toryism and the Tory Democracy*, in which he sought to reconcile feudal and aristocratic values with the realities of modern society, became the inspiration of Russell who nevertheless was uninterested in the Irish gentry retaining ascendancy in Ireland. The historical reality of an Ireland in the 1900s, in which the cultural activities of the Literary Revival were divorced from socio-economic reality and in which that reality was bourgeois materialist in form, ensured the inevitable marginalisation of O'Grady's vision of imaginative-historical unity. His retreat into the nightmarish view of history as contingency (without the necessity of causality) was, in this sense, the result of historical necessity rendering his work contingent to the movement it spawned.

Nevertheless, if the movement made by Yeats and Russell beyond O'Grady was historically inevitable, it was not in the direction of a materialist but an imaginative response to history. If O'Grady's insistence on the necessity of grounding the imagination in the cement of empirical fact was rendered contingent by the force of historical necessity, it was also the case that Yeats's insistence on the primacy of imaginative contingency superseded O'Grady's position by force of historical necessity. In other words, the dialectic of necessity and contingency continued to structure Yeats's work as it did O'Grady's but in an inverse manner. Russell's ideology of co-operation was located at an interim point between O'Grady and Yeats. Indebted to O'Grady in his determination to invest the practical economic circumstances of Ireland with the imaginative zeal he identified in O'Grady's work, Russell nevertheless shared with Yeats the view that O'Grady's criticism of the dramas of the Abbey Theatre were ill-founded. Like Yeats, Russell believed this criticism indicated O'Grady's nervousness at the possibility of the Red Branch cycle of legends receiving a more imaginatively liberated treatment than his own. However, Russell's advancement beyond O'Grady's conservative orientation never entirely surpassed the contradiction of history and the imagination, as the split between the pragmatism of his co-operative writing and the mysticism of his poetry testifies to.

O'Grady's contemporary relevance is evident in how his work undermines various assumptions commonplace in studies of Ireland's history, culture and politics. First, his work undermines the view that the Irish Literary Revival was predominantly an expression of Arnold's opinion that the Celtic race was feminine. The masculine force of O'Grady's Cuchulainn ran throughout the Revival as a counter to the effeminate Celticism of Oscar Wilde, Fiona MacLeod (William Sharp), and James Stephens. When Yeats found in Nietzsche the philosophical pretext for a more masculine treatment of his themes and images, O'Grady's Cuchulainn provided a motif perfectly suited to the Nietzschean voice Yeats developed after 1900. Second, the historiographic context within which O'Grady developed his cultural and political positions, challenges the assumption that the Revival involved a wholescale turning away from material historical circumstances. On the contrary, it illustrates that the Revival was deeply implicated in a general crisis of historical representation becoming evident in European culture towards the end of the nineteenth century that would develop into a full-blown literary modernism in the first decades of the twentieth century. The commonly felt sense that the Revival was somehow outside this is due in part to the tendency to view it exclusively within an Irish-British framework and in part to the fact that the mythical subject-matter predominant in the literature of the Revival often had the effect of veiling this crisis. In taking up O'Grady's narratives for their own literary purposes, later writers were engaging in subject-matter formed out of a passionate labour at integrating empirical history and the imagination; separating that labour from the subject-matter was simply impossible – it was written into its very form.

Of course, O'Grady's writing is separated from us today by a century of traumatic cultural and political changes in Ireland and, more generally, in Europe. His style is very much in a Victorian mode and the barbarities associated with militaristic heroism during the twentieth century make ethically impossible today any uncritical identification with the heroic sentiment pervading his work. Viewed in terms of the contradictions running through his writing that this book has attempted to highlight, O'Grady becomes relevant not only to any rethinking of the Literary Revival but also to the modes by which the Revival, along with many other aspects of Irish cultural and political history, are understood in contemporary Irish Studies. Those contradictions circulate around history, race, science and the relations between these; in so far as they foreground the experience of modernity as a rupture in temporal continuity, their effects continue to ruffle the foundations of contemporary scholarship, thereby implicating such scholarship in the objects of its analysis.

This is made all the more serious by the complex line of descent through which the Revival connects up to contemporary scholarship – the history of twentieth-century Europe. Neil Belton's assessment of fascism in an *Irish Times* supplement marking the millennium is pertinent here: 'The Nazi project lies at the very centre of our time, and is irreducible. It will not be made more understandable by distance or comparative analysis.'[3] Belton, in other words, locates fascism at the centre of modernity conceived as rupture, a historical development that produces a crisis of historical representation, thereby implicating the empirical-scientific strategies of contemporary historical scholarship in the legitimacy it grants to knowledge claims made on the basis of systematically organised documentary evidence. The claims of contemporary historical revisionism are implicated on this point, particularly when considering writers like O'Grady, Æ and Yeats, whose work is so closely bound up with broader developments in European cultural history. To the extent to which revisionism can be seen as part of the attempt to render historical scholarship more rigorous by emptying it of mythic and culturalist baggage, it becomes unconsciously complicit in the general systematisation of human experience most evident in global economic integration; a project that has emerged in part from a liberal humanist reaction to a fascism *rationally* understood as the outpouring of aberrant, irrational, nationalist fanaticism.

The radical scepticism of postmodernism, the negative dialectical moment of such systematisation, forms the underside of this humanist reaction to the fascist legacy in Europe. In one sense, postmodernism can be conceived as a displaced meditation on the incomprehensibity of a fascism comprehended as a violation of modes of comprehension foundational to modern European civilisation, the scientific and the cultural. Key concepts in the Enlightenment tradition – causality, clear and distinct ideas, the rationality of the real – are rendered incomprehensible by postmodernism through a foregrounding of their rhetoricity. In an ironic twist of fate, this strategy accommodates a new form of nationalism in the provision it makes for a postcolonial critique of Eurocentricism. The magical, communalist and irrational aspects of subaltern cultural formations are championed as forces incomprehensible to the liberal humanist disposition and a refutation of Enlightenment universalism. Heroic irrationalism, hysteria, communal ritual – once associated culturally with *Götterdämmerung* and *Volkgeist* – achieve postmodern legitimacy under the guise of New Age *chic* as post-Enlightenment *jouissance*.

The force of contradiction flowing through O'Grady's writing and its formal recurrence in Æ and Yeats traces a precedent for this general contemporary situation (this is not to overstate his case – his work is a particular instance of broader European patterns). On the basis of the historiographic paradigm O'Grady contributed to the Revival and the pressures that frustrated its coherent realisation, a pretext exists for a renewed assertion of dialectical consciousness in Irish literary, political and historical scholarship; not in the direction of some hopelessly outdated scientific socialism, however, but towards a form of critique that locates historical causal necessity *within* the instability generated by contradiction rather than beyond it. Such a form of critique would be – of necessity – revolutionary (and not revolting). The challenge that O'Grady's work and its influence presents for contemporary Irish Studies is how to submit to dialectical liberation, how to recognise the determining force of historical necessity simultaneous with the disruptive force of imaginative contingency. The shifts in Irish cultural and political discourse in recent times may point to such a possibility. In any case, as with O'Grady's prophetic or Walter Benjamin's messianic history, in the future it is already an historic *event*.

Notes

INTRODUCTION

1 Joep Leerssen, *Mere Irish and Fíor-Ghael: Studies in the idea of Irish Nationality, its development and literary expression prior to the Nineteenth-Century*. (Amsterdam: John Benjamin, 1986).

2 David Cairns and Shaun Richards, *Writing Ireland: Colonialism, Nationalism and Culture*. (Manchester: Manchester University Press, 1988).

3 Terence Brown, *Ireland: A Social and Cultural History, 1922–1979*. (London: Fontana, 1981). W.J. McCormack, *From Burke to Beckett: Ascendancy, Tradition and Betrayal in Literary History* (Cork: Cork University Press, 1994).

4 R.F. Foster, *Paddy and Mr Punch: Connections in Irish and English History* (London: Penguin, 1993).

5 Edna Longley, *The Living Stream: Literature and Revisionism in Ireland* (Newcastle: Bloodaxe, 1994). Terry Eagleton, *Heathcliff and the Great Hunger: Studies in Irish Culture* (London: Verso, 1995). Declan Kiberd, *Inventing Ireland* (London: Jonathan Cape, 1995). Joep Leerssen, *Remembrance and Imagination: Patterns in Historical and Literary Representation* (Cork: Cork University Press, 1996). Seamus Deane, *Strange Country: Modernity and Nationhood in Irish Writing since 1790*. (Oxford: Clarendon, 1997).

6 The phrase is taken up by Ernest Boyd in his affirmative assessment of O'Grady. See 'A Fenian-Unionist', *Appreciations and Depreciations* (London: Fisher Unwin, 1917), pp.5–22.

7 Terry Eagleton, *Heathcliff and the Great Hunger*, p.101. Seamus Deane, *Celtic Revivals* (London: Faber, 1985), p.25.

8 R.F. Foster, *The Story of Ireland* (Oxford: Clarendon, 1995), pp.14–15.

9 Jacques Derrida, 'Structure, Sign, and Play in the Discourse of the Human Sciences', Richard Macksey and Eugenio Donato, (eds) *The Language of Criticism and the Sciences of Man* (Baltimore: Johns Hopkins University Press, 1970), p.248.

10 Norman Geras, 'Althusser's Marxism: An Account and Assessment', *NLR*, 71 (1972), p.80. More recently Neil Larsen has expressed an implacable hostility to the incursions of postmodern ideas on the left while Martei Calinescu bemoans the absence of a current specifically Marxist criticism and the loss of genuine historicity within contemporary neo-Marxist theory. See Neil Larsen – 'Postmodernism and Imperialism', *Essays in Postmodern Culture* (London: Oxford University Press, 1993), pp.270–3. See also Martie Calinescu, 'Marxism, "Theory", and History', *Stanford Literature Review*, 3, 2 (1986), pp.173–82. Peter Vilar takes a softer approach, recognising the legitimacy of certain claims in Althusserian and Foucaultian theory, but insisting on the need to retain empirical

historical practice. 'Marxist History, a History in the Making: Towards a Dialogue with Althusser', *NLR*, 80 (1973) pp.74, 80, 101.

11   Tony Bennett, *Formalism and Marxism* (London: Methuen, 1979).

12   Tony Bennett describes post-Marxism as 'a heterogeneous assembly of theoretical and political positions which, although socialist in aspiration, have registered a definite break with Marxist thought while also remaining substantially indebted to and affected by the Marxist tradition', *Outside Literature* (London: Routledge, 1990), p.17.

13   Calinescu, 'Marxism, "Theory", and History'. 176–8.

14   Judith Butler, 'Poststructuralism and Postmarxism'. *Diacritics*, 23, 4 (1993). p.5.

15   Fredric Jameson, *The Political Unconscious* (London: Methuen, 1981), p.100.

16   Ibid., p.35.

17   Alex Honneth defines Althusser's concept of 'structural causality' governing this idea of relative autonomy in terms of the view of social systems as 'hierarchical matrices of relations based on an economic sub-system, within which the non-economic sub-divisions are only determined in terms of the scope of their influence, and not in terms of their internal modes of production', 'History and Interaction: On the Structuralist Interpretation of Historical Materialism', in Gregory Elliot (ed.) *Althusser: A Critical Reader* (Oxford: Blackwell, 1984) pp.87–8.

18   Karl Marx, *Capital*, Vol. 1. Ernest Mandel, Introd., Ben Fowkes, Trans. Rpt. (London: Penguin, 1990), p.286.

19   In criticising their work, Geoff Bennington makes the point that history functions as a transhistorical principle in the work of Jameson and Eagleton. Geoff Bennington, 'Demanding History', in Derek Attridge, Geoff Bennington and Robert Young (eds), *Poststructuralism and the Question of History* (Cambridge: Cambridge University Press, 1987), p.20. However, Nicos Poulantzas pre-empts Bennington in observing that history functions this way in the work of Marx himself. See Anne Reilly and Próspero Saíz, 'Volosinov, Bennett, and the Politics of Writing', *Contemporary Literature*, 22, 4 (1981), p.527.

20   'History and Interaction: On the Structuralist Interpretation of Historical Materialism', p.98. This argument echoes Foucault's claim that Marxism is epistemologically defined by the nineteenth century. See Michèle Barrett, *The Politics of Truth: From Marx to Foucault* (Cambridge: Polity, 1991), p.139.

21   Terence Brown is categorical in his view that Yeats understood symbolism in the 1890s in logocentric terms, i.e. as a magical gateway to a spiritual reality. Terence Brown, *The Life of W.B. Yeats: A Critical Biography* (Oxford: Blackwell, 1999), p.73. There is, however, a contradiction at work here that undermines the view of symbolism as simply an escape from material history – in conceiving it as magical, the empirical view of language as an instrument in communicating material reality is refuted. In contradistinction to Victorian empiricism, the symbol is opaque, though spiritually, it is transparent. Thus a dialectic of opacity–transparency resides at the heart of Yeats's symbolism, even in the 1890s.

22   Jameson, *The Political Unconscious*, p.102.

23   Bennett, *Outside Literature*, p. 214. Jameson, *The Political Unconscious*, p.102.

24   Perhaps the most sustained revisionist critique of postcolonialism on this basis is located in the introduction to Edna Longley's *The Living Stream*, pp.9–68.

25   Seamus Deane, *Strange Country*, p.183

26 Ibid., pp.190–1.

27 R.F. Foster comments that historical revisionism is simply 'a desire to eliminate as much as possible of the retrospectively "Whig" view of history which sees every event and process in the light of what followed it rather than what went before: the effort to get behind hindsight'. 'We are all Revisionists now', *The Irish Review*, No. 1 (1986), p.2. On this basis Foster states that 'to say "revisionist" should just be another way of saying "historian"' Ibid. p.5. For a comprehensive statement of the falsifiability thesis, see Karl Popper, *Conjectures and Refutations: the Growth of Scientific Knowledge*, 4th edn (London: Routledge, 1972).

28 *Outside Literature*, p.215.

29 *The Political Unconscious*, p.36.

30 *Hegemony and Socialist Strategy*, p.86.

31 Ibid, p.86.

32 Ernesto Laclau, *New Reflections on the Revolution of Our Time* (London: Verso, 1990), p.26.

33 Karl Marx, *Capital*, Vol. 1. Introd. Ernest Mandel. Trans. Ben Fowkes (London: Penguin, 1990), p.103. For a discussion of significance of this passage, see Louis Althusser, *For Marx*, Ben Brewster, Trans. (London: Penguin, 1969), pp.89–94. Arguing from a standpoint very distant from that of Marx, Sören Kierkegaard also points to the necessary connection between reason and irrationality in his attack on Hegel's dialectical method, claiming that 'the supreme paradox of all thought is the attempt to discover something that thought cannot think', an argument re-echoed in Gerard Raulet's claim that Adorno's negative dialectics '*thinks the unthinkable*'. Sören Kierkegaard, *Philosophical Fragments* (Princeton University Press, 1936), p.46. Gerard Raulet, 'Marxism and the Post-Modern Condition', *Telos*, 67 (1986), p.153.

34 *New Reflections on the Revolution of Our Time*. 270, pp.30–1. Judith Butler observes that the Hegelian notion of universal history remains as 'the negated but necessary condition for the inauguration of a posthistorical time' in the work of Laclau, 'Poststructuralism and PostMarxism', p.7.

35 'Marxism and the Post-Modern Condition', p.147.

36 Ibid., pp.147, 150–5.

37 Declan Kiberd expresses this view when he links the attitude of revisionists to the history of British involvement in Ireland to the widely accepted view of the role of the military in Northern Ireland – both views deny any colonial or imperial dimension, instead identifying a 'well-meaning, occasionally inept, but rarely malevolent' exercise, *Inventing Ireland*, p.652.

38 An Irish nationalist agenda under a liberal multicultural guise might be suspected by revisionists in the link Kiberd draws between the rights of Irish language speakers and the rights of unionists. An official accommodation of the former, he implies, might make unionists feel more secure about entering an 'agreed Ireland' because it would be evidence of a toleration of minority rights. It is difficult to resist the feeling here that the old language restoration project is being brought in through the backdoor, hidden under a multicultured quilt -*b'fheidir*, *Inventing Ireland*, p.652.

39 Colin Graham, '"... maybe that's just Blarney": Irish Culture and the Persistence of Authenticity', in Colin Graham and Richard Kirkland (eds) *Ireland and Cultural Theory* (London: Macmillan, 1999), pp.7–28.

Notes

1 Christopher Murray, *Twentieth-Century Irish Drama: Mirror Up To Nation* (Manchester: Manchester University Press, 1997), p.1.
2 Seamus Deane, *Celtic Revivals: Essays in Modern Irish Literature 1880–1980*, p.20.
3 Ibid., p.21.
4 Terry Eagleton, *Scholars and Rebels* (Oxford: Blackwell, 1999).
5 Jerry C.M. Nolan, 'O'Grady's Cultural Nationalism', *Irish Studies Review*, Vol. 7, No. 3 (1999), pp.352–3.
6 Mercier, Vivian. *Modern Irish Literature: Sources and Founders* (Oxford: Clarendon, 1994), 16.
7 Standish O'Grady, 'A Wet Day', *The Irish Homestead*, Vol. V, No. 47 (Christmas issue. 1899), p.12.
8 Peter Denman, *Samuel Ferguson: The Literary Achievement* (Gerrards Cross: Colin Smythe: 1990), p.113.
9 Aubrey De Vere, *The Foray of Queen Maeve* (London: Kegan Paul, 1882), p.116. De Vere refers to Standish O'Grady's 'brilliant bardic "History of Ireland"' and to 'the genius of Sir Samuel Ferguson' in his introduction to the poem. Ibid., p.xxiv. Malcolm Browne notes that in his youth Standish O'Grady was a regular at the Ferguson weekly at-homes. *Sir Samuel Ferguson* (Lewisbury: Bucknell University Press, 1973), p.16.
10 Standish O'Grady, 'A Wet Day', p.12.
11 W.B. Yeats, 'The Poetry of Sir Samuel Ferguson – II' (Dublin University Review, 1886). *Uncollected Prose by W.B. Yeats*, John P. Frayne (ed.), Vol. I (London: Macmillan, 1970), p.103.
12 M.A.G. O'Tuathaigh, 'Sir Samuel Ferguson – Poet and Ideologue', in Terence Brown and Barbara Hayley (eds), *Samuel Ferguson: A Centenary Tribute* (Dublin: Royal Irish Academy, 1987), p.23.
13 Peter Denman, *Samuel Ferguson: The Literary Achievement* (Gerrards Cross: Colin Smythe, 1990), p.2.
14 David Lloyd, *Nationalism and Minor Literature: James Clarence Mangan and the Emergence of Irish Cultural Nationalism* (Berkeley: University of California Press, 1987), p.84.
15 Peter Denman, *Samuel Ferguson: The Literary Achievement*, p.178.
16 Whatever about the general tenability of the distinction Joep Leerssen draws between patriotism and nationalism in Ireland's cultural and political history of the nineteenth century, it is useful in this context – if applied with qualification – in distinguishing the tenor of Ferguson's work from that of O'Grady. See *Remembrance and Imagination: Patterns in Historical and Literary Representation* (Cork: Cork University Press, 1996), 8–32.
17 Standish O'Grady, *History of Ireland: Critical and Philosophical*, Vol. I (London, 1881), p.61.
18 Edward Hagan, '*High Nonsensical Words: A Study of the Works of Standish James O'Grady* (New York: Whitson, 1986), p.1.
19 In what is probably a nodding reference to Hegel's *Lectures on the Philosophy of World History* that appeared three years before the essays on Hardiman's work, Ferguson wryly comments: 'Now to give him [Hardiman] a wrinkle in "the Philosophy of History", 'Hardiman's Irish Minstrelsy, No. IV, *Dublin University*

157

Magazine, Vol. IV, No. 23 (1834), p.518.

20   Peter Denman, *Samuel Ferguson: The Literary Achievement*, p.42.

21   Perhaps the most notable exceptions are the 'Hardiman' essays that, at one point, bring to the surface the contradiction that Hegel raised and immediately reduced in his teleological view of history. In seeking to explain the dynamic of Irish history in teleological terms, Ferguson finds himself voicing the view that early nineteenth century society was simultaneously rude and refined, thus anomalous to the teleological model of historical development (effectively, if unintentionally, anticipating Marx's concept of structurally uneven development). 'Hardiman's Irish Minstrelsy, No III', *Dublin University Magazine*. Vol. IV, No. 22 (1834), p.451.

22   Standish O'Grady, *History of Ireland: Critical and Philosophical*, pp.56–7.

23   Oscar Wilde, 'The Decay of Lying', *De Profundis and Other Writings* (London: Penguin, 1973).

24   The success of Greek legend lay, for Arnold, in the addition of a sense of measure to the perceptive, emotional temperament characteristic of the Celt. The reason for what Arnold believed to be the inferior nature of Celtic literature lay in the absence of this sense of measure in the Celtic character, 'its chafing against the despotism of fact'. O'Grady's attempt to lend a historical sense to Gaelic legend, and the analogies he draws, implicitly and explicitly, between Gaelic and Greek legend, particularly in *History of Ireland: Critical and Philosophical*, indicate that he is responding to Arnold's criticism. Matthew Arnold, *On the Study of Celtic Literature* (London, 1867), p.103.

25   Friedrich Nietzsche, 'On the Uses and Disadvantages of History for Life', in Daniel Breazeale (ed.), R.J. Hollingdale, trans. *Untimely Meditations* (Cambridge University Press, 1997), pp.95–6. O'Grady's concept persists in contemporary literary theory. Rodolphe Gasché focuses on Alexander Gottlieb Baumgarten's dissertation of 1735, *Meditationes philosophicae de nonnullis ad poema pertinentibus*, to argue that the contemporary discourses of aesthetics and history share the same point of origin: 'Historically speaking, the rise of the historical view of life in the eighteenth century is intimately linked to the appearance of aesthetics . . . Historical and aesthetical knowledge, then, are the two new modes of non-rationalist cognition that correspond to individualities constituted in analogy to reason through extensive determinateness into concrete and sensible unities.' 'Of aesthetic and historical determination', in Derek Attridge, Geoff Bennington and Robert Young (eds) *Post-structuralism and the Question of History* (Cambridge University Press, 1987), pp.139–61.

26   Thomas Carlyle, 'On History', *Critical and Miscellaneous Essays*, Vol. II, 3rd edn (London, 1888), p.154. For an account of Carlyle's attack on utilitarianism, particularly the thought of John Locke, see Emery Neff, *Carlyle and Mill* (New York: Octagon, 1974), pp.202–7.

27   Thomas Carlyle, *Past and Present* (London, 1897), p.152.

28   Thomas Carlyle, *Sartor Resartus* and *On Heroes, Hero-Worship and the Heroic in History* (London, 1863), p.194.

29   John Rosenberg notes the revolutionary nature of this approach to history when he claims that Carlyle's account of the French Revolution was itself revolutionary, 'a kind of French Revolution' in historiography', *Carlyle and the Burden of History* (Oxford: Clarendon, 1985) p.31.

30 Standish O'Grady, *History of Ireland: The Heroic Period*, Vol. 1 (1878). New York: Lemma, 1970), p.13.

31 Ibid., p.15. For a consideration of racial ideas in O'Grady's work, see Edward Hagan, 'The Aryan Myth: A Nineteenth Century Anglo-Irish Will to Power', *Ideology and Ireland in the Nineteenth Century* (Dublin: Four Courts Press), pp.198–205.

32 The motive behind this claim for the cultural parity of Gaelic with Greek legend sheds some light on the preoccupation with classical Greek models in the Irish Literary Revival, most notably in Joyce's *Ulysses* and the Hellenistic, Platonist and Pythagorean allusions of Yeats's later poetry. Frank O'Connor makes a similar claim to that of O'Grady when he argues that Irish culture is, along with Hebrew and Greek, a 'primary' culture distinctive from all others, which O'Connor sees as derivative. *The Backward Look* (London: Macmillan, 1967), pp.41–52.

33 James Anthony Froude, *The English in Ireland in the Eighteenth Century*, Vol. I (1881). Rpt. (London: Longmans, Green & Co., 1906), p.24.

34 Ibid., p.23.

35 The racial interpretation of Irish pre-history that O'Grady proposes here can be seen in terms of necessity and contingency at two levels. The northern Turanians can be viewed as representing historical necessity and the southern Sythians as representing the contingency of the imagination. Furthermore, O'Grady's attempt to unify both can be seen as a form of Hegelian rational necessity in contradistinction to the view that their irreconcilability is emblematic of the fragmentation of contingency. From this it is clear that the dialectic of necessity and contingency determines O'Grady's work from the outset, thereby making the relevance of his work to the theoretical question considered in my introduction unquestionable.

36 *History of Ireland: The Heroic Period*, p.27.

37 Michel Foucault, 'Nietzsche, Genealogy, History', in Paul Rainbow (ed.), *The Foucault Reader*. (London: Penguin, 1991), p.79.

38 The relationship between history and death is evidence of the influence of O'Grady on Yeats, considered in Chapter 6 of this volume. In considering Hamlet's ghost as a hovering 'presence' in *The Communist Manifesto*, Jacques Derrida locates spectrality at the centre of Marx's writing, suggesting that historical necessity is inextricable from the contingency of spectrality in Marx's thought. *Specters of Marx*, Trans. Peggy Kamuf (London: Routledge, 1994), pp.3–29.

39 *History of Ireland: The Heroic Period*, p.39. A trace of Samuel Ferguson's thought can be observed here, in the line of progress from tribalism to civic constitutionalism that Ferguson draws in his response to Hardiman's *Irish Minstrelsy*. See 'Hardiman's Irish Minstrelsy, No. 3', *Dublin University Magazine*, Vol. IV, No. 22 (October 1834), p.452.

40 From this perspective, O'Grady's work is marked by the rupture that Gerard Raulet identifes in Marx as the sign of modernity in his work, a sign that becomes more explicit in Walter Benjamin and reaches its zenith in Theodor Adorno's *Negative Dialectics*, 'Marxism and the Post-Modern Condition', *Telos*, 67 (1986), pp.150–5. In Hegel's dialectical method, origin is violently marked by rupture: 'God, become Nature, has spread himself out in the splendour and mute periodicity of his formations, becomes aware of the expansion, of lost punctuality,

and is enraged by it. This fury is the forming, the gathering together into the empty point'. Quoted in Robert Heiss, *Hegel, Kierkegaard, Marx* (New York: Delacorte, 1975), p.39.

41   The concept of the feminine as Other in this context refers not to an essentialist notion of femininity as irrational, but to an integral element of the discursive form of the subject–object split within which O'Grady writes but which he attempts to transcend. Toril Moi's criticism of Evelyn Keller's gender critique of the subject–object split pre-supposed in scientific practices illustrates how the view of the feminine as Other refers not to femininity as essentially irrational but as constructed as such within discourse. 'Patriarchal thought and the desire for knowledge', in Teresa Brennan (ed.) *Between Feminism and Psychoanalysis* (London: Routledge, 1989), pp.189–94.

42   *History of Ireland: The Heroic Period*, p.32.

43   Ibid., p.40.

44   Mikhail Bakhtin, *Rabelais and His World*. Trans. Helene Iswolsky (Cambridge, MA: MIT, 1968), p.11. Constrained by his Victorian moralism, O'Grady's work is less receptive to the transgressive features of medieval carnival as presented by Bakhtin than Yeats's would be subsequently. O'Grady's attempt to accommodate the imaginative free-play that this transgression involves without capitulating to what he believed to be decadent, is symptomatic of the crisis pervading his work.

45   *History of Ireland: The Heroic Period*, p.48.

46   Benjamin conceives of truth not as beyond 'intention and knowledge', or the subject–object split that is the pre-condition for rationality, but as the experience of language *as* language, revealed in the act of naming. *The Origins of German Tragic Drama*. Trans. John Osborne (London: New Left Books, 1977), p.36. Benjamin suggests that this experience of language in its immediacy can be called magic and the magic of language points to its infinity. 'On Language as Such and on the Language of Man', *One-Way Street and Other Writings*. Trans. Edmund Jephcott and Kingsley Shorter (London: Verso, 1985), p.109. In collapsing the form-content opposition by referring only to itself, O'Grady's invocation is an instance of this linguistic magic and can, therefore, be viewed as a redemptive moment.

47   'On Language as Such and on the Language of Man', p.114. In the Gaelic language column of the *All-Ireland Review* of 3 Feb. 1900, O'Grady placed sound before light in the hierarchy of original substance. *All-Ireland Review*, Vol. I, No. 5 (3 Feb. 1900), p.3. Three weeks later he wrote of his hope that the Irish dramatic movement would dispense with stage scenery, 'and trust unreservedly to the mighty and all-compelling power of Sound...' *All-Ireland Review*, Vol. I, No. 8 (24 Feb. 1900), p.5.

48   For an insightful consideration of the occult and invocatory form of Yeats's poem see Terence Brown, *The Life of W.B. Yeats: A Critical Biography*, pp.229–34.

49   Eric Auerbach, *Mimesis* (Princeton: Princeton University Press, 1968), pp.3–11.

50   Ibid., p.18.

51   *History of Ireland: The Heroic Period*, p.62.

52   Ibid., p.xii.

53   *Past and Present*, p.38.

54   Craivetheena's magical spell anticipates the spell that is cast on the Red Branch Knights during their war with the forces of Queen Maeve that forms the central

narrative of *History of Ireland*. However, in this case it is employed to restore the patriarchal order whereas in the war of the Táin Bo Cuailgne it is employed to disrupt it. O'Grady's contradictory attitudes to the practice of druidism that these contrary effects suggest, indicates the precarious nature of his attempt to combine the imaginative and the historical, the imagination containing both the possibility of redeeming history from mechanistic vacuousness of scientific rationality and of plunging the mind into a vertiginousness where any sense of historical reality is abandoned.

55 Ibid, p.14.
56 W.B. Yeats, *A Vision* (London: Macmillan, 1962), pp.71–3.
57 Julia Kristeva, 'Women's Time', in Toril Moi (ed.) *The Kristeva Reader* (Oxford: Basil Blackwell, 1986), pp.188–90.
58 Hélène Cixous argues that femininity is presented as threatening within patriarchal thought in order to satisfy masculine sexual desire. However, Cixous also celebrates woman's 'art of living her abysses, of loving them, of making them sing', subverting the subjectivity that designates her as threatening within patriarchal thought by making it the site of *jouissance*. 'The Laugh of the Medusa', in Elaine Marks and Isabelle de Courtivon (eds) and Introd. *New French Feminisms* (London: Harvester Wheatsheaf, 1981), p.255. 'La – The (Feminine)', *The Hélène Cixous Reader* (London: Routledge, 1994) p.59. If this strategy reveals the precariousness of patriarchy in its *necessary* construction of feminine subjectivity as other, it also indicates the danger of feminism prolonging the orthodoxies of the patriarchy it denounces in a celebration of contingency. As suggested below, Maeve becomes most threatening when she moves from the realm of subjectivity to the public arena of politics.
59 *History of Ireland: The Heroic Period*, p.88.
60 Samuel Weber, 'Capitalizing History: Notes on *The Political Unconscious*', p.26.
61 *History of Ireland: The Heroic Period*, p.110.
62 Thomas Carlyle, *On Heroes, Hero-Worship and the Heroic in History* (London, 1872), p.26.
63 Ibid., p.18. The relationship between power and sacred knowledge that Carlyle sees here anticipates the magical power of language suggested in O'Grady's invocation in the first volume of *History of Ireland*, referred to above.
64 Ibid., p.42.
65 *History of Ireland: The Heroic Period*, p.116.
66 Ibid., p.117.
67 Ibid., p.118.
68 *'High Nonsensical Words'*, p.78.
69 Ibid., p.24. An inversion of this dualistic attitude to the druids can be detected in 'The Wanderings of Oisin' where the druidism of a pagan Celtic world is presented in a positive fashion by Yeats in contrast to his depiction of St Patrick, who is presented as a Victorian moralist out of tune with the imaginative richness of Oisin's paganism. The moral basis of Patrick's hostility to the druidic world of Oisin echos O'Grady's sense of the potential for immorality in druidic magic. See Chapter 6 for a consideration of 'The Wanderings of Oisin'.
70 'The Newly Born Woman', *The Hélène Cixous Reader*, pp.37–8.
71 Toril Moi, 'Patriarchal thought and the desire for knowledge,' in Teresa Brennan (ed.), *Between Feminism and Psychoanalysis* (London: Routledge, 1989), p.194.

72 Cixous recognises this fear in hieratic institutions as the trace of their patriarchal form: 'Let the priests tremble, we're going to show them our sexts!', 'The Laugh of the Medusa', p.255.

73 The influence of Irish antiquarian scholarship, particularly of Ferguson, is registered in this interest in Ogham letters. See Pròinsèas Nì Chathàin, 'Sir Samuel Ferguson and the Ogham Inscriptions', *Irish University Review*, Vol. 16, No. 2 (1986), pp.159–69.

74 Derrida rcognises that a purely phonetic writing is impossible, but the opposite is equally valid. The constitution of language as opaque, a governing ethos of poststructuralism, necessarily posits linguistic transparency as its Other. Therefore linguistic transparency and opacity are dialectical, a claim that Derrida intimates, notwithstanding his general disavowal of dialectics, when he writes that 'the distinction between phonetic and non-phonetic writing, although completely indispensible and legitimate, remains very derivative with regard to what may be called a synergy and a fundamental synesthesia', Jacques Derrida, *Of Grammatology*. Trans. Gayatri Spivak (London: Johns Hopkins University Press, 1976), p.89.

75 'Druidism', *Dublin University Magazine*, 86 (1875), pp.524, 530–1. *Of Grammatology*, p.90. Derrida describes phonocentric writing as pneumatological and hieratic which suggests that the primacy of the invocation in *History of Ireland* is phonocentric. This phonocentricism, combined with the linguistic opacity of the Ogham letters, reveals druidism as the crisis point of patriarchy, the ground of masculine presence and feminine absence.

76 Kristeva claims that in hysterical discourse, an unnamed real remains beyond narrative, 'setting the field of speech ablaze only to reduce it to cold ashes, fixing in this way an hallucinatory and untouchable *jouissance*'. 'The True-Real', *The Kristeva Reader*, p.27.

77 *History of Ireland: The Heroic Period*, p.37.

78 Ibid., p.152.

79 Ibid., p.152.

80 Ibid., p.139.

81 Ibid., p.231.

82 Ibid., p.235.

83 Ibid., p.238.

84 Ibid., p.267.

CHAPTER TWO

1 This attitude to *History of Ireland* persists today. Patricia Boyne describes O'Grady's *History of Ireland* as 'a novel in the guise of history'. 'Thank You, Eoin O'Curry: From Mangan, O'Grady and Others', *Studies,* Vol. LXXII (1983), p.76.

2 Standish O'Grady, *History of Ireland: Cuculain and His Contemporaries*, Vol. II (1880), (New York: Lemma, 1970), p.32.

3 Ibid., p.32.

4 In *Autobiographies*, Yeats also employs the biblical analogy for the origin of his autobiography as a work of art and for his own artistic origin. *Autobiographies* (London: Macmillan, 1980), p.5.

5 Quoted in Hagan, *'High Nonsensical Words'*, p.93. The determination to refute Froude undoubtedly motivated O'Grady's attempt to produce an Irish epic. Froude's comments on epic work in Irish literature reveal the influence of Matthew Arnold: 'Their [the Irish] lyrical melodies are exquisite, their epic poetry is ridiculous bombast.' *The English in Ireland in the Eighteenth Century*, Vol. I, p.23.

6 *History of Ireland: Cuculain and His Contemporaries*, p.6.

7 Ibid., p.68.

8 Ibid., p.51. Like the deathly quality O'Grady attributes to Irish history prior to Emain Macha in the first volume of *History of Ireland*, the skeleton image is another reminder of the residual spectrality haunting his historiography.

9 Ibid., p.56.

10 Ibid., p.56.

11 This point of separation structurally corresponds to the synchronic origin that Rodolpe Gasché attributes to the discourses of aesthetics and empirical history in 'Of Aesthetic and Historical Determination'. See Chapter 1 note 5.

12 *History of Ireland: Cuculain and His Contemporaries*, p.65.

13 *'High Nonsensical Words'*, p.93.

14 Ibid., p.95.

15 *Past and Present.* 74.

16 Ibid., p.48.

17 *History of Ireland: Critical and Philosophical*, p.46.

18 W.J. McCormack, *From Burke to Beckett: Ascendancy, Tradition and Betrayal in Literary History*, p.235.

19 *History of Ireland: Cuculain and His Contemporaries*, p. 119.

20 Ibid., p.140.

21 Elizabeth Cullingford claims that W.B. Yeats 'readily accepted the Amazonic and queenly woman of suffrage propaganda as types of Maeve, Aoife, Scathach, and Emer'; *Gender and History in Yeats's Love Poetry* (Cambridge: Cambridge University Press, 1993), p.77. Although this seems an inversion of O'Grady's attitude, it is nevertheless important to acknowledge the precedent he establishes for Yeats's 'Amazonic' picture of Maeve.

22 *History of Ireland: Cuculain and His Contemporaries*, p.141.

23 Ibid., pp.174–77.

24 Ibid., p.178.

25 Ibid., p.76.

26 Ibid., p.77. This points once more to the sense of death and spectrality residual in O'Grady's historiography.

27 Julie Sparks, 'At the Intersection of Victorian Science and Fiction: Andrew Lang's "Romance of the First Radical"', *English Literature in Transition 1880–1920*, Vol. 42, No. 2 (1999), p.127. For a discussion of the controversy between Müller, Lang, Alfred Nutt and other scholars of folklore, and on the influence of this controversy on Yeats's investigations into Gaelic folklore, see Angela Jenkins, 'W.B. Yeats and Irish Mythology', MA Thesis, University of Kent at Canterbury (1980), pp.17–21.

28 Ibid., p.128.

29 Ibid., p.174.

30 *'High Nonsensical Words'*, p.100.

31 *Past and Present*, p.6.

32 Throughout his philosophical *œuvre*, Theodor Adorno warns that the affirmation,

without reference to their opposites, of contingency and particularism merely repeats, under the sign of absolute non-identity, the authoritarianism associated with rational self-identity. He attacks the glorification of contingency in the music of Strauss, for example, as a mask for 'the anarchy of commodity production and the brutality of those who run it', in Gretel Adorno and Rolf Tiedemann, *Aesthetic Theory*, Trans. C. Lenhardt (London: Routledge & Kegan Paul, 1984), p.306. His dialectical method reveals how absolute contingency is another form of the authoritarian rationality it destroys. Terry Eagleton identifies the problem Adorno confronts through the method of negative dialectics as 'how to prise loose the grip of an insane rationality without allowing the slightest opening to some barbarous irrationalism', 'Art After Auschwitz', *The Significance of Theory* (Oxford: Blackwell, 1990), p.45.

33 Julia Kristeva observes that because certain trends of contemporary feminism identify themselves with cyclical temporality, this does not make it incompatible with 'masculine' values. This suggests what the case of the restoration of patriarchy in *History of Ireland* illustrates; the cyclical model is both oppressive and liberating in relation to femininity. 'Women's Time', *The Kristeva Reader*, p.193.

34 *Hegemony and Socialist Strategy*, p.111.

35 Highlighting what he regards as the 'booby-trapped' nature of the concept of difference in postmodernism, Fredric Jameson asks whether 'the difference between the Same and the Other [is] the same as the difference between the Other and the Same, or is it different?' Fredric Jameson, *Postmodernism, or, The Cultural Logic of Late Capitalism* (London: Verso, 1991), p.341. In a similar vein, it may be asked of Laclau and Mouffe whether it is necessarily the case that necessity is a mere check on contingency or whether that view is merely contingent.

36 Theodor Adorno, *Minima Moralia*. Trans. E.F.N. Jephcott (London: New Left Books, 1974), p.245.

37 Ibid., pp.245-6.

38 Ibid., p.247.

39 Theodor Adorno, *Negative Dialectics*, *The Adorno Reader*, Brian O'Connor (ed.) (London: Blackwell, 2000), p.57.

40 *'High Nonsensical Words'*, p.95.

41 *History of Ireland: Cuculain and His Contemporaries*, pp.190–1.

42 Ibid., p.218.

43 *History of Ireland: The Heroic Period*, p.152.

44 *History of Ireland: Cuculain and His Contemporaries*, p.267.

45 Ibid., p.267.

46 Ibid., p.278.

47 Ibid., p.279.

48 Steven Lukes notes the 'immense and confusing variety of usage' to which the term 'individualism' has been put since the Enlightenment. *Individualism* (Oxford: Basil Blackwell, 1973), p. 42.

49 Atomistic individualism in this instance refers to the concept of human beings reduced to autonomous monads in a mechanistic form of social order. The distinction Lukes attributes to Balzac between *individualism* as social atomisation and *individualité* as self-realisation is useful in this instance. *Individualism*, p.8.

50 Wên-Kuei Liao, *The Individual and the Community* (London: Kegan Paul, 1933), p.121.

51 Williams, Raymond. *The Long Revolution* (London: Chatto & Windus, 1961), p.77. Owen Chadwick. *The Secularization of the European Mind in the 19th Century* (Cambridge: Cambridge University Press, 1975), p.25.
52 *The Long Revolution*, pp.93–6.
53 Georg Lukács, *The Theory of the Novel* (London: Merlin, 1978), p.66.
54 *History of Ireland: Cuculain and His Contemporaries*, pp.291–2.
55 The context of contemporary urban masses necessary to the depiction of Cuchulainn as the exceptional hero in this scene from *History of Ireland* indicates the proximity of O'Grady's hero to Nietzsche's Overman, but only when this is thought of in dialectical relation to Nietzsche's concept of the Herd. The Overman emerges out of the Herd as its Other, just as Cuchulainn appears as Other to the Dublin 'crowd' from which he is alienated.
56 *Individualism*, pp. 3–22.
57 *The Long Revolution*, p.76.
58 Lukes, *Individualism*, pp.19–22. These two forms of Romanticism are indicated in the opposing principles that Adorno claims have governed art since Baudelaire: in France, of *l'art pour l'art* and in Germany of art as 'a moral institution'. *Aesthetic Theory*, p.336.
59 This form of individualism stresses 'the supreme value of subjectivity, solitude and introspection', Lukes, *Individualism*, p.19. However, O'Grady implies that this form is not tautologous with aristocracy since the latter only appears in this form in the context of the decline of feudalism. This view calls into question Ervin Laszlo's claim that aristocracy is by definintion individualist. *Individualism, Collectivism and Political Power* (The Hague: Nijhoff, 1963), p.49.
60 Standish O'Grady, *Selected Essays and Passages*, A.P. Graves, William Magennis and Douglas Hyde (eds) (Dublin: Talbot, 1918), p.251.
61 Notwithstanding the enormous gulf separating O'Grady's feudalism and Marx's materialism, the proximity of this understanding of alienation to Marx's suggests both the radical potential of O'Grady's thought and the historical specificity of Marx's concept of alienation. Significantly, Bertell Ollman identifies the separation of man from his fellow man as a central aspect of Marx's theory of alienation, *Alienation: Marx's Conception of Man in Capitalist Society* (Cambridge: Cambridge University Press, 1976), p.134.
62 Lawrence Stone, *The Family, Sex and Marriage in England, 1500–1800* (London: Weidenfeld & Nicolson, 1977), pp.221–39.
63 Ibid., p.125.
64 *History of Ireland: The Heroic Period*, pp.84–6.
65 *History of Ireland: Cuculain and His Contemporaries*, p.126.
66 *Selected Essays and Passages*, p.251.
67 Ibid., pp.252–3.
68 Ibid., p.252.
69 Ibid., pp.250–1. The relationship O'Grady draws here between fact and genealogical patriarchy reinforces the observation that by history he means patriarchy and by enchantment he means its erosion throughout *History of Ireland*.
70 Although opposed to Froude on his general attitude to Ireland, O'Grady is very close to Froude's view that rebellion was against the natural order because 'the superior part has a natural right to govern; the inferior part has a natural right to be governed', *The English in Ireland in the Eighteenth Century*, Vol. I, p.3. Donal

McCartney claims that this work came to be re-read in the late 1880s as a blue-print for the Balfourian policy of killing Home Rule with kindness. 'James Anthony Froude and Ireland: A Historiographical Controversy of the Nineteenth Century', *Irish University Review*, Vol. 1, No. 2 (1971), p.256.

71   Thomas Carlyle, *On Heroes, Hero-Worship and the Heroic in History* (London, 1872), pp.50–1.

72   *The Family, Sex and Marriage in England 1500–1800*, p.134.

73   Ibid., p.135.

74   Ibid., p.239.

75   *'High Nonsensical Words'*, p.93.

76   *History of Ireland: The Heroic Period*, p.244.

77   Ibid., pp.249–50.

CHAPTER THREE

1   *History of Ireland: Critical and Philosophical*, p.57.

2   Ibid., p.10.

3   Ibid., p.14.

4   Ibid., p.15. This view is expressed again the following year by Aubrey de Vere, who found the same 'mark of truthfulness' in the characters of the Tàin saga as in the characters of Homer. See Introduction to *The Foray of Queen Maeve*, p.x.

5   Ibid., p.21.

6   Ibid., p.31.

7   Ibid., p.87.

8   Ibid., p.87.

9   Gillian Beer notes how Darwin, in the use he made of the tree image in the Notebooks and in *The Origin of the Species*, called into question the opposition between the Trees of Life and Knowledge in religious tradition: 'In his argument and its expression he found a means of condensing this image so that the two opposed trees could prove to be one', *Darwin's Plots: Evolutionary Narrative in Darwin, George Eliot and Nineteenth-Century Fiction* (London: Routledge, 1983), p.37. Beer reinforces her claims for a link between the scientific and the mythical in Darwin in observing the paradox that Darwin's thought is both fragmentary in terms of categorisation and unifying in terms of tracing common ancestry. Ibid., p.94.

10   This emphasises the importance of Jacques Barzun's observation that the notion of race for the man who influenced Nietzsche most, Richard Wagner, was not only cultural but also scientific. *Darwin, Marx, Wagner*, 2nd edn (New York: Doubleday Anchor, 1958), p.5.

11   *History of Ireland: Critical and Philosophical*, pp.153–4.

12   Ibid., p.166.

13   Ibid., p.247.

14   Ibid., p.252.

15   Ibid., p.391.

16   Ibid., p.41.

17   *History of Ireland: Critical and Philosophical*, p.45

18   Colin Graham, *Ideologies of Epic: Nation Empire and Victorian Epic Poetry*

(Manchester: Manchester University Press, 1998), p.9.

19 Mikhail Bakhtin, *The Dialogic Imagination*, Michael Holquist (ed.) Trans. Carlyl Emerson and Michael Holquist (Austin: Texas University Press, 1981), p.15.

20 Ibid., p.15.

21 Ibid., p.19.

22 This is aptly illustrated in O'Grady's attitude to the Atticottic revolt which, he argues, is not historical, and in his general belief in revolt as 'satanic', *History of Ireland: Critical and Philosophical*, p. 323. An intrinsic relationship between morality and history emerges in O'Grady's attitude to disruptions of patriarchal tradition throughout the volumes of *History of Ireland*.

23 *Ideologies of Epic*, pp.13–14. This assessment is arrived at with reference to Benedict Anderson's *Imagined Communities*, Ernest Gellner's *Nations and Nationalism* and, from the nineteenth century, Ernest Renan's 'What is a Nation?'

24 *Ideologies of Epic*, p.74.

25 *History of Ireland: Critical and Philosophical*, p.55.

26 Charles Darwin, *The Descent of Man* (1871). *The Darwin Reader*, Marston Bates and Philip Humphrey (London: Macmillan, 1957), p.365.

27 It is significant that morality was the one aspect of human society that challenged Darwin's belief that the individual rather than the group was the key element in the evolutionary mechanism. As Michael Ruse points out, however, Darwin did not abandon the principle of individual selection as a result, though he did tend towards group selection theory on this question. *The Darwinian Paradigm* (London: Routledge, 1989), pp.47–52.

28 Taking Derrida's notion of the supplement and, following Balibar, applying it to nationalism, Morash argues that while racialism compensates the lack of universality in nationalism by extending its identity beyond national boundaries (as in the Aryan myth), it also threatened the stability of the nation by the specificity of its racial identification. 'Celticism: Between Race and Nation', *Ideology and Ireland in the Nineteenth Century*, pp.206–13.

29 Edward Hagan, 'The Aryan Myth: A Nineteenth-Century Anglo-Irish Will to Power', p.199.

30 Ibid., p.200. Although O'Grady used the myth in this way, Hagan argues that O'Grady's use of the myth was inherently anti-Catholic, thus inscribing the sectarian division it was ostensibly employed to overcome. Ibid., pp.198–9.

31 Louis Althusser, *For Marx*, p.34.

32 Karl Marx, *The German Ideology. Karl Marx: Selected Writings*, David McLellan (ed.) (Oxford University Press, 1977), p.164.

33 'If eternal means, not transcendent to all (temporal) history, but omnipresent, trans-historical and therefore immutable in form throughout the extent of history, I shall adopt Freud's expression word for word, and write *ideology is eternal*, exactly like the unconscious', Louis Althusser, 'Ideology and Ideological State Apparatuses', *Lenin and Philosophy and Other Essays*. Trans. Ben Brewster (London: New Left Books, 1977), p.152.

34 *The German Ideology*, p.165. This conceptualisation of history as beyond the division between empiricism and idealism bears a strong resemblance to O'Grady's attempt to integrate fact and imagination in his own treatment of history. This is indicative not just of Marx's historical specificity but also of the problematical nature of O'Grady's political ideology.

35 Ibid., p.165.

36 Norman Geras, 'Althusser's Marxism: An Account and Assessment', p.68.

37 Louis Althusser, *For Marx*, p.36.

38 Althusser interprets history as the process by which the subject is ideologically 'interpellated' so as to necessarily misrecognise historical reality – history is the process of the occlusion of history. 'Ideology and Ideological State Apparatuses', pp.169–70.

39 'Ideology and Ideological State Apparatuses', p.154.

40 Yeats describes O'Grady as the only Irish historian 'who is anything of an artist', 'Irish National Literature, II' in John P. Frayne (ed.) *Uncollected Prose*, Vol. I (New York: Columbia University Press, 1970), p.367. The narrative aspects of O'Grady's treatment of the Elizabethan period recall Ferguson's 'Hibernian Nights' Entertainments', *Dublin University Magazine*, Vol, V, No. I–IV (Jan–April) (1835).

41 Standish O'Grady, *The Coming of Cuculain: A Romance of the Heroic Age of Ireland* (London, 1894), pp.v–vi.

42 Standish O'Grady, *In the Gates of the North* (Dublin: Talbot, 1901), p.ix.

43 W.J. McCormack identifies this indeterminacy as the source of O'Grady's importance to the extent that he 'symbolized in an uncanny way the incompleteness of social character which is highly relevant to the consequences of the ideology of Protestant Ascendancy', *From Burke to Beckett*, p.235.

44 Roland Barthes, *Mythologies* (1957). Trans. Annett Lavers (London: Vintage, 1993), p.109.

45 Seamus Deane, *Celtic Revivals: Essays in Modern Irish Literature*, p.32.

46 This position is signifcantly at variance with Deane's more recent work, *Strange Country*, where he rejects the assumption in a seminal essay of Irish historical revisionism, T.W. Moody's 'Irish History and Irish Mythology' in which an epistemological priority is granted to the 'scientific' history of the professional historian in opposition to the 'myth' of popular views of history. *Strange Country: Modernity and Nationhood in Irish Writing since 1790*, pp.185–9.

47 *Lost on Du-Corrig*, p.22.

48 This connection between phantasmagoria and hunger is one instance of the general relationship O'Grady draws between illusion and the material impoverishment he identifies with the rise of capitalism, echoing once more the thought of Thomas Carlyle.

49 *Mythologies*, p.115.

50 Ibid., p.117.

51 Among the concepts Weber roots in predestinarianism are individualism (the absence of mediating support for man's salvation), the absence of magic and the rationalisation of the world, *The Protestant Ethic and the Spirit of Capitalism* (London: Allen & Unwin, 1930), pp.98–128. Gianfranco Poggi illuminates this as an embryonic capitalist thought process when he writes that 'the spirit of capitalism enjoins the entrepreneur to consider his economic activity as a calling', *Calvinism and the Capitalist Spirit: Max Weber's Protestant Ethic* (London: Macmillan, 1983), pp.40–1.

52 Standish O'Grady, *Lost on Du-Corrig or 'Twixt Earth and Ocean*, p.276

53 *Mythologies*, p.119.

54 The specifically moral attitude underpinning the historical imperative informing O'Grady's work is suggested if this free-play of the imagination is thought of as a

deference to magic. Weber argues that Puritanism was most advanced among religions in eliminating magic from the world. *The Protestant Ethic and the Spirit of Capitalism*, p.117. W.J. McCormack makes an interesting comparison between a work of O'Grady's contemporary, W.E.H. Lecky, *The History of the Rise and Influence of Rationalism in Europe* (1865) and Weber's work; Lecky's argument for religious decline is considered against Weber's argument for the persistence of its paradigm in modernisation, *From Burke to Beckett*, pp.215–19.

55   *The Chain of Gold*, p.4.

56   R.F. Foster considers gothic influences on Yeats in terms of the socio-political conditions specific to the Anglo-Irish ascendancy, *Paddy and Mr Punch: Connections in Irish and English History*, p.220. Seamus Deane recognises O'Grady's work as part of 'the long discourse of Protestant Gothic' but claims that his 'Gothic settings are less obliquely political than those of his contemporaries', *Strange Country*, p.85.

57   *The Chain of Gold*, p.216.

58   Stjepan Mestrovic's analysis of Thorstein Veblen's *The Theory of the Leisure Class*. (1899) , provides a telling insight into the degree to which the last *fin de siècle* was informed not only by practices Veblen identifed as barbaric but also by a blurring of the barbarism–civilisation binary. See *The Barbarian Temperament: Towards a Postmodern Critical Theory* (London: Routledge, 1993). Such a blurring is also evidence of the continuing and pervasive influence of Darwinism for writers like O'Grady.

59   *The Chain of Gold*, p.171.

60   'Capitalizing History: Notes on *The Political Unconscious*', p.23.

61   Oscar Wilde equates Nature with formlessness and genders it as feminine in 'The Decay of Lying'. His sentiments express a masculine need to 'cultivate' that Edward's gardening symbolises. See 'The Decay of Lying', *De Profundis and Other Writings*, p.57.

62   See Ciaran Brady (ed.), *Interpreting Irish History: The Debate on Historical Revisionism* (Dublin: Irish Academic P, 1994). This provides a thorough presentation of the genesis of Irish historical revisionism and the controversies emanating from it.

63   *The Bog of Stars and Other Stories and Sketches of Elizabethan Ireland*, Dublin, 1893 (New York: Books for Libraries, 1973), p.69.

64   Nioclás Ó'Cearnaigh's poem, 'Cumha na máthara fá anbhás a linbh', first published in the journal of the Young Ireland Movement, *The Nation*, is one of the most striking depictions of this image. See *Fios Feasa 3* (Dublin: Comhlucht Oidheacais na hÉireann, 1974), pp.256–58.

65   Standish O'Grady, *Pacata Hibernia or A History of The Wars in Ireland during the reign of Queen Elizabeth*, Vol. I, (London, 1896), p.xxx. It is one of the ironies of O'Grady's influence on the Irish Literary Revival that the father of Irish Ireland philosophy, D.P. Moran, implicitly concedes the truth of O'Grady's argument in claiming that Irish nationalism was Anglicised since the seventeenth century. Moran, however, locates the fall of Limerick in 1691 rather than the earlier period of the Plantations as the beginning of the disappearance of 'the Gael', 'The Pale and the Gael', *The New Ireland Review*, Vol. XI (Dublin, 1899), pp.230–33.

66   *Pacata Hibernia*, p.xxxii–xxxiii.

67   Standish O'Grady, *The Bog of Stars*, p.131. Sean O'Faolain makes a similar case

many years later when highlighting the kinship between Irish and Anglo-Irish noblemen up to the end of the seventeenth century, *King of the Beggars* (London: Nelson, 1938), pp.15–16. This is evidence of the influence of the genealogical method of *History of Ireland: Critical and Philosophical* on the Literary Revival.

68   Standish O'Grady, *Red Hugh's Captivity: A Picture of Ireland, Social and Political during the Reign of Queen Elizabeth* (London, 1899), p.3.

69   *The Bog of Stars*, p.104.

CHAPTER FOUR

1   'High Nonsensical Words', p.156.

2   Standish O'Grady, *Toryism and Tory Democracy* (London, 1886), p.191.

3   Perhaps the most strenuous advocate of the social importance of religion during the Victorian age was Matthew Arnold who argued vehemently against the individualising tendencies of Nonconformism in England that produced what he regarded as a provincialism of 'a bitter type and a smug type'. This arises, according to Arnold, because it is not 'in contact with the main current of national life, like the member of an Establishment. In a matter of such deep and vital concern as religion, this separation from the main current of the national life has peculiar importance', *Culture and Anarchy*, J.D. Wilson (ed.) (Cambridge, Cambridge University Press, 1946), p.14.

4   *Toryism and Tory Democracy*, p.105.

5   The millenarian attitude that O'Grady adopts to the emergence of a dominant pecuniary ethos in industrial England reveals once more the influence of Carlyle, particularly in his essay 'Chartism': 'O reader, to what shifts is poor Society reduced, struggling to give still some account of herself, in epochs when Cash Payment has become the sole nexus of man to man! On the whole, we will advise Society not to talk at all about what she exists for; but rather with her whole industry to exist, to try how she can keep existing!' *Critical and Miscellaneous Essays*, Vol. III (London, 1869), p.293.

6   *Toryism and Tory Democracy*, p.144.

7   'Henry George (1839–1897), the American political economist who had previously been a gold prospector, sailor, cowboy and campaigner for the Democratic Party, was a leading figure in the Liberal land question. He owed this to his book *Progress and Poverty* which was published in America in 1879 and in England two years later. It was followed by speaking tours in Britain and strife-torn Ireland and by the establishment of the Land Reform Union in London in 1883. George played an important part in the growth of collectivism because he provided a theoretical underpinning for Radical anti-landlordism', Matthew Fforde, *Conservatism and Collectivism 1886–1914* (Edinburgh, Edinburgh University Press, 1990), p.46.

8   *Toryism and Tory Democracy*, p.117.

9   Ibid., p.117.

10   The Conservative's Allotments Bill was proposed in 1886 by Henry Broadhurst, parliamentary champion of the Leaseholds Enfranchisement Association, an organisation established to promote the policy of giving occupiers the compulsory right to purchase their freeholds. The bill, which proposed that power be given to

local authorities to buy land, by voluntary or compulsory means, and let it out to suitable tenants, initially failed to win the support of Lord Salisbury who was generally suspicious of the Tory Democracy movement. However, the bill became law through the Allotments Acts of 1887 and 1890, *Conservatism and Collectivism 1886–1914*, pp.46, 69, 76.

11   *Toryism and Tory Democracy*, p.140.
12   Ibid., p.142.
13   Ibid., p.143.
14   Ibid., p.159.
15   Ibid., pp.172–3.
16   Ibid., p.132.
17   Ibid., p.163.
18   Ibid., p. 189.
19   Ibid., p.194.
20   Matthew Arnold, 'Democracy.' *The Works of Matthew Arnold*, Vol. X (London: Macmillan, 1904), p.26.
21   John Ruskin, *The Political Economy of Art* (London: Macmillan, 1912), pp.25–6.
22   P.J. Keating, 'Arnold's Social and Political Thought', in Kenneth Allcott (ed.), *Matthew Arnold* (London: Bell, 1975), p.223.
23   The all-pervasive influence of statist ideology in the latter half of the nineteenth century is illustrated in the fact that possibly Marx's most important statements on the organisation of future society are made in his critique of the Gotha Programme. This programme was the product of an agreement between two wings of German socialism, Liebknechtians (disciples of Marx) and Lassalleans made in May 1875. Marx's criticism of this programme indicates the extent to which it was pervaded by statism: 'The German workers' party – at least if it adopts the programme – shows that its socialist ideas are not even skin-deep; in that, instead of treating existing society (and this holds good for any future society), it treats the state rather as an independent entity that possesses its own intellectual, ethical and libertarian bases', David McLellan, (ed.), *Karl Marx: Selected Writings*, p.564.
24   Chantal Mouffe, 'Hegemony and Ideology in Gramsci', in Chantal Mouffe (ed.), *Gramsci and Marxist Theory* (London, Routledge, 1979), pp.168–204.
25   This indicates that the opposite of economic reductionism, the infinite indeterminacy of the field of discourse, is equally inadequate in understanding O'Grady's politics. See Introduction to this volume for discussion of this in relation to Fredric Jameson and Ernesto Laclau/Mouffe.
26   Jean Baudrillard's 'simulative' critique of just about everything hardly privileges nationalism, considering its Enlightenment attachment. 'Symbolic Exchange and Death', *Selected Writings* Mark Poster (ed.), (Cambridge: Polity, 1988). For a postmodernist acknowledgement of the contemporary relevance of nationalism see Barry Smart, *Postmodernity* (London: Routledge, 1993), pp.142–5.
27   Etienne Balibar, 'The Nation Form: History and Ideology', in *Race, Nation, Class* (London: Verso, 1991), p.89.
28   Ibid., p.88
29   Ibid., pp.88–9
30   Ibid., p.89
31   Ibid., p.90

32   Ibid., p.93

33   A.D. Smith, *The Ethnic Revival* (Cambridge: Cambridge University Press, 1981), p.8.

34   Ibid., p.18

35   Nikos Poulantzas, *Poltical Power and Social Classes* (London: New Left Books, 1973). Mouffe, *Gramsci and Marxist Theory*, pp.172–6.

36   Ernesto Laclau and Chantal Mouffe, *Hegemony and Socialist Strategy: Towards A Radical Democratic Politics* (London: Verso, 1985), pp.56–7.

37   Ibid., p.111. Michele Barrett views this move as evidence of the poststructuralist nature of their general argument, *The Politics of Truth*, p.68.

38   Quintin Hoare and Geoffrey Nowell Smith (eds), *Selections from the Prison Notebooks of Antonio Gramsci* (London: Lawrence & Wishhart, 1971), p.79.

39   Ibid., p.80.

40   *Selections from the Prison Notebooks of Antonio Gramsci*, p.53

41   Vincenzo Gioberti (1801–52) was a leading moderate during the *Risorgimento*. Alessandro Manzoni (1785–1873) was an Italian novelist and poet, brought up on the ideas of the French and Italian Enlightenment but converted to Catholicism around 1810. They were leading members of a liberal Catholic movement in Italy in the first half of the nineteenth century known as Neo-Guelphism. This movement had as its goal an Italian federation under the Pope. *Selections from the Prison Notebooks of Antonio Gramsci*, pp.58, 375, 399.

42   *Selections from the Prison Notebooks of Antonio Gramsci*, pp.59–60.

43   *Toryism and Tory Democracy*, p.145.

44   *Selected Essays and Passages*, p.231.

45   Standish O'Grady, *All-Ireland* (London, 1898), p.11.

46   Conor Cruise O'Brien, *Parnell and his Party* (London: Oxford University Press: 1957), p.349.

47   Ibid., p.350.

48   R.F. Foster, *Paddy and Mr Punch: Connections in Irish and English History*, p.63.

49   Ibid., p.71. George Boyce writes that although he was a member of the Anglo-Irish ruling class and although the bulk of that class were Unionist, 'that did not prevent Parnell (like Jonathan Swift before him) possessing that hearty contempt for the English establishment that any well-connected Irish Protestant worth his salt was capable of harbouring', *Nationalism in Ireland* (London: Routledge, 1990), p.208. F.S.L. Lyons writes of 'the extreme dislike of "Englishness" which rapidly became an obsession with him', *Charles Stewart Parnell* (London: Collins, 1977), p.31. Joseph Lee argues that he 'certainly despised the Irish at least as much as the English, but the supercilious Saxon air keenly rankled the Anglo-Irish artistocrat', *The Modernisation of Irish Society 1848–1918* (Dublin: Gill & Macmillan, 1973), p.76.

50   John Hutchinson, *The Dynamics of Cultural Nationalism* (London: Allen & Unwin, 1987), p.9.

51   Ernest Gellner, *Nations and Nationalism* (Oxford: Basil Blackwell, 1983), p.1.

52   *The Ethnic Revival*, p.13.

53   E.J. Hobsbawm, *Nations and Nationalism since 1780* (Cambridge: Cambridge University Press, 1990), p.64.

54   Ibid., p.65.

55   'Yet the genetic approach to ethnicity is plainly irrelevant, since the crucial base

of an ethnic group as a form of social organization is cultural rather than biological', *Nations and Nationalism since 1780*, p.63. Granted that this position is invoked to attack the use of genetic ideas of ethnicity by the Nazis against the Jews, it nevertheless appears contradictory when considered in the context of the importance he attributes to physical ethnicity in modern nationalism.

56   The validity or otherwise of demands for political independence made by political representatives of these ethnic minorities is not at issue here. Political autonomy can express itself in terms other than national.

57   Benedict Anderson, *Imagined Communities* (London: Verso, 1983), p.15.

58   Ibid., pp.76–9.

59   Ibid., p.82.

60   Ibid., p.103.

61   Ibid., p.103.

62   Hugh Kearney provides a succinct account of the tension between ethnic and civic concepts of national identity. 'Contested Ideas of Nationhood 1800–1995', *The Irish Review*, 20 (1997), pp.1–22.

63   Yeats disagrees with O'Grady's 'conclusions too constantly and sees the armed hand of nationality in too many places where he but sees the clash of ancient with modern institutions…' 'Irish National Literature II', *Bookman* (1895), *Uncollected Prose*, Vol. I, p.369. Yet it is hardly necessary to refer to the importance of the idealised Irish Peasant in Yeats's literature.

64   *Hegemony and Socialist Strategy*, p.63.

65   Ibid., p.64.

66   Ibid., p.86.

67   Judith Butler's criticism of a later essay by Laclau, 'Beyond Emancipation', illustrates how necessity, in the logical sense, remains in Laclau's theory of social practices. She asks 'Whether the theoretical demarcation of "the logically possible" can suffice as a normative ideal for social practices, when the assumption of a radical ontological divide between the logical and the social precludes from the start the realizability of a logical norm within the domain of the social', 'Poststructuralism and Postmarxism', p.10.

CHAPTER FIVE

1   Ernest Boyd, *Appreciations and Depreciations*, p.21.

2   Standish O'Grady, *The Coming of Cuculain*, 2nd edn (London: Methuen, 1919), p.xiv.

3   Ibid., p.xx.

4   Peter Kuch, *Yeats and Æ: The antagonism that unites dear friends* (Gerrards Cross: Colin Smythe, 1986). Kuch claims that Russell, unlike Yeats, remained a poet of the Celtic Twilight throughout his career.

5   Darrell Figgis, *AE* (London: Maunsel, 1916), p.84.

6   F.S.L. Lyons, *Ireland Since the Famine* (London: Fontana, 1973), p.32.

7   In an article on the Irish Creamery System, Cormac O'Gráda also argues that the co-operative ideal envisaged by Plunkett and Æ failed to materialise but he argues that the reason lay not in a sense of nationalist loyalty on the part of Irish farmers but simply because of their hard-nosed attitude to co-operation. He quotes from

the IAOS records for Killasnet co-op, 5th July 1900, in which the manager informs Æ: 'The farmers look at it solely as a matter of £.s.d. They do not concern themselves in the least about measures of co-operation, etc., etc., but if Lonsdale [a private firm] or the market pays us a higher price, there is where we will go. This is the way with them, they are the greatest niggers [sic] I have ever met where a penny is concerned.' 'The Beginnings of the Irish Creamery System, 1880–1914', *Economic History Review*, xxx, 2nd series (Welwyn Garden City: Popper, 1977), p.300.

8   F.S.L. Lyons, *Ireland Since The Famine*, p.216.

9   Paul Bew, *Conflict and Conciliation in Ireland, 1890–1910* (Oxford: Clarendon, 1987), p.27.

10   In *The Irish Homestead* (28 Jan. 1899) an account is given of speeches delivered in Manchester by Plunkett and Finlay on the subject of co-operation. In his speech Finlay acknowledged that as Plunkett was identified with the landlord class, and as a Protestant Unionist, he would encounter great difficulty in convincing the Home Rule Munster landlords. He also said that it was no bad thing if the drinks trade in Ireland was destroyed but that this would not necessarily lead to the destruction of Irish small towns, an argument that was opposed by a powerful group in middle-class Irish nationalism, publicans. Trevor West identifies the friendship between Finlay, Plunkett, Russell and R.A. Anderson as the combination that drove the Co-operative Movement intellectually (Plunkett), organisationally (Anderson), morally (Finlay), and imaginatively (Russell). Trevor West, *Horace Plunkett: Co-operation and Politics, An Irish Biography* (Gerrards Cross: Colin Smythe, 1986), For an assessment of the relationship of the Co-operative Movement to Irish Catholicism, see Liam Kennedy, 'The Early Response of the Irish Catholic Clergy to the Co-operative Movement', *Reactions to Irish Nationalism* (Dublin: Gill & Macmillan, 1987), pp.170–85.

11   *Conflict and Conciliation in Ireland, 1890–1910*, pp.76–7.

12   Ibid., p.79.

13   *The Irish Homestead*, Vol. V, No. 5 (4 Feb. 1899), p.3.

14   In *The Freeman's Journal*, 2nd May 1906, it was argued that the IAOS should receive no financial assistance from The Department of Agriculture and Technical Instruction (of which Plunkett was vice-president) since it was largely engaged in trade. This is but one example of the many attacks launched by the newspaper against the movement.

15   *The Irish Homestead*, Vol. XII, No. 22 (2 June 1906), p.3.

16   Antonio Gramsci, 'Notes on Italian History', in *Selections from the Prison Notebooks of Antonio Gramsci*. Gramsci argues that the success of the French Revolution lay in the willingness of rural France to unite their interests with those of the Jacobins, thus producing a 'national-popular' movement. Chantal Mouffe and Ernesto Laclau have interpreted Gramsci's analysis as a coded attack on the economism of the Second International. See 'Hegemony and ideology in Gramsci', *Gramsci and Marxist Theory*.

17   For an account of the genesis of the Co-operative Wholesale Society see G.D.H. Cole, *A Century of Co-operation* (London: Allen & Unwin, 1945), pp. 128–47.

18   *The Freeman's Journal* (4 May 1907), pp.4–5.

19   *The Irish Homestead* (1 Feb. 1908), p.18.

20   Henry Summerfield, (ed.) *Selections from the Contributions to The Irish Homestead* (Gerrards Cross: Colin Smythe, 1978), p.131.

21   Bew, *Conflict and Conciliation in Ireland, 1890–1910*, p.203.

22   Ibid., p.63.

23   *The Irish Homestead* (1 Feb. 1908), p.3.

24   Ibid., p.4.

25   Thomas A. Boylan, and Timothy P. Foley, *Political Economy and Colonial Ireland* (London: Routledge, 1992), p.2.

26   Ibid., p.116.

27   *The Irish Homestead*, (11 April 1896), p.4.

28   Cole, *A Century of Co-operation*, pp.244–5.

29   Ibid., p.245–9.

30   *The Irish Homestead* (23 May 1896), pp.8–9.

31   Ibid. (23 Jan. 1897), p.9. G.D.H. Cole argues that the disagreement between the CWS and the IAOS lay in the perception rather than the reality of profiteering motives being exercised by the former in their Irish projects. Furthermore, he points out that the CWS in turn suspected the IAOS of 'seeking to build up something analogous to a capitalist monopoly', *A Century of Co-operation*, p.251.

32   *Ireland in the New Century*, p.21.

33   *The Irish Homestead* (18 April 1896), p.5.

34   Ibid. (25 April 1896), pp.2–3.

35   Mary Daly makes the point that, in any case, the impact of Whately's political economy in Ireland must have been slight. Given the erratic nature of school attendance during the nineteenth century and the virtual inevitability of emigration for the vast majority of Catholic teachers, she argues, political economy rarely reached the Catholic masses. Review of *Political Economy and Colonial Ireland*, *Irish Historical Studies*, Vol. XXIX, No. 114 (1994), p.268.

36   In an open letter to John Dillon published in *The Irish Homestead* Russell attacked him on the basis of his rural middle-class background rather than his nationalism. The Dillon family business, originally a small shop started early in the nineteenth century by John's uncle Thomas Dillon, had flourished and expanded under the management of his cousin Anne Deane, from whom he inherited it around 1905. In the light of this, Russell's attack may seem to carry a certain tone of aristocratic condescension but, more importantly, it exposed the class politics operating beneath Dillon's nationalism: 'For many years the present writer believed that it was possible your opposition was only political. But when you descend to the methods of your speech in Parliament, when you deliberately deceive and mislead, the suspicion, long kept under, that you have in you merely the soul of a little country trader defending his class under the guise of high politics arises in one's mind', *Selections from the Contributions to The Irish Homestead*, p.317.

37   Æ, *The National Being* (London: Maunsel, 1916) p.128.

38   Ibid., p.12.

39   *The Irish Homestead*, Vol. III No. 3 (19 Jan. 1901), p.3.

40   *The National Being*, pp.60–1.

41   Although writing on a subject as alien to that of *The National Being* as the crisis of representation in twentieth century avant-garde literature, Jameson's logic is peculiarly similar to Æ's: 'So a strange malediction hangs over art in our time,

and for the writer this dilemma is felt as an increasing (structural) incapacity to generalize or universalize private or lived experience. The dictates, not only of realism, but of narrative in general, tend gradually to restrict writing to sheer autobiography, at the same time that they transform even autobiographical discourse itself into one more private language among others: reduced to the telling of the truth of a private situation alone, that no longer engages the fate of a nation, but merely a single locality...' 'Demystifing the Ideology of Modernism', in Francis Mulhern (ed.) *Contemporary Marxist Literary Criticism* (New York: Longman, 1992), p.185.

42   *The National Being*, p.23. The metaphor used here recalls Plato's cave analogy in Book VII of *The Republic* and it suggests the residual influence of Darwinism on Russell's thought, thereby recalling the Darwinism latent within O'Grady's *History of Ireland: Critical and Philosophical*. Plato, *The Republic*. Trans. A.D. Lindsay (London: Dent, 1976), pp.207–10. In *The Candle of Vision* Platonic formalism and Darwinism meet in Russell's description of a vision he once had, in which an ape fashions clouds into a certain form, telling Russell that this was what he was trying to do. *The Candle of Vision* (London: Macmillan, 1919), p.69. It is symptomatic of Russell's efforts to overcome the opposition between idealism and materialism, significantly motivating his involvement with the Irish Co-operative Movement. In this he was clearly influenced by O'Grady.

43   A Hegelian strain in Russell's thought is evident in this understanding of independence of character. His awareness of Hegel's thought is indicated in *Song and its Fountains*, where he recalls a criticism of Hegel's doctrine of the Absolute becoming self-conscious in the unfolding of the universe. *Song and its Fountains* (London: Macmillan, 1932), pp.69–70.

44   *Ireland in the New Century*, p.44. For Hegel's notion of the individual will as realisable only through the rational ends of the state, see Adrian Oldfield, *Citizenship and Community: Civic Republicanism and the Modern World* (London: Routledge, 1990), pp.105–6.

45   *Citizenship and Community*, p.82.

46   F.M. Barnard, *Herder's Social and Political Thought* (Oxford: Clarendon, 1987), p.67.

47   Ibid., p.80.

48   Ibid., p.63.

49   *The National Being*, p.2.

50   Ibid., p.53.

51   See George Moore, *The Untilled Field* (London: Fisher Unwin, 1903). This provides the most graphic fictional account of stagnation in rural Ireland at the turn of the century.

52   *The National Being*, p.33.

53   Æ, *Co-operation and Nationality* (1912) (Dublin: Irish Academic Press, 1982), pp.7–8.

54   *The Irish Homestead*, Vol. VIII, No. 26 (28 June 1902), pp.3–4.

55   *The Irish Homestead*, Vol. XV, No. 43 (24 Oct. 1908), p.5.

56   *The Dynamics of Cultural Nationalism*, pp.152–3.

57   Ibid., pp.152–3.

58   Andrew Gailey, *Ireland and the Death of Kindness* (Cork: Cork University Press, 1987), p.65.

59   Ibid., pp.63–4.
60   By discursive determination I have in mind the form which Foucault attributes to contradiction: '... it is because contradiction is always anterior to the discourse, and because it can never therefore entirely escape it, that discourse changes, undergoes transformation, and escapes of itself from its own continuity. Contradiction, then, functions throughout discourse, as the principle of its historicity', Michel Foucault, *The Archaeology of Knowledge* (London: Flamingo, 1983), p.151.
61   Raymond Williams, *The Country and the City* (London: Chatto & Windus, 1973), p.78.
62   Ibid., p.79. Terry Eagleton criticises Williams for turning to 'the Romantic radical-conservative lineage of nineteenth-century England' in the attempt to create a 'socialist humanism'. 'Criticism and Politics: The Work of Raymond Williams' (*NLR*, 95, 1976), p.10. Anthony Barrett implies that Eagleton's criticism is undialectical in missing the dual nature of Williams's thought, stating that the paradox of Williams is 'that while he has been idealist in the roles which he assigns to culture within society, he has at the same time been materialist in his treatment of practices within culture', 'Raymond Williams and Marxism: a rejoinder to Terry Eagleton' (*NLR*, 99, 1976), p.60.
63   *The National Being*, pp.23–4.
64   Ibid., pp.68–9. Desmond Fennell considers the relationship of Russell's thought to Connolly's. 'James Connolly and George Russell', *The Crane Bag*, 9, 1 (1985), pp.57–62.
65   Russell is keen to point out that co-operation is not socialism and he is wary of socialist utopias not grounded in reality: 'The extraordinary propensity of a number of Irishmen to take up lost causes, causes which were hopelessly lost before they were even found, has been manifested in the way in which some Irishmen are advocating Socialism for Ireland', *The Irish Homestead*, Vol. XVI, No. 46, (13 Nov. 1909), p.4.
66   *Ireland in the New Century*, p.58.
67   *Co-operation and Nationality*, p.47.
68   Ibid., p.48.
69   Ibid., p.49.
70   Ibid., p.50.
71   Ibid., p.51.
72   Ibid., p.51 (my italics).
73   Hugh Brody, *Inishkillane* (London: Penguin, 1973), p.45
74   Ibid., p.209. Brody's analysis casts doubt on Kevin Whelan's claim that, between 1850 and 1960, '"country" triumphed over "town" in ideological terms in southern Ireland...' 'Town and Village in Ireland: A socio-cultural perspective', *The Irish Review*, No. 5 (1988), p.41.
75   Ibid., p.131–2.
76   Liam O'Dowd contends that community is the dominant characteristic of Irish social ideology. This, he claims, is not because communalism has consistently reflected Irish social reality but because it has been successfully employed by class/sectional interests resulting in the marginalisation of ideologies challenging communalism. 'Town and Country in Irish Ideology', *Canadian Journal of Irish Studies*. Vol. 13, No. 2 (1987), pp.44–5. Given Russell's commitment to community,

O'Dowd's praise for him on the grounds that he represents a challenge to the dominant cultural ideology of an 'imagined community', is at variance with O'Dowd's own critique of communalism.

77   Nicos Mouzelis, *Post-Marxist Alternatives* (London: Macmillan, 1990), p.173.

78   *Outside Literature*, p.214. John Frow, 'Marxism after Structuralism', *Southern Review*, 17 (1984), p.39.

79   Samuel Weber, 'Capitalizing History: Notes on *The Political Unconscious*', *Diacritics*, 13, 2 (1983), pp.20–1.

80   *Outside Literature*, pp.208–9.

81   *The All-Ireland Review*, Vol. VII, No. 38 (18 Nov. 1905), p.1.

82   Ibid., Vol. VI, No. 44 (13 Jan. 1906), p.5.

83   *The Irish Homestead*, Vol. XII, No. 2 (13 Jan. 1906), p.8. For Russell's criticisms of O'Grady's 'New Order' see *The Irish Homestead*, Vol. XI, No. 51 (30 Dec. 1905), pp.3–4.

84   Ernest Boyd, '"A Fenian Unionist", Standish O'Grady', *Appreciations and Depreciations*.

85   In a letter to *The Irish Homestead* O'Grady compares the difference between his Commune and the Co-operative Society as that between Christianity and the marketplace. This reputed difference, however, turns out merely to be the very organicism that Æ promotes throughout *The National Being*: 'The Commune takes all into itself, into its own organic unity, cherishing, feeding, sustaining all; just as the one life, which is in our own bodies, cherishes, feeds, and sustains every atom and fibre of our corporeal being. The ideal and exemplar of the Commune is just that: just the body of man. There is no resemblance at all between the Commune and the Co-operative Society. The Co-operative Society aims and exerts itself towards Money: the Commune does not aim towards Money at all.' *The Irish Homestead* (2 April 1910), pp.9–10. Predictably, Russell's response is to point out the unworkability of a project that aims to accommodate drunkards and idlers, *The Irish Homestead* (2 April 1910), p.9.

86   This claim recurs throughout Æ's economic writings. See particularly *Co-operation and Nationality*, pp.20–1, 46–51.

87   Liam O'Dowd, 'Neglecting the Material Dimension: Irish Intellectuals and the Problem of Identity', *The Irish Review*, 3 (1988), p.10.

88   Ibid., p.11.

89   Liam O'Dowd, 'Intellectuals in 20th Century Ireland: And the case of George Russell (Æ)', *The Crane Bag*, 9, 1 (1985), p.19.

90   Ibid., p.19.

91   Henry Summerfield, *That Myriad-Minded Man* (Gerrards Cross: Colin Smythe, 1975), p.88.

92   Darrell Figgis, *Æ*, p.84.

93   Robert Davis, *George William Russell ('Æ')* (Boston: Twayne, 1977), p.90.

94   A.J. Balfour was deeply impressed by the ethos of self-help and modernisation that inspired the IAOS. He particularly admired Plunkett, writing that 'if others of [Plunkett's] class would imitate his example, more could be done to knit classes together than is possible by any amount of legislation or any strength of administration'. See Catherine B. Shannon. *Arthur J. Balfour and Ireland* (Washington: Catholic University of America Press, 1988), p.55. However, the principle of individualism predominated his thought and his support for the

activities of the Congested Districts Board and the IAOS was predicated on the assumption that they would produce the conditions in Ireland to stimulate individual enterprise. Ibid., p.74. This is at variance with Æ's perspective on co-operation which was concerned with producing a communalist society very different to that of Victorian England. See *The Irish Homestead* (30 July 1898), p.11.

95   Raymond Williams, *The Country and The City*, pp.69–78. Terry Eagleton has argued that during the latter half of the nineteenth century, Victorian capitalism looked to the organicism of romantic humanism as source for cultural forms particular to its ideological requirements. He sees Matthew Arnold as a key intellectual in this process. Implicit in Eagleton's position is the belief that organicism is an essentially conservative, if not reactionary, doctrine. His stinging criticism of Yeats on organicist grounds suggests that no concession would be made to Russell's use of organicism either. See *Criticism and Ideology*, 2nd edn (London: Verso, 1978), pp.102–110, and 'Politics and Sexuality in W.B. Yeats', *The Crane Bag*, 9, 2 (1985), p.139.

CHAPTER SIX

1   W.B. Yeats, 'A General Introduction to My Work', *Essays and Introductions* (London: Papermac, 1989), p.512.

2   Quoted in Phillip Marcus, *Standish O'Grady* (Lewisburg, Bucknell University Press, 1970), p.76.

3   'Irish National Literature, II: Contemporary Prose Writers', *Bookman*. Aug. 1895) *Uncollected Prose*, Vol. I, p.369.

4   Estella Ruth Taylor, *The Modern Irish Writers: Cross Currents of Criticism* (Connecticut: Greenwood, 1954), p.103.

5   *All-Ireland Review and Irish Industrial Gazette* III, No. 6 (12 April 1902), p.2. O'Grady viewed the Irish Theatre movement critically. He regarded it in the same manner as the tourist trade in Ireland, something to which he was deeply hostile. See *All-Ireland Review*, Vol. I, No. 8 (24 Feb. 1900), p.5. He was critical of Yeats's *The King's Threshold* which he accused of depicting an unnatural and unrealistic event. See *All-Ireland Review*, Vol. IV, No. 32 (24 Oct. 1903), p.6. Daniel J. O'Sullivan notes that these disagreements led to O'Grady's estrangement from the literary and dramatic movement, indicated by the fact that the *All-Ireland Review* devoted less space and attention to the activities of the movement. 'Standish James O'Grady's *All-Ireland Review*', *Studia Hibernica*, No. 69 (1969), p.134.

6   Æ, 'The Dramatic Treatment of Heroic Literature', *Samhain*, No. 2 (1902), p.11.

7   Ibid., p.12.

8   *All-Ireland Review and Irish Industrial Gazette*, Vol. III, No. 35 (1 November 1902), p.5. For an example of those cultural imperatives Yeats associated with literary propaganda see D.P. Moran, *The Philosophy of Irish Ireland* (Dublin: Duffy, 1905).

9   Endnote to 'The Dramatic Treatment of Heroic Literature', *Samhain*, No. 2 9 (1902), p. 12.

10   Ibid., p.12. The heuristic power Yeats attributes to sound here recalls the primacy

O'Grady attributes to sound in his use of invocation in *History of Ireland: The Heroic Period* . See Chapter 1 of this volume. For evidence of the importance of sound to Yeats's understanding of art, see 'Literature and the Living Voice', *Explorations* (London: Macmillan, 1962), pp.202–21.

11 Ibid., p.13. The influence of Wagner is clearly evident here in Yeats's references to music and warriors. Although, unlike Maud Gonne, George Moore and Edward Martyn, Yeats never attended the Wagner music festival at Bayreuth, the influence of Wagner on him cannot be underestimated. In January 1898 he wrote enthusiastically to Lady Gregory of Maud Gonne's invitation to attend the Bayreuth festival with her the following year. John Kelly and Ronald Schuchard. *The Collected Letters of W.B. Yeats*. Vol. III (1901–1904) (Oxford: Clarendon, 1994), p.178. In a letter to Frank Fay in April 1902 he looked to Wagner's 'Communication to my friends' (1852), laying out his plans for a German National Theatre, as an important precedent for the establishment of a National Theatre in Ireland. *The Collected Letters of W.B. Yeats*, Vol. III, p.175. In the face of John Eglinton's criticism, he promotes Wagner's work, along with that of Ibsen, as the standard to be pursued by the Irish Dramatic Movement. See the consideration of the *Daily Express* controversy below.

12 W.B. Yeats, *Bealtaine*, No. 1 (1899), p.21.

13 For O'Grady's criticism of Yeats's cosmopolitanism, see *All-Ireland Review*, Vol. I, No. 48 (1 Dec. 1900), p.6.

14 *Autobiographies*, pp.193–4.

15 *Samhain*, No. 3 (1903), p.6.

16 Walter Benjamin, *The Origins of German Tragic Drama*, p.16.

17 Ibid., p.36.

18 In July 1916, Benjamin wrote to Martin Buber: 'I can understand writing as such as poetic, prophetic, objective in terms of its effect, but in any case only as *magical*, that is as un-mediated ... In however many forms language may prove to be effective, it will not be so through the transmission of content, but rather through the purest disclosure of its dignity and its nature, Gershom Scholem and Theodor Adorno, *The Correspondence of Walter Benjamin*. Trans. Manfred R. Jacobson and Evelyne M. Jacobson (London: Chicago University Press, 1994), p.80.

19 Benjamin's own work epitomises this apparent dichotomy. George Steiner perceives Mallarméan and Gnostic influences in his philosophy of language, arguing that Benjamin subscribes to the concept of universal language while recognising the fragmentary nature of language as it is used. *After Babel* (London: Oxford University Press, 1975), p.64.

20 Richard Ellmann observes the influence of Kabbalist doctrine on the Golden Dawn, a doctrine that gained interest among cults that grew up in Europe during the nineteenth century. *Yeats: The Man and the Masks* (London: Faber, 1961), pp.89–90.

21 Richard Wolin, *Walter Benjamin: An Aesthetic of Redemption* (Berkeley: California University Press, 1994), pp.37–42.

22 *The Origins of German Tragic Drama*, p.13.

23 'The Tragic Theatre', *Essays and Introductions*, p.245. While it is necessary not to forget the specifically Kabbalistic origin of the imagery used here, a trace can undoubtedly be made to the influence of the Life-Tree Idgrasil on O'Grady's

genealogical method of *History of Ireland: Critical and Philosophical*. This indicates that, as with the relationship between Darwinism and myth in O'Grady's work, this Kabbalistic form of Yeats's occultism reveals that Yeats's relationship to science is not simplistically negative.

24   Friedrich Nietzsche, *The Birth of Tragedy and The Genealogy of Morals*. Trans. Francis Golffing (New York: Doubleday, 1956), p.53. (My italics.)

25   Malcolm Humble points to the influence of Wagner's musicology on Yeats's dramaturgy. See 'German Contacts and Influences in the Lives and Works of W.B. Yeats and D.H. Lawrence, with Special Reference to Friederich Nietzsche', PhD Thesis (Cambridge University, 1969), pp.27–8. Benjamin identifies the symbolic nature of language with sound. 'On Language as Such and on the Language of Man', *One-Way Street and Other Writings*, p.114.

26   *The Birth of Tragedy*, p. 27.

27   Ibid., p.66.

28   'The Tragic Theatre', *Essays and Introductions*, p.243. Nietzsche and Yeats's understanding of individuation is evidently Oedipal in this context. However, it can also be legitimately viewed in terms of O'Grady's valorisation of a unity conceived as feudal beyond the subject–object split pre-supposed in the method of empirical science. See Chapter 2 of this volume for a consideration of this in terms of O'Grady's depiction of Cuchulainn in *History of Ireland: Cuchulainn and His Contemporaries*.

29   Frances Nesbitt Oppel refers to Eric Bentley's *A Century of Hero-Worship: A Study of the Idea of Heroism in Carlyle and Nietzsche* in pointing out the influence of Carlyle on Nietzsche, and of both on Yeats. *Mask and Tragedy: Yeats and Nietzsche, 1902–10* (Charlotsville: Virginia University Press, 1987), p.8.

30   *The Origins of German Tragic Drama*, p.106.

31   Peter Bürger argues that Benjamin's redemptive critique is distinguished from a conservative historical attitude because it is grounded in the present. Following Bürger, it can be stated that the 'redemptive' concept of language is always split; it appears as redemptive only within the context of the 'fallen-redeemed' dialectic, *The Decline of Modernism*. Trans. Nicholas Walker (Cambridge: Polity, 1992), pp.19–30.

32   It can be argued that the distance between Symons/Wilde and O'Grady depends on the degree to which their work is construed as a flight from history or as a re-conceptualisation of the meaning of history. While the 'art for art's sake' ethos of 'The Decay of Lying' invites an interpretation in the former sense, Symons's articles on Wagner and Nietzsche after 1900, suggest a sense of *engagé* in 1890s decadence that became more overt in the new century, given the concern for an understanding of history alternative to empiricism in Nietzsche's work. See Arthur Symons, 'Nietzsche on Tragedy', *The Academy and Literature* (30 Aug. 1902) 'The New Bayreuth', *The Academy and Literature* (27 Sept. 1902), 'The Ideas of Richard Wagner', *The Quarterly Review*, Vol. 203, p.404 (London: John Murray, 1905). For the purposes of this work, however, the literary sense of decadence is taken to mean a flight from historical reality into the realm of pure imagination, as O'Grady understood it.

33   'Nationality and Literature', *United Ireland* (27 May 1893). *Uncollected Prose*. Vol. I, pp.270–1.

34   Ibid., pp.273–4. Terence Brown observes that in the early 1890s Yeats was editing

the works of William Blake with the poet and painter Edwin Ellis; a Blakean obscurity combined with a sense of O'Grady's bardic energy informed Yeats's writing on a Celtic past, *The Life of W.B. Yeats*, p.67.

35   For a detailed examination of Yeats's critique of the propagandist literature of The Young Ireland Movement see John Kelly, 'The Political and Intellectual Background to the Irish Literary Revival to 1901', PhD thesis (Cambridge University, 1971), pp.244–6, 262, 281–5.

36   *All-Ireland Review*. Vol I, No. 48 (1 Dec. 1900), p.6.

37   'Nationality and Literature', *United Ireland* (27 May 1893). *Uncollected Prose*. Vol. I, p.268.

38   John Kelly, 'The Political, Social and Intellectual Background of the Irish Literary Revival to 1901', p.187.

39   'Irish National Literature', *United Ireland* (27 May 1893). *Uncollected Prose*. Vol. I, p.367.

40   W.B. Yeats, 'The Fisherman', *Collected Poems*. 2nd edn (London: Picador, 1990), p.166.

41   Daniel Hoffman, *Barbarous Knowledge* (Oxford: Oxford University Press, 1967), p.84.

42   George Bornstein, 'Last Romantic or Last Victorian: Yeats, Tennyson and Browning', *Yeats Annual*, Vol. 1 (Dublin: Macmillan, 1982), p.129.

43   Ibid., p.120.

44   Deborah Anne Sherman, 'Yeats Talk: The Critical Theory of W.B. Yeats and the Victorian Background', PhD thesis (Brown University, 1982), p.34. Edward Engelberg, *The Vast Design: Patterns in W.B. Yeats's Aesthetic*, 2nd edn. (Washington: Catholic University of America, 1988), p.3. See also Stan Smith, *The Origins of Modernism: Eliot, Pound, Yeats and the Rhetorics of Renewal* (London: Harvester-Wheatsheaf, 1994), p.157. Herbert J. Levine also sheds light on the extent of this Victorian influence in his consideration of the importance of Ruskin to Yeats's aesthetics. See 'Yeats's Ruskinian Byzantium', *Yeats Annual*, 2 (Dublin: Macmillan, 1983), pp.25–34.

45   Deborah Sherman, 'Yeats Talk: The Critical Theory of W.B. Yeats and the Victorian Background', p.35.

46   Introduction to Standish O'Grady, *The Coming of Cuculain*, pp.xiii–xiv.

47   'No Second Troy', *Collected Poems*, p.101; 'Vacillation', *Collected Poems*, p.282; 'In Memory of Major Robert Gregory', *Collected Poems*, p.148; 'A Prayer On Going Into My House', *Collected Poems*, p.183; 'The Second Coming', *Collected Poems*, p.210; 'Byzantium', *Collected Poems*, p.280.

48   'Yeats Talk', p.142.

49   Ibid., p.142.

50   *Gender and History in Yeats's Love Poetry*, p.15.

51   In *History of Ireland: The Heroic Period*, p. 139, the Red Branch Knights are 'stricken by the insane mist', signalling the emergence of a state of anarchy marked by the demise of patriarchy. In an analogous fashion, the insane mist represents the fatality of enchantment, an aspect of Victorian aesthetics that finds its ideological corollary in O'Grady's 'The Great Enchantment'. With regard to gender, O'Grady's epic is formally and thematically dominated by a valorisation of masculinity, particularly in the form of Cuchulainn, as has been considered in Chapter 1 of this volume.

52   *History of Ireland: Critical and Philosophical*, p.321.

53   Ibid., p.61. Daniel J. Sullivan describes the poem as 'the one outstanding exception' to the failure of O'Grady's *History of Ireland* to inspire an outpouring of Anglo-Irish epic poetry. 'The Literary Periodical and the Anglo-Irish Revival, 1894–1914', PhD thesis (University College, Dublin. 1969).

54   *The Origins of Modernism*, pp.180–1.

55   Harold Bloom, *Yeats* (Oxford: Oxford University Press, 1972), p.87.

56   *Collected Poems*, p.409. Observing the lack of historical awareness in what he regards as Harold Bloom's otherwise impressive reading of Yeats's poem, Terence Brown claims that history is represented by St Patrick in 'The Wanderings of Oisin'. This has the value of centring St Patrick in the dynamic between Niamh and Oisin. *The Life of W.B. Yeats*, p.45. It is more accurate, however, to identify history with the set of relations between all three characters in the poem, for that is to recognise the imaginative dimension of historical development itself.

57   Robert Welch describes 'The Island of Forgetfulness' as 'the most aesthetic of the islands; indeed it is an epitome of certain dominant moods of aesthetic indulgence Yeats was to find in himself and in the Rhymers club of the nineties, moods that Yeats never surrendered himself to, even here, in this narrative poem written in his early twenties before the nineties began', *Irish Poetry from Moore to Yeats* (Gerrards Cross: Colin Smythe, 1980), p.221.

58   *Collected Poems*, p.436.

59   Ibid., p.204.

60   *History of Ireland: The Heroic Period*, p.62. For O'Grady's interest in the mystical quality of stone, see 'Stone Worship: Ireland', *Dublin University Magazine*, p.85 (1875).

61   *Collected Poems*, p.421.

62   Conor Cruise O'Brien argues that the Nietzschean influence on Yeats was essentially fascist, *Passion and Cunning and Other Essays* (London: Grafton, 1990), pp.18–86; *The Suspecting Glance* (London: Faber, 1972), pp.72–84. W.J. McCormack also points to what he sees as evidence of fascism in the later Yeats and is scathing of those post-colonial critics who ignore this in order to 'save Yeats for the Third World', *From Burke to Beckett*, pp.18, 364–71. For a refutation of the fascist argument see Elizabeth Butler Cullingford, *Yeats, Ireland and fascism* (London: Macmillan, 1982).

63   *Collected Poems*, pp.437–9.

64   John Reed. *Decadent Style* (Athens, Ohio: Ohio University Press, 1985), p.92.

65   Seamus Deane, 'The Literary Myths of the Revival: A Case for their Abandonment', in Joseph Ronsley (ed.) *Myth and Reality in Irish Literature* (Ontario: Wilfrid Laurier University Press, 1977), p.319. Deane's criticism of myth in Yeats's work contradicts his criticism of the opposition of historical revisionism to myth making, *Strange Country*, pp.185–94.

66   *Paddy and Mr Punch*, p.232.

67   *Mimesis*, pp.10–11.

68   Ibid., pp.10–11.

69   This suggests a blind spot in Foucault's thought when he attempts to dissociate language from power. Michel Foucault, *Power/Knowledge: Selected Interviews and Other Writings 1972-1977*, Colin Gordon (ed) (Brighton: Harvester, 1980), pp.114–15. Benjamin's conception of language as magic in 'On Language as Such

and on the Language of Man', referred to earlier, also expresses it as power, in the sense that magic is inseparable from the concept of power.

70   *Mimesis*, p.11.

71   *History of Ireland: The Heroic Period*, pp.218–23.

72   'The Wanderings of Oisin', *Collected Poems*, p.418.

73   *Mimesis*, p.20.

74   Mircea Eliade, *Myth and Reality* (London: Allen & Unwin, 1964), p.6.

75   Myth, in this sense, is a practice; it has no existence outside its enactment. This, of course, anticipates the structural anthropology of Claude Lévi-Strauss's *Mythology* but also (more significantly in this context) the view of practice as defined by Althusser in which the most important aspect is neither the raw material used nor the final product but 'the *labour of transformation* itself', *For Marx*, p.166. Myth in this instance is a primary instance of practice since its raw material and its product have no existence outside of this 'labour of transformation'. Althusser specifically refers to ritual as the practice of ideology, manifesting the '*material existence of an ideological apparatus...*', 'Ideology and Ideological State Apparatus', p.158.

76   Ibid., p.19. Martin Heidegger, *Being and Time*. Trans. John Macquarrie & Edward Robinson (London: SCM, 1962), p.477.

77   Vivien Mercier, 'Victorian Evangelicalism and the Anglo-Irish Revival', in Peter Connolly (ed.) *Literature and the Changing Ireland* (Gerrards Cross: Colin Smythe, 1982), 85.

78   Ibid., pp.59, 86.

79   Sherman, 'Yeats Talk', pp.54–6.

80   Angela Jenkins, 'W.B. Yeats and Irish Mythology', MA thesis, p.48.

81   'The Political, Social and Intellectual Background to the Irish Literary Revival to 1901', pp.290–1.

82   *Yeats: The Man and the Masks*, p.125.

83   'The Literary Movement in Ireland', *North American Review* (Dec. 1899). *Uncollected Prose*, Vol. II, pp.193–4. *Toryism and Tory Democracy*, p.106.

84   *Collected Poems*, p.446.

85   'The Literary Movement in Ireland', *North American Review* (Dec. 1899). *Uncollected Prose*, Vol. II, p.185.

86   Edward Hagan notes the moral conservatism governing O'Grady's editing from his source material for *History of Ireland*, '*High Nonsensical Words*', pp.80–3. Rosalind Clark notes the same conservatism that leads him to downplay the significance of the Morrígan, one of the ancient Irish goddesses, in *History of Ireland. The Great Queens: Irish Goddess from the Morrígan to Cathleen Ní Houlihan* (Gerrards Cross: Colin Smythe, 1991), pp.56–7.

87   See Chapter 2 of this volume for consideration of O'Grady's treatment of individualism.

88   'The Literary Movement in Ireland', *North American Review* (Dec. 1899). *Uncollected Prose*, Vol. II, p.185.

89   Ibid., p.193.

90   *Autobiographies*, p.220. For criticism of Yeats's praise of O'Grady see 'The Best Irish Books', *New Ireland Review*, Vol. III (1895), pp.122–6.

91   John Eglinton, *et al. Literary Ideals in Ireland* (London, 1899), p.24.

92   Ibid., p.27.

93   Ibid., p.35.

94   Ibid., p.36.

95   Ibid., p.51.

96   Ibid., p.58.

97   Ibid., p.80.

98   Ibid., pp.86–7.

99   Æ, 'The Cuchullin Saga', *New Ireland Review*, Vol. X (1899), pp.3–4.

100   *Yeats and Æ: 'The Antagonism that Unites Dear Friends'*, pp.14–16: 'Russell was more concerned with the purpose of poetry than he was with a poem qua poem.'

101   Ibid., p.168.

102   Kelly, 'The Political, Social and Intellectual Background of the Irish Literary Revival to 1901', p.294. Significantly, Terence Brown notes that in a dispute with George Moore over *Hail and Farewell* some years later, Yeats claimed that he did not mean bourgeois to refer so much to a particular class as to a way of thinking and living contrary to artistic values and practices. *The Life of W.B. Yeats*, p.206.

103   'The Symbolism of Poetry', *Essays and Introductions*, p.163.

104   Ibid., p.164.

CONCLUSION

1   Hugh Art O'Grady, *Standish James O'Grady: The Man and The Writer* (Dublin: Talbot, 1921), p.46.

2   *All-Ireland Review*, Vol. VII, No. 3. (Jan. 1907), p.2.

3   Neil Belton, 'Killing on an Assembly Line Basis', *Irish Times* (30 Dec. 1999), p.10.

Bibliography

O'Grady, Standish, *All-Ireland* (London, 1898).
O'Grady, Standish, 'A Wet Day', *The Irish Homestead*, Vol. V, No. 47 (Christmas, 1899).
O'Grady, Standish, 'Druidism', *Dublin University Magazine*, 86 (Dublin, 1875).
O'Grady, Standish, *History of Ireland: Critical and Philosophical*, Vol. I (London, 1881).
O'Grady, Standish, *History of Ireland: Cuculain and His Contemporaries*, Vol. II. 1880 (New York: Lemma, 1970).
O'Grady, Standish, *History of Ireland: The Heroic Period*, Vol. I (1878) (New York: Lemma, 1970).
O'Grady, Standish, *In The Gates of the North* (Dublin: Talbot, 1901).
O'Grady, Standish, *Lost on Du-Corrig or 'Twixt Earth and Ocean* (London, 1894).
O'Grady, Standish, *Red Hugh's Captivity: A Picture of Ireland, Social and Political, In the Reign of Queen Elizabeth* (London, 1889).
O'Grady, Standish, *Selected Essays and Passages*, A.P. Graves, William Magennis and Douglas Hyde (eds) (Dublin: Talbot, 1918).
O'Grady, Standish, 'Stone Worship: Ireland', *Dublin University Magazine*, 85 (1875).
O'Grady, Standish, *The Bog of Stars and Other Stories and Sketches of Elizabethan Ireland* (1893) (New York: Books for Libraries Press, 1973).
O'Grady, Standish, *The Chain of Gold: A Tale on the West Coast of Ireland* (Dublin, 1895).
O'Grady, Standish, *The Coming of Cuculain* (London, 1894).
O'Grady, Standish, *The Coming of Cuculain*, 2nd. edn (Dublin: Talbot, 1919).
O'Grady, Standish, *The Story of Ireland* (London, 1894).
O'Grady, Standish, *Toryism and the Tory Democracy* (London, 1886).

Works edited by O'Grady:
Pacata Hibernia or A History of The Wars in Ireland during the reign of Queen Elizabeth, Vol. I (London, 1896).
All-Ireland Review, Vol. I, No. 1 (6 Jan. 1900) – Vol. VII, No. 3 (Jan. 1907).

Russell, George *(Æ)*, *Co-operation and Nationality* (1912). (Dublin: Irish Academic Press, 1982).
Russell, George, *Song and its Fountains* (London: Macmillan, 1932).
Russell, George, 'The Cuchullin Saga', *New Ireland Review*, Vol. X (1899).
Russell, George, *The Candle of Vision* (London: Macmillan, 1919).
Russell, George, *The National Being* (London: Maunsel, 1916).

Works edited by Russell:
The Irish Homestead. Vol. II, No. 1 (7 Mar. 1896) – Vol. XXIX, No. 51 (30 Dec. 1922).

Yeats, W.B., *A Vision* (London: Macmillan, 1962).
Yeats, W.B., *Autobiographies* (London: Macmillan, 1980).
Yeats, W.B., *Collected Poems* 2nd. edn (London: Picador, 1990).
Yeats, W.B., *Essays and Introductions* (London: Papermac, 1989).
Yeats, W.B., *Explorations* (London: Macmillan, 1962).
Yeats, W.B., *The Collected Letters of W.B. Yeats 1901–1904*, John Kelly and Ronald

Schuchard (eds) (Oxford: Clarendon, 1994).
Yeats, W.B., *Uncollected Prose*. Vol. I, John P. Frayne (ed.) (New York: Columbia University Press, 1970).

Works edited by Yeats.
Bealtaine, Nos. 1–2 (1899–1900).
Samhain. Nos. 1–8 (1901–1908).

Other works:
Adorno, Theodor, *Minima Moralia*. Trans. E.F.N. Jephcott (London: New Left Books, 1974).
Adorno, Theodor, *Aesthetic Theory*, Gretel Adorno and Rolf Tiedemann (eds). Trans. C. Lenhardt (London: Routledge, 1984).
Alexander, Edward, *Matthew Arnold, John Ruskin, and the Modern Temper* (Columbus: Ohio State University Press, 1973).
Althusser, Louis, *For Marx*. Trans. Ben Brewster (London: Penguin, 1969).
Althusser, Louis, 'Ideology and Ideological State Apparatuses', *Lenin and Philosophy and other essays*. Trans. Ben Brewster (London: New Left Books, 1977).
Anderson, Benedict, *Imagined Communities* (London: Verso, 1983).
Arnold, Matthew, 'Democracy', *The Works of Matthew Arnold*, Vol. X (London: Macmillan, 1904), p.26.
Arnold, Matthew, *Culture and Anarchy*, J.D. Wilson (ed.) (Cambridge University Press, 1946).
Arnold, Matthew, *On the Study of Celtic Literature* (London, 1867).
Aronowitz, Stanley, 'Theory and Socialist Strategy', *Social Text* (1986–7).
Auerbach, Eric, *Mimesis* (Princeton: Princeton University Press, 1968).
Bakhtin, Mikhail, *Rabelais and His World*. Trans. Helene Iswolsky (Cambridge, MA: MIT, 1968).
Bakhtin, Mikhail, *The Dialogic Imagination*, Michael Holquist (ed.). Trans. Caryl Emerson and Michael Holquist (Austin: Texas University Press, 1981).
Balibar, Etienne, 'The Nation Form: History and Ideology'. *Race, Nation, Class*. Trans. Chris Turner, in Etienne Balibar and Immanuel Wallerstein (eds) (London: Verso, 1991).
Barnard, F.M., *Herder's Social and Political Thought* (Oxford: Clarendon, 1965).
Barrett, Anthony, 'Raymond Williams and Marxism: A Rejoinder to Terry Eagleton', *The New Left Review (NLR)*, 99 (1976).
Barrett, Michèle, *The Politics of Truth: From Marx to Foucault* (Cambridge: Polity, 1991).
Barthes, Roland, *Mythologies* (1957). Trans. Annette Lavers (London: Vintage, 1993).
Barzun, Jacques, *Darwin, Marx, Wagner*, 2nd edn (New York: Doubleday, 1958).
Baudrillard, Jean, *Selected Writings*, Mark Poster (ed.) (Cambridge: Polity, 1988).
Beer, Gillian, *Darwin's Plots: Evolutionary Narrative in Darwin, George Eliot and Nineteenth-Century Fiction* (London: Routledge, 1983).
Benjamin, Walter, 'On Language as Such and on the Language of Man', *One-Way Street and Other Writings*. Trans. Edmund Jephcott and Kingsley Shorter (London: Verso, 1985).
Benjamin, Walter, *The Origins of German Tragic Drama*. Trans. John Osborne (London: New Left Books, 1977).
Benjamin, Walter, 'Theses on the Philosophy of History', XVII, *Illuminations*, Hannah Arendt (ed.). Trans. Harry Zohn (London: Fontana, 1992).
Bennett, Tony, *Formalism and Marxism* (London: Methuen, 1979).
Bennett, Tony, *Outside Literature* (London: Routledge, 1990).
Bennington, Geoff, 'Demanding History', in Derek Attridge, Geoff Bennington and Robert Young (eds), *Poststructuralism and the Question of History* (Cambridge: Cambridge University Press, 1987).
Bentley, Eric, *A Century of Hero Worship: A Study of the Idea of Heroism in Carlyle and Nietzsche* (Boston: Beacon, 1957).

Bibliography

Bew, Paul, *Conflict and Conciliation in Ireland, 1890–1910* (Oxford: Clarendon, 1987).

Bloom, Harold, *Yeats* (Oxford: Oxford University Press, 1972).

Bohlmann, Otto, *Yeats and Nietzsche* (London: Macmillan, 1982).

Bornstein, George, 'Last Romantic or Last Victorian: Yeats, Tennyson and Browning', *Yeats Annual*, Vol. 1 (Dublin: Macmillan, 1982).

Boyce, George, *Nationalism in Ireland* (London: Routledge, 1991).

Boyd, Ernest, *Appreciations and Depreciations* (London: Fisher Unwin, 1917).

Boylan, Thomas A. and Timothy P. Foley, *Political Economy and Colonial Ireland* (London: Routledge, 1992).

Boyne, Patricia, 'Thank You, Eoin O'Curry: From Mangan, O'Grady and Others', *Studies*, Vol. LXXII (1983).

Brady, Ciaran (ed.) *Interpreting Irish History: The Debate on Historical Revisionism 1938–1994* (Dublin: Irish Academic Press, 1994).

Brody, Hugh, *Inishkillane* (London: Penguin, 1973).

Browne, Malcolm, *Sir Samuel Ferguson* (Lewisbury: Bucknell University Press, 1973).

Brown, Terence, *Ireland: A Social and Cultural History, 1922–1979* (London: Fontana, 1981).

Bürger, Peter, *The Decline of Modernism*. Trans. Nicholas Walker (Cambridge, Polity, 1992).

Butler, Judith, 'Poststructuralism and Post-Marxism', *Diacritics*, 23, 4 (1993).

Cairns, David and Shaun Richards, *Writing Ireland: Colonialism, Nationalism and Culture* (Manchester: Manchester University Press, 1988).

Calinescu, Matei, 'Marxism, "Theory' and History"', *Stanford Literature Review*, Vol. 3, No. 2 (1986).

Carlyle, Thomas, 'Chartism', *Critical and Miscellaneous Essays*. Vol. III (London, 1869).

Carlyle, Thomas, *On Heroes, Hero-Worship and the Heroic in History* (London, 1872).

Carlyle, Thomas, 'On History', *Critical and Miscellaneous Essays*. Vol. II, 3rd edn (London, 1888).

Carlyle, Thomas, *Past and Present* (London, 1897).

Carlyle, Thomas, *Sartor Resartus* and *On Heroes, Hero-Worship and the Heroic in History* (London, 1863).

Chadwick, Owen, *The Secularization of the European Mind in the 19th Century* (Cambridge: Cambridge University Press, 1975).

Cixous, Hélène, 'The Laugh of Medusa', in Elaine Marks and Isabelle de Courtivon (eds) *New French Feminisms* (London: Harvester Wheatsheaf, 1981).

Clark, Rosalind. *The Great Queens: Irish Goddess from the Morrígan to Cathleen Ní Houlihan* (Gerrards Cross: Colin Smythe, 1991).

Cole, G.D.H., *A Century of Co-operation* (London: Allen & Unwin, 1945).

Cullingford, Elizabeth Butler, *Gender and History in Yeats's Love Poetry* (Cambridge: Cambridge University Press, 1993).

Cullingford, Elizabeth Butler, *Yeats, Ireland and fascism* (London: Macmillan, 1982).

Daly, Mary, Review of *Political Economy and Colonial Ireland, Irish Historical Studies*, Vol. XXIX (Nov. 1994).

Darwin, Charles, *The Descent of Man* (1871). *The Darwin Reader*, Marston Bates & Phillip Humphrey (eds) (London: Macmillan, 1957).

Davidson, Alastair, Review of *Hegemony and Socialist Strategy. Thesis Eleven*, 16 (1987).

Davis, Robert, *George William Russell ('Æ')* (Boston: Twayne, 1977).

Deane, Seamus, *Celtic Revivals* (London: Faber, 1985).

Deane, Seamus, *Strange Country: Modernity and Nationhood in Irish Writing since 1790* (Oxford: Clarendon, 1997).

Deane, Seamus, 'The Literary Myths of the Revival: A Case for their Abandonment', in Joseph Ronsley (ed.), *Myth and Reality in Irish Literature* (Ontario: Wilfrid Laurier University Press, 1977).

Denman, Peter, *Samuel Ferguson: The Literary Achievement* (Colin Smythe: Gerrards Cross, 1990).

De Vere, Aubrey, *The Foray of Queen Maeve* (London: Kegan Paul, 1882).

Derrida, Jacques, *Of Grammatology*. Trans. Gayatri Spivak (London: Johns Hopkins University Press, 1976).

Derrida, Jacques, *Specters of Marx*. Trans. Peggy Kamuf (London: Routledge, 1994).

Derrida, Jacques, 'Structure, Sign, and Play in the Discourse of the Human Sciences', in Richard Mackey and Eugenio Donato (eds), *The Language of Criticism and the Sciences of Man* (Baltimore: Johns Hopkins University Press, 1970).

Diggory, Terence, 'De Man And Yeats', *Yeats Annual of Critical and Textual Studies*, Vol. 8 (1990).

Donoghue, Denis, 'Yeats: The Question of Symbolism', in Joseph Ronsley (ed.) *Myth and Reality in Irish Literature* (Ontario: Wilfrid Laurier University Press, 1977), p.105.

Dorn, Karen, *Players and Painted Stage: The Theatre of W.B. Yeats* (Sussex: Harvester, 1984).

Eagleton, Terry, 'Art after Auschwitz', *The Significance of Theory* (Oxford: Blackwell, 1990).

Eagleton, Terry, 'Criticism and Politics: The Work of Raymond Williams', *The New Left Review*, 95 (1976).

Eagleton, Terry, *Criticism and Ideology*, 2nd edn (London: Verso, 1978).

Eagleton, Terry, *Heathcliff and the Great Hunger* (London: Verso, 1995).

Eagleton, Terry, 'Politics and Sexuality in W.B. Yeats', *The Crane Bag*, 9, 2 (1985).

Eagleton, Terry, *Scholars and Rebels* (Oxford: Blackwell, 1999).

Eliade, Mircea, *Myth and Reality* (London: Allen & Unwin, 1964).

Eglinton, John, et al., *Literary Ideals in Ireland* (London, 1899).

Ellmann, Richard, *Yeats: The Man and the Masks* (London: Faber, 1961).

Engelberg, Edward, *The Vast Design: Patterns in W.B. Yeats's Aesthetic*, 2nd edn. (Washington: Catholic University of America, 1988).

Fennell, Desmond, 'James Connolly and George Russell', *The Crane Bag*, 9, 1 (1985).

Ferguson, Samuel, 'Hardiman's Irish Minstrelsy, 1–4', *Dublin University Magazine*, Vol. IV, pp.19–23 (1834).

Fforde, Matthew, *Conservatism and Collectivism 1886–1914* (Edinburgh: Edinburgh University Press, 1990).

Figgis, Darrell, *Æ* (London: Maunsel, 1916).

Foster, John Wilson, '"The Interpreters": A Handbook to Æ and the Irish Revival', *Ariel* XI, 3 (1980).

Foster, R.F., *Paddy and Mr Punch: Connections in Irish and English History* (London: Penguin, 1993).

Foster, R.F., *The Story of Ireland* (Oxford: Clarendon, 1995).

Foster, R.F., *W.B. Yeats: A Life*, Vol. 1 (Oxford: Oxford University Press, 1997).

Foucault, Michel, *Madness and Civilization*. Trans. Richard Howard (London: Tavistock, 1967).

Foucault, Michel, 'Nietzsche, Genealogy, History', in Paul Rainbow (ed.), *The Foucault Reader* (London: Penguin, 1991).

Foucault, Michel, *Power/Knowledge: Selected Interviews and Other Writings 1972–1977*, Colin Gordon (ed.) (Brighton: Harvester, 1980).

Foucault, Michel, *The Archaeology of Knowledge* (London: Flamingo, 1983).

Froude, James Anthony, *The English in Ireland in the Eighteenth Century*, Vol. I (1881) (London: Longmans, Green & Co., 1906).

Frow, John, 'Marxism after Structuralism', *Southern Review*, 17 (1984).

Gailey, Andrew, *Ireland and the Death of Kindness* (Cork: Cork University Press, 1987).

Gasché, Rodolphe, 'Of Aesthetic and Historical Determination', in Derek Attridge, Geoff Bennington and Robert Young (eds), *Post-structuralism and the Question of History* (Cambridge: Cambridge University Press, 1987).

Gellner, Ernest, *Nations and Nationalism* (Oxford: Basil Blackwell, 1983).

Geras, Norman, 'Althusser's Marxism: An Account and Assessment', *New Left Review*, 71 (1972).

Geras, Norman, 'Post-Marxism?', *New Left Review*, 163 (1987).

Goldstein, Philip, 'Marxism Meets Foucault: Will the Real Marx Please Stand Up', *The Minnesota Review*, 4 (1993).

Graham, Colin, *Ideologies of Epic: Nation, Empire and Victorian Epic Poetry* (Manchester: Manchester University Press, 1998).

Graham, Colin, '"…maybe that's just Blarney": Irish Culture and the Persistence of Authenticity', in Colin Graham and Richard Kirkland (eds), *Ireland and Cultural Theory* (London: Macmillan, 1999).

Greene, Catherine, 'The Cuchulain Legend in the Plays of W.B. Yeats', MA thesis (Liverpool University, 1973).

Hagan, Edward, *'High Nonsensical Words': A Study of the Works of Standish James O'Grady* (New York: Whitson, 1986).

Hagan, Edward, 'The Aryan Myth: A Nineteenth Century Anglo-Irish Will to Power', in Tadhg Foley (ed.), *Ideology and Ireland in the Nineteenth Century* (Dublin: Four Courts, 1998).

Heiss, Robert. *Hegel, Kierkegaard, Marx* (New York: Delacorte, 1975).

Heidegger, Martin, *Being and Time*. Trans. John Macquarrie and Edward Robinson (London: SCM, 1962).

Henn, Thomas, 'The Sainthood of A.E.', *Last Essays* (Colin Smythe, Gerrards Cross, 1976).

Hoare, Quintin and Geoffrey Nowell Smith (eds), *Selections from the Prison Notebooks of Antonio Gramsci* (London: Lawrence & Wishhart, 1971).

Hobsbawm, E.J., *Nations and Nationalism since 1780* (Cambridge: Cambridge University Press, 1990).

Hoffman, Daniel, *Barbarous Knowledge* (Oxford: Oxford University Press, 1967).

Honneth, Alex. 'History and Interaction: On the Structuralist Interpretation of Historical Materialism', in Gregory Elliot (ed.), *Althusser: A Critical Reader* (Oxford: Blackwell, 1984).

Humble, Malcolm, 'German Contacts and Influences in the Lives and Works of W.B. Yeats and D.H. Lawrence, with Special Reference to Friedrich Nietzsche', PhD thesis (Cambridge University. 1969).

Hutchinson, John, *The Dynamics of Cultural Nationalism* (London: Allen & Unwin, 1987).

Jameson, Fredric, 'Demystifying the Ideology of Modernism', in Francis Mulhern (ed.), *Contemporary Marxist Literary Criticism* (New York: Longman, 1992).

Jameson, Fredric, *Postmodernism, or, The Cultural Logic of Late Capitalism* (London: Verso, 1991).

Jameson, Fredric, *The Political Unconscious* (London: Methuen, 1981).

Jenkins, Angela, 'W.B. Yeats and Irish Mythology', MA thesis (University of Kent at Canterbury, 1980).

Kain, Richard and James O'Brien, *George Russell (Æ)* (Lewisburg, Bucknell University Press, 1976).

Kearney, Hugh, 'Contested Ideas of Nationhood 1800–1995', *The Irish Review*, 20 (1997).

Keating, P.J., 'Arnold's Social and Political Thought', in Kenneth Allcott (ed.) *Matthew Arnold* (London: Bell, 1975).

Kelly, John, 'The Political and Intellectual Background to the Irish Literary Revival to 1901', PhD thesis (Cambridge University, 1971).

Kennedy, Liam, 'The Early Response of the Irish Catholic Clergy to the Co-operative Movement', *Reactions to Irish Nationalism* (Dublin: Gill & Macmillan, 1987).

Kiberd, Declan, *Inventing Ireland* (London: Jonathan Cape, 1995).

Kiberd, Declan, Review of *Celtic Revivals. Yeats Annual*, 5 (London: Macmillan, 1987).

Kierkegaard, Sören, *Philosophical Fragments* (Princeton University Press, 1936).

Krause, David, 'The De-Yeatsification Cabal', *Irish Literary Supplement*, Vol. 8, 1 (1990).

Kuch, Peter, *Yeats and A.E.: 'The Antagonism that Unites Dear Friends'* (Gerrards Cross: Colin Smythe, 1986).

Laclau, Ernesto, *New Reflections on the Revolution of Our Time* (London: Verso, 1990).

Laclau, Ernesto and Chantal Mouffe, *Hegemony and Socialist Strategy: Towards A Radical Democratic Politics* (London: Verso, 1985).

Laclau, Ernesto and Chantal Mouffe, 'Post-Marxism Without Apologies', *New Left Review*, 166 (1987).

Larsen, Neil, 'Postmodernism and Imperialism', *Essays in Postmodern Culture* (London: Oxford University Press, 1993).

Laszlo, Ervin, *Individualism, Collectivism and Political Power* (The Hague: Nijoff, 1963).

Lee, Joseph, *The Modernisation of Irish Society 1848–1918* (Dublin: Gill & Macmillan, 1973).

Leerssen, Joep, *Mere Irish and Fíor-Ghael: Studies in the Idea of Irish Nationality, its Development and Literary Expression prior to the Nineteenth-Century* (Amsterdam: John Benjamin, 1986).

Leerssen, Joep, *Remembrance and Imagination: Patterns in Historical and Literary Representation* (Cork: Cork University Press, 1996).

Levine, Herbert J., 'Yeats's Ruskinian Byzantium', *Yeats Annual*, 2 (Dublin: Macmillan, 1983).

Liao, Wên-Kuei, *The Individual and the Community* (London: Kegan Paul, 1933).

Lloyd, David, *Nationalism and Minor Literature: James Clarence Mangan and the Emergence of Irish Cultural Nationalism* (Berkeley: University of California Press, 1987).

Lukács, Georg, *The Theory of the Novel* (London: Merlin, 1978).

Lukes, Steven, *Individualism* (Oxford: Basil Blackwell, 1973).

Lyons, F.S.L., *Charles Stewart Parnell* (London: Collins, 1977).

Lyons, F.S.L., *Ireland Since The Famine* (London: Fontana, 1973).

Marcus, Phillip, *Standish O'Grady* (Lewisburg: Bucknell University Press, 1970).

Marx, Karl, *Capital*, Vol. 1. Introd. Ernest Mandel. Trans. Ben Fowkes (London: Penguin, 1990).

Marx, Karl, and Friedrich Engels, *The Communist Manifesto* (London: Penguin, 1967).

McCartney, Donal, 'James Anthony Froude and Ireland: A Historiographical Controversy of the Nineteenth Century', *Irish University Review*, Vol. 1, 2 (1971).

McCormack, W.J., *From Burke to Beckett: Ascendancy, Tradition and Betrayal in Literary History* (Cork: Cork University Press, 1994).

McFate, Patricia, 'The Interpreters: AE's Symposium and Roman à Clef', *Éire-Ireland* XI, 3 (1976).

McLellan, David (ed.), *Karl Marx: Selected Writings* (London: Oxford University Press, 1977).

Mercier, Vivien, 'Victorian Evangelicalism and the Anglo-Irish Revival', in Peter Connolly (ed.), *Literature and the Changing Ireland* (Gerrards Cross: Colin Smythe, 1982).

Mercier, Vivien, *Modern Irish Literature: Sources and Founders* (Oxford: Clarendon, 1994).

Mêstrovic, Stjepan, *The Barbarian Temperament: Toward a Postmodern Critical Theory* (London: Routledge, 1993).

Moi, Toril, 'Patriarchal Thought and the Desire for Knowledge', in Teresa Brennan (ed.), *Between Feminism and Psychoanalysis* (London: Routledge, 1989).

Moi, Toril, (ed.), *The Kristeva Reader* (Oxford: Basil Blackwell, 1986).

Moore, George, *Hail and Farewell*, Richard Cave (ed.) (Toronto: Macmillan, 1976).

Moore, George, *The Untilled Field* (London: Fisher Unwin, 1903).

Moran, D.P., 'The Pale and the Gael', *The New Ireland Review*, Vol. XI (Dublin, 1899).

Moran, D.P., *The Philosophy of Irish Ireland* (Dublin: J. Duffy, 1905).

Morash, Christopher, 'Celticism: Between Race and Nation', in Tadhg Foley (ed.), *Ideology and Ireland in the Nineteenth Century* (Dublin: Four Courts, 1998).

Mouffe, Chantal, 'Hegemony and ideology in Gramsci', in Chantal Mouffe, *Gramsci and Marxist Theory* (London: Routledge & Kegan Paul, 1979).

Mouzelis, Nicos, *Post-Marxist Alternatives* (London: Macmillan, 1990).

Bibliography

Murray, Christopher, *Twentieth-Century Irish Drama: Mirror Up To Nation* (Manchester: Manchester University Press, 1997).

Neff, Emery, *Carlyle and Mill* (New York: Octagon, 1974).

Nietzsche, Friedrich, *Beyond Good and Evil* (London: Penguin, 1973).

Nietzsche, Friedrich, 'On the Uses and Disadvantages of History for Life', in Daniel Breazeale (ed.), *Untimely Meditations*. Trans. R.J. Hollingdale (Cambridge University Press, 1997).

Nietzsche, Friedrich, *The Birth of Tragedy and The Genealogy of Morals*. Trans. Francis Golffing (New York: Doubleday, 1956).

Nolan, Jerry C.M., 'O'Grady's Cultural Nationalism', *Irish Studies Review*, 7, 3 (1999).

O'Brien, Conor Cruise, *Parnell and his Party* (London: Oxford University Press: 19570.

O'Brien, Conor Cruise, *Passion and Cunning and Other Essays* (London: Grafton, 1990).

O'Cearnaigh, Nioclás, 'Cumha na máthara fá anbhás a linbh', *Fios Feasa 3* (Dublin: Comhlucht Oidheacais na hÉireann, 1974).

O'Connor, Frank, *The Backward Look* (London: Macmillan, 1967).

O'Dowd, Liam, 'Intellectuals in 20th Century Ireland: And the case of George Russell (Æ)', *The Crane Bag*, 9, 1 (1985).

O'Dowd, Liam, 'Neglecting the Material Dimension: Irish Intellectuals and the Problem of Identity', *The Irish Review*, No. 3 (1988).

O'Dowd, Liam, 'Town and Country in Irish Ideology', *Canadian Journal of Irish Studies*, 13, 2 (1987).

O'Faolain, Sean, *King of the Beggars* (London: Nelson, 1938).

O'Gráda, Cormac, 'The Beginnings of the Irish Creamery System, 1880–1914', *Economic History Review*, p.xxx, 2nd series (Welwyn Garden City: Popper, 1977).

O'Grady, Hugh Art, *Standish James O'Grady: the Man and the Writer* (Dublin: Talbot, 1921).

Oldfield, Adrian, *Citizenship and Community: Civic Republicanism and the Modern World* (London: Routledge, 1990).

Ollman, Bertell, *Alienation: Marx's Conception of Man in Capitalist Society* (Cambridge: Cambridge University Press, 1976).

Oppel, Francis Nesbitt, *Mask and Tragedy: Yeats and Nietzsche, 1902–10* (Charlottesville: Virginia University Press, 1987).

O'Sullivan, Daniel J., 'Standish James O'Grady's *All-Ireland Review*', *Studia Hibernica*, 69 (1969).

O'Sullivan, Daniel J. 'The Literary Periodical and the Anglo-Irish Revival, 1894–1914', PhD thesis (University College, Dublin. 1969).

O'Tuathaigh, M.A.G., 'Sir Samuel Ferguson – Poet and Ideologue', in Terence Brown and Barbara Hayley (eds), *Samuel Ferguson: A Centenary Tribute* (Dublin: Royal Irish Academy, 1987).

Paulin, Tom, 'Yeats's Hunger-Strike Poem', *Minotaur: Poetry and the Nation State* (London: Faber, 1992).

Plato, *The Republic*. Trans. A.D. Lindsay (London: Dent, 1976).

Poggi, Gianfranco, *Calvinism and the Capitalist Spirit: Max Weber's Protestant Ethic* (London: Macmillan, 1983).

Poulantzas, Nikos *Political Power and Social Classes*. London: New Left Books, 1973.

Raulet, Gerard, 'Marxism and the Post-Modern Condition', *Telos*, 67 (1986).

Reed, John, *Decadent Style* (Athens, Ohio: Ohio University Press, 1985).

Reilly, Anne & Próspero Saíz, 'Volosinov, Bennett, and the Politics of Writing', *Contemporary Literature*, 22, 4 (1981).

Rosenberg, John, *Carlyle and the Burden of History* (Oxford: Clarendon, 1985).

Ross, Andrew, Review of *Hegemony and Socialist Strategy*, *M/F*. 11–12 (1986).

Ruse, Michael, *The Darwinian Paradigm* (London: Routledge, 1989).

Ruskin, John, *The Political Economy of Art* (London: Macmillan, 1912).

Scholem, Gershom, and Theodor Adorno, *The Correspondence of Walter Benjamin*. Trans. Manfred R. Jacobson and Evelyne M. Jacobson (London: Chicago University Press, 1994).

Sellers, Susan (ed.), *The Hélène Cixous Reader* (London: Routledge, 1994).

Shannon, Catherine B., *Arthur J. Balfour and Ireland* (Washington: Catholic University of America Press, 1988).

Sherman, Deborah Anne, 'Yeats Talk: The Critical Theory of W.B. Yeats and the Victorian Background' (Brown University, PhD thesis, 1982).

Smart, Barry, *Postmodernity* (London: Routledge, 1993).

Smith, A.D., *The Ethnic Revival* (Cambridge: Cambridge University Press, 1981).

Smith, Stan, *The Origins of Modernism* (New York: Harvester Wheatsheaf, 1994).

Sparks, Julie, 'At the Intersection of Victorian Science and Fiction: Andrew Lang's 'Romance of First Radical', *English Literature in Transition 1880–1920*, 42, 2 (1999).

Steiner, George, *After Babel* (London: Oxford University Press, 1975).

Stone, Lawrence, *The Family, Sex and Marriage in England, 1500–1800* (London: Weidenfeld & Nicolson, 1977).

Summerfield, Henry (ed.), *Selections from the Contributions to The Irish Homestead*, 2 vols (Gerrards Cross: Colin Smythe, 1978).

Summerfield, Henry, *That Myriad-Minded Man* (Colin Smythe, Gerrards Cross, 1975).

Summerfield, Henry, 'Unpublished Letters from AE to John Eglinton', *Malahat Review*, Vol. 14 (1970).

Symons, Arthur, 'Nietzsche on Tragedy', *The Academy and Literature* (London: 30 Aug. 1902).

Symons, Arthur, 'The New Bayreuth', *The Academy and Literature* (London: 27 Sept. 1902).

Symons, Arthur, 'The Ideas of Richard Wagner', *The Quarterly Review*, Vol. 203, 404 (London: John Murray, 1905).

Taylor, Estella Ruth, *The Modern Irish Writers: Cross Currents of Criticism* (Connecticut: Greenwood, 1954).

Vilar, Peter, 'Marxist History, a History in the Making: Towards a Dialogue with Althusser', *New Left Review*, 80 (1973).

Weber, Max, *The Protestant Ethic and the Spirit of Capitalism* (London: Allen & Unwin, 1930).

Weber, Samuel, 'Capitalizing History: Notes on *The Political Unconscious*', *Diacritics*, 13, 2 (1983).

Welch, Robert. *Irish Poetry from Moore to Yeats* (Gerrards Cross: Colin Smythe, 1980).

West, Trevor, *Horace Plunkett: Co-operation and Politics, An Irish Biography* (Gerrards Cross: Colin Smythe, 1986).

Whelan, Kevin, 'Town and Village in Ireland: A Socio-Cultural Perspective.' *The Irish Review*, No. 5 (1988).

Wilde, Oscar, 'The Decay of Lying', *De Profundis and Other Writings* (London: Penguin, 1973).

Williams, Raymond, 'Base and Superstructure in Marxist Cultural Theory', *New Left Review*, 82 (1973).

Williams, Raymond, *Culture and Society* (London: Chatto & Windus, 1958).

Williams, Raymond, *Keywords*, 2nd edn (London: Flamingo, 1983).

Williams, Raymond, *The Country and the City* (London: Chatto & Windus, 1973).

Williams, Raymond, *The Long Revolution* (London: Chatto & Windus, 1961).

Wolin, Richard, *Walter Benjamin: An Aesthetic of Redemption* (Berkeley: California University Press, 1994).

Wood, Ellen Meiksins, 'The Retreat From Class', *New Left Review*, 163 (1987).

Index

Adorno, Theodor 12, 47, 49, 160n40,
    164n32
Æ *see* Russell, George W.
Ahrimail 42–3, 55
Aileel Finn 41
Aileel More 28, 33, 50
All-Ireland Review 149
Allotments Bill 171n10
Althusser, Louis 3–6, 9, 71–2, 121,
    154–5n10, 155n17, 168nn33,38,
    185n75
Anderson, Benedict 98–9
Anderson, R.A. 175n10
Anly 30
Annals of the Four Masters 64
Ardan 30
Arnold, Matthew 17, 18, 20, 61, 68, 91,
    135, 158n24, 170–1n3
art, and history 18–19
Aryan Myth 60, 70, 168n30
Ath-a-Cliath *see* Dublin
atomistic individualism 52, 165n49
Atticottic revolt 63–4, 66, 90, 167n22
Auerbach, Eric 24–5, 140–2

Bakhtin, Mikhail 23, 65–7
Balfour, A.J. 116–17, 125, 179–80n94
Balibar, Etienne 4, 70, 92, 168n28
banquet scenes 55
bardic history 36–8
bards, status of 41–3
Barnard, F.M. 114
Barrett, Anthony 178n62
Barthes, Roland 74, 76–8
Barzun, Jacques 167n10
Baudrillard, Jean 7, 172n26
Beer, Gillian 167n9
Belton, Neil 152
Benjamin, Walter 12, 130–1, 160nn40,46,
    181nn18,19, 184–5n69
Bennett, Tony 4, 7, 8, 121–2, 155n12
Bennington, Geoff 155n19

Bentham, Jeremy 52
Bew, Paul 105–6, 108
Bhaba, Homi K. 2
Bingham, Richard 81
Blake, William 182–3n34
Bloom, Harold 137, 184n56
Bornstein, George 135
Boyce, George 173n49
Boyd, Ernest 15, 104
Boylan, Thomas 109, 111
Brigamba 57
Broadhurst, Henry 88, 171n10
Brody, Hugh 120–1
Brooke, Charlotte, Lady Morgan 14
Browne, Malcolm 16, 157n9
Brown, Terence 1, 155n21, 182–3n34,
    184n56, 186n102
Bunting, Edward 14
Bürger, Peter 182n31
Burke, Edmund 15
Butler, Judith 4, 156n34, 174n67

Cailitin 42–3, 44–5, 55
Cairns, David 1
Calinescu, Matei 4, 154–5n10
Carlyle, Thomas 17, 19–20, 29–30,
    39–40, 159n29, 171n5
Castlemahon Co-operative Creamery 110
Cathvah 30, 32, 45
Celtic Revivals 14–15
Chadwick, Owen 52
Churchill, Lord Randolph 86, 89
Cixous, Hélène 31, 161n58, 162n72
Clarke, Austin 17
Clark, Rosalind 185n86
Colingas, Cormac 44
communalism 51–2, 58–9, 120–1, 178n76
Concobhar MacNessa 30–2, 51
Co-operative Movement *see* Irish Co-
    operative Movement
Co-operative Wholesale Society (CWS)
    107, 110–11, 176n31

Corac 24–7, 55, 141
Corbet, W.J. 96
Craivetheena 26, 27, 31, 33, 161n54
Croothean 57–8
Cuchulainn 29, 33–5, 50–4, 57, 59,
    141–2, 146, 151
Cullingford, Elizabeth 136, 163–4n21

Daly, Mary 176n35
Darwin, Charles 62–3, 68–70, 167nn9,27,
    177n42
Davis, Robert 124
Deane, Seamus 1, 2, 7–8, 14–15, 74,
    139–40, 169nn46,56, 184n65
decadence, Yeats's views 133–5
Deirdre 30–2
Denman, Peter 16, 17
Denson, Alan 124
Department of Agriculture and Technical
    Instruction (DATI) 107–8
Derrida, Jacques 32, 162nn74,75, 168n28
De Vere, Aubrey 16, 17, 166n4
dialectical discourse 10–13, 49
Dillon, John 106–7, 117, 176n36
Dionysius 133
Dowden, Edward 146
dramatisation, of legends 128–9, 180n5
druids 31–3, 162n69
Dublin, and Cuchulainn 52–4, 57, 59,
    165n55
Dun-Rie 24, 26, 27
Duras House 14

Eadâne 28, 29
Eagleton, Terry 1, 2, 15, 178n62, 180n95
education, role of 109, 176n35
Eglinton, John 145, 181n11
Eliade, Mircea 142
Elizabethan period, O'Grady's treatment
    of 72, 81–5
Ellis, Edwin 182–3n34
Ellmann, Richard 143, 181n20
Emain Macha 21, 24, 55, 61
enchantment 45, 50, 51, 183n51
Engelberg, Edward 136
English Co-operative movement 107,
    110–11
English Romanticism 134
epic form 24–5, 65–7, 136, 139–41
Esmonde, Thomas 96
ethnicity, and nationalism 97–9, 173n55
evangelical revivalism 142

Fardia 34
feminine subjectivity 46–7, 138
femininity
    Maeve 48
    malign influence 137, 138
    as the Other 28, 32, 138, 160n41
    see also gender
Fergus MacRoy 30–3, 51, 138
Ferguson, Samuel 15–18, 67, 157n9,
    159–60n39
Festus Rufus 61
feudal communalism 58–9
Figgis, Darrell 104, 124
Filmer, Robert 57
Finlay, Fr 105, 175n10
Fionn McCool 22
Firbolgs 43
Fleeas, Queen 41–2, 55
Foley, Timothy 109, 111
Fomorians 43
forgetfulness 137, 138–9
Foster, R.F. 1, 2, 96, 140, 156n27, 169n56
Foucault, Michel 21, 177–8n60,
    184–5n69
Freeman, John 75–6, 78–80
The Freeman's Journal 106–7
French Revolution 93–4
Froude, James Anthony 20, 163n5,
    166n70
Furbisher, Frank 78–9

Gadelian legend 63–4
Gaelic origins, O'Grady's view 20–1,
    159n35
Gailey, Andrew 116
Gasché, Rodolphe 158n25
Gellner, Ernest 97
gender
    aspects of 27–8, 31, 161n58, 183n51
    see also femininity
George, Henry 88, 171n7
Geras, Norman 3
Gilson, John 81
Gonne, Maud 136, 143, 181n11
Graham, Colin 13, 65, 66–7
Gramsci, Antonio 4, 93–4, 101, 175n16
Greek culture 20, 159n32
Greek literature 68
Gregory, Augusta 2

Hagan, Edward 31, 38–9, 70, 185n86
Hardiman, James 17, 158n21
Heber 25

Hegel, Georg 11–12, 114, 156n33, 160n40, 177n43
hegemony, theory of 93–4, 101
Heidegger, Martin 142
Herder, Johann 114, 118
Hermetic Students of the Golden Dawn 131, 181n20
Herodotus 98
heroism, notion of 22, 29–30, 51
history, and myth 37–44, 74–5, 133, 142, 146–7
Hobsbawm, E.J. 98
Hoffman, Daniel 135
Homer, comparison with 24–5, 61, 67–8, 141
Home Rule movement 106, 116–17
Honneth, Alex 6, 155n17
hospitality 55–6
Hull, Eleanor 146
Humble, Malcolm 182n25
Hutchinson, John 97, 115–16, 117

Ibsen, Henrik, influence of 145
ideology, and science 70–1
individualism 52–4, 113–14, 165nn49,59
'insane mist' 34, 46, 47, 50, 51, 183n51
Ioldana 51
Irish Agricultural Organisation Society (IAOS) 105, 107–8, 110–11, 112–13, 174n7, 175n14, 176n31, 179–80n94
Irish Co-operative Movement
  and English Co-operative movement 110–11, 176n31
  history of 105–8, 175n10
  ideology of 106–7, 111–12
  and nationalism 105–6
  objectives of 108–9
  and Russell 13, 102–3, 108–15, 124–5
Irish Creamery System 174n7
The Irish Homestead 105, 106–7, 111
Irish Literary Revival
location of 14
  O'Grady's influence on 1–3, 151, 170n65
  origins 14–16
  personal rivalries 127
Irish Literary Theatre 14
Irish nationalism 12–13, 156–7n38
Island of Forgetfulness 138, 139, 184n57
Italy, *Risorgimento* 94, 173n41

Jameson, Fredric 4–5, 6–9, 29, 78–9, 113, 121–2, 176n41

Jenkins, Angela 142–3

Kabbalist influence 131, 181nn20,23
Kearney, Hugh 174n62
Keller, Evelyn 160n41
Kelly, John 143, 147
Kiberd, Declan 1, 156nn37,38
Kierkegaard, Sören 156n33
Kimbay MacFiontann 21, 24, 55, 61
kinship, decline 56
Kristeva, Julia 27, 32, 162n76, 164n33

Laclau, Ernesto 4, 10–11, 48–9, 93, 101–2, 174n67
Laeg 34–5, 57–8
landlords, O'Grady's views of 46, 53–4, 55–6, 85, 95
land reform, O'Grady's views 88–90
Lang, Andrew 43–4, 135
Lara 24–7, 55, 141
Larminie, William 146
Larsen, Neil 154–5n10
Lee, Joseph 173n49
Leerssen, Joep 1, 157n16
Lemass, Sean 124
Lia Fáil 138–9
Lloyd, David 16–17
Locke, John 52, 57
Longley, Edna 1
Lorc 24
Lowcram 30
Lu 51
Lukács, Georg 52
Lyons, F.S.L. 105, 173n49

Macheray, Pierre 4
MacLeod, Fiona 151
Maeve, Queen 28–35, 41–2, 44–7, 49–50, 55, 137, 138, 161n54
Maloney, Patrick 113
Manzoni, Alessandro 94, 173n41
Martyn, Edward 181n11
Marxism 121
Marxist theories of history 3–5, 11–12, 154–5n10
Marx, Karl
  alienation theory 166n61
  on Gotha Programme 172n23
  science and ideology 70–1
McCartney, Donal 166n70
McCormack, W.J. 1, 40, 168n43, 184n62
Mercier, Vivian 15, 142
Mestrovic, Stjepan 169n58

Milesian clan 24, 25, 37, 61, 63, 139
mode of production, and history 5, 8–9
Moi, Toril 31, 160n41
Moody, T.W. 8
Moore, George 127, 181n11, 186n102
Moore, Thomas 14
Moran, D.P. 170n65
Morash, Christopher 70, 168n28
Moreea 26, 55
More, Ugainey 24, 28
Mouffe, Chantal 10–11, 48–9, 91, 93,
    101–2
Mouzelis, Nicos 121
Müller, Max 43, 44
Murphy, William Martin 119
Murray, Christopher 14
music, influence of 132–3
mythology
    and history 37–44, 74–5, 133, 142,
        146–7
    and narrative 75–8
    and ritual 142–3, 185n75

nationalism
    and ethnicity 97–9, 173n55
    and Irish Co-operative Movement
        105–6
    nation-state, O'Grady's views on
        89–103
Naysi 30
neo-Marxism 4
Niall of the Nine Hostages 61
Niamh, and Oisin 136–8, 140
Nietzsche, Friedrich 18–19, 63, 132–3,
    165n55
Nolan, Jerry C.M. 15
Norman, H.F. 105

O'Brien, Conor Cruise 96, 184n62
O'Connell, Daniel 14
O'Curry, Eugene 15, 56
Odin 29
O'Dowd, Liam 123–4, 178n76
Ogham letters 32
O'Grady, Standish Hayes 40
O'Grady, Standish James
    and *All-Ireland Review* 149
    concept of history 4, 5–6, 18–20, 36–7,
        149–50
    contemporary relevance 151–3
    and Co-operative Movement 105,
        179n85
    on dramatisation 128–9, 180n5

on Elizabethan period 72, 81–5
and epic form 24–5, 65–7
and Ferguson, Samuel 16–18
futurism 149
Irish Literary Revival originator 15
on landlords 46, 53–4, 55–6, 85, 95
life of 1–2
literary/historical/political levels of
    work 9–10
mythology and history 37–44, 146–7
nation-state views 89–103
novels of 73–85
on Parnell 95–6
patriarchy views 57
politics of 2–3, 13, 86–7, 122–3
racial views 60–2, 70, 72
and religion 87
All-Ireland (1898) 99
The Bog of Stars 81–2, 84
The Chain of Gold 74, 75, 78–9, 83
The Coming of Cuculain (1894) 73
Early Bardic Literature, Ireland (1879)
    37
History of Ireland: The Heroic Period
    (1878)
    banquet scenes 55
    Cuchulainn saga 29, 33–5
    emergence of hero 22, 141
    Gaelic origins 20–2
    Maeve story 28–35
    responses to 36–7
    Slieve Mish legend 24–8
*History of Ireland: Cuculain and His
    Contemporaries* (1880)
    banquet scenes 55
    bards 41–3
    capitalism 58
    Cuchulainn 50–4
    dialectical form 59
    enchantment 50
    Maeve story 44–5, 49–50
*History of Ireland: Critical and
    Philosophical* (1881)
    Atticottic revolt 63–4, 66, 90,
        167n22
    concept of history 18, 60
    gender issues 137
    genealogy 61–3, 68–70
In The Gates of the North (1901) 73
Lost on Du-Corrig 74, 75–8
Pacata Hibernia 81, 83
The Queen of the World 149
Red Hugh's Captivity 82, 83–4

Toryism and The Tory Democracy
  (1886) 86–103, 121, 125, 143, 150
O'Gràda, Cormac 174n7
O'Halloran, Sylvester 1, 15
Oisin 42, 135–42, 162n69
Oldfield, Adrian 114
Old Testament, epics 24–5, 141–2
O'Neill, Hugh 83–4
Order of the Golden Dawn 131, 143,
  181n20
O'Rourke, Brian Ogue 82, 84–5
the Other
  femininity 28, 32, 138, 160n41
  historical discourse 10
O'Tuathaigh, M.A.G. 16

Pan-Celticism 97–8
Parnell, Charles Stewart 95–6, 173n49
patriarchy 30, 33, 46–7, 56–7
Patrick, St, Yeats's treatment of 137–8,
  143, 184n56
Piast myth 75–7
Plunkett, Horace 105, 107–11, 114, 117,
  125, 175n10
Popper, Karl 8
postcolonialism 1, 2–3, 6, 7–8, 13
post-Marxism 4, 7, 10–11, 48, 102,
  121–2, 155n12
postmodernism 152, 164n35
poststructuralism 3, 4–5
Poulantzas, Nicos 4, 93, 155n19
Ptolemy 61

race, O'Grady's views 60–2, 70, 72
Raulet, Gerard 12, 160n40
Red Branch Knights 24, 30, 33–4, 45, 50,
  161n54, 183n51
Red Hand of Ulster 50
Redmond, John 96, 107–8
Reed, John 139
religion, O'Grady's views 87
revisionism 1, 2–3, 6, 7–8, 13, 156n27
Richards, Shaun 1
ritual 142–3, 185n75
Rolleston, T.W. 17, 107
Rosenberg, John 159n29
rurality 118–20
Rury the Great 28
Ruse, Michael 167n27
Ruskin, John 86, 91
Russell, George W.
  futurism 149
  and individualism 113–14

and Irish Co-operative Movement 13,
  102–3, 108–15, 124–5
mythology and history 146–7
O'Grady's influence on 6, 13, 104,
  123, 136
and socialism 119, 178n65
and Yeats 126–7, 145–6
The Candle of Vision 177n42
Co-operation and Nationality 111–12,
  119–20, 125
The National Being 109–10, 111–13,
  115, 117, 119
Song and its Fountains 177n43

science, and ideology 70–1
Sherman, Deborah 136
Slieve Mish 24–8
Smith, A.D. 92–3, 97
Smith, Stan 137
socialism, Russell's views 119, 178n65
Sparks, Julie 43
Stafford, Thomas 81
St Edmundsbury 39–40
Steiner, George 131, 181n19
Stephens, James 151
stone, metaphor of 138–9
Stone, Lawrence 54–5, 56–7
Sullivan, Daniel J. 184n53
symbolism 6, 147–8, 155n21
Symons, Arthur 134, 182n32

Táin Bo Cuailgne 32, 35, 128, 161n54
Tara 22–3, 61
Taylor, Estella Ruth 127
Techtmar, Tuatha 61
Tierna 21
Todhunter, John 17
Tory Democracy movement 86–7
tragedy, dramaturgy 131–2
Tree of Life 62, 131, 167n9
Tuatha De Danann 25, 26, 28, 37, 38

United Irish League 106
Usna 30

Vilar, Peter 154–5n10
Vincenzo, Gioberti 94, 173n41
Volk concept 114–15, 118–19, 120

Wagner, Richard, influence of 145,
  181n11, 182n25
Wallerstein, Immanuel 92
Watkins, Samuel 75–6

Weber, Max 77, 83, 169nn51,54
Weber, Samuel 79–80, 122
Welch, Robert 184n57
Wên-Kuei Liao 52
West, Trevor 175n10
Whateley, Richard 109, 110, 176n35
Wilde, Oscar 18, 134, 151, 170n61
Williams, Raymond 52, 118, 125, 178n62, 180n95
Wordsworthian idea of the poet 42–3, 145
Wyndham, George 125

Yeats, W.B.
    Amazonic women 163–4n21
    on decadence 133–5
    on dramatisation of legends 128–9
    myth and history 74–5, 133, 142
    and the occult 130, 140
    O'Grady's influence on 2, 10, 126–48
    and Order of the Golden Dawn 131, 143
    and Russell 126–7, 145–6
    symbolism 6, 147–8, 155n21
    on tragedy 131–2
    Wagner's influence 145, 181n11, 182n25
    'The Wanderings of Oisin' 42, 135–42, 162n69
Yeoha Faydleeah 28
Young Ireland Movement 143